Terry Brincell 94

Human Resource Management in Europe

Emerging principally from the Third Conference on International Personnel and Human Resources Management held at Ashridge Management College in 1992, this volume aims to address, head on, the issues of European HRM. The ramifications of the 'new' Europe are discussed as walls come down in the political and commercial sense, and liberated ex-Communist countries get to grips with Western business practices. Particular reference is made to the HR manager who wants to become conversant with the particular issues of transnational HRM.

These collected papers, drawn from experts in Europe and the USA, arranged in thematic order, make a timely contribution to the burgeoning debate concerning the nature of European HRM. In the opening section, the contributors recognize the state of flux in which continental Europe finds itself, and from their various perspectives, attempt to discern a European HRM model specific to the region. In contrast to the American or Japanese models, European HRM is dissected to discover the essential components which make it unique.

Part II contains a detailed discussion of the implications of EC developments for European HRM and traces the contours of emerging HR trends within both EC and non-EC countries within Europe. One of the most important themes to emerge in Part III is the need for understanding when dealing with the embryonic human resource structures existent behind the defunct iron curtain. The clash of the West and East is seen in a positive light, a catalyst for producing creativity and innovation, and the emphasis within this section's chapters is upon knowledge sharing and the impact a market economy will have for human resource management in eastern Europe. Finally, Part IV discusses, with case examples, the rise of cross-border business within Europe and the associated need for the recruitment and development of a new breed of Euro-manager with a distinct international competence.

The issues raised by this important collection of opinions are relevant not only to the professional HR manager, but also for the student of European management and business. It is broad ranging and authoritative and should become an essential element in the European debate.

Professor Paul S. Kirkbride is a Programme Director at Ashridge Management College, leading the academic team responsible for HRM, leadership and change. He is also a visiting Professor at the University of Hertfordshire.

Human Resource Management in Europe

Perspectives for the 1990s

Edited by Paul S. Kirkbride

London and New York

First published 1994
by Routledge
11 New Fetter Lane, London EC4P 4EE

Simultaneously published in the USA and Canada
by Routledge
29 West 35th Street, New York, NY 10001

Typeset in Times by
Ponting–Green Publishing Services, Chesham, Bucks

Printed and bound in Great Britain by
Mackays of Chatham PLC, Chatham, Kent

British Library Cataloguing in Publication Data
A catalogue record for this book is available from the British
Library

Library of Congress Cataloging in Publication Data
Has been applied for

ISBN 0–415–08658–2 (hbk)
ISBN 0–415–08659–0 (pbk)

Contents

Part III Developments in Eastern Europe

Part IV Creating the pan-European manager

Part V Conclusions

Figures

Tables

Contributors

Kevin Barham is Research and Development Partner with the International Institute for Organizational Change, IOC-Ashridge based in Archamps, France. Kevin holds a BA in international relations from the University of Sussex, an MSc in international relations from the London School of Economics and an MBA in finance from the City University Business School. His research interests are in the areas of international management development and international organizational change. His recent co-authored publications include *The International Manager* (Business Books 1991) and *Management Across Frontiers* (Ashridge Management Research Group – Foundation for Management Education 1992).

Peter Benkovič is a Research Scientist in the Institute of Creativity at the Slovak Academy of Sciences in Bratislava where he directs a funded research programme. He obtained his MA in psychology from Comenius University, Bratislava. His research interests include creativity in organizations and managing change through stimulating creativity and training.

Ariane Berthoin Antal is Director of the International Institute for Organizational Change, IOC-Ashridge in Archamps, France. Ariane obtained her BA in foreign languages from Pomona College, California, her MA in international relations from Boston University, and her doctorate from the Technical University of Berlin. Previously she was Senior Fellow at the Wissenschaftzentrum Berlin für Sozialforschung. Her research and consulting are international and focus on innovation in organizations and promoting individual and organizational learning. Her recent publications include *Comparative Policy Research: Learning from Experience* (edited with M. Dierkes and H. Weiler, Gower) and *Corporate Social Performance: Rediscovering Actors in their Organizational Contexts* (Campus Verlag).

Chris Brewster is Senior Lecturer in Human Resource Management at the Cranfield School of Management, Cranfield Institute of Technology. He has extensive experience in trade unions, government and management and consults widely on human resource management. Chris obtained his PhD from the London School of Economics. His research interests are in the areas of expatriation and international human resource management. He is currently directing a major research programme on strategic human resource management, assessing developments across Europe and a study of the development of human resource management in the Eastern Länder of Germany. His most recent publications include *The European Human Resource Management Guide* (co-editor, Academic Press 1992); *International Comparisons in Human Resource Management* (Pitman 1991), and *The Management of Expatriates* (Kogan Page 1991).

Jim Durcan is a Programme/Client Director at Ashridge Management College where he directs the Leadership Development Programme and the Leadership Across Frontiers Programme. Jim holds a BA (Hons) in economics from the University of Essex; an MSc in quantitative economics and econometrics from the University of Bristol; and an MA from Oxford University. His past research interests have included industrial conflict, collective bargaining structures, reward systems, and industrial relations power. He is co-author of *Strikes in Post-War Britain* (Allen & Unwin 1983) which remains the seminal work in the area. Currently his research interests are focused on issues of leadership in the European context; on empowerment and its implications for managerial roles and behaviour; and on strategic HRM and the development of a contingency model of the relationship between business strategy, human resource policies and practices and market performance.

Ariane Hegewisch is a Senior Researcher at the Centre for European Human Resource Management at the Cranfield School of Management. Ariane obtained her undergraduate economics degree from the London School of Economics and her MPhil from the Institute of Development Studies at the University of Sussex. Her research interests centre around European developments in the areas of remuneration policies, equal opportunity and flexible working practices. Her current research focuses on HRM developments in East Germany after reunification. She has recently co-edited the *European Human Resource Management Guide* (Academic Press 1992) and *Developments in European Human Resource Management* (Kogan Page 1993).

Chris Hendry is Principal Research Fellow and Associate Director of the Centre for Corporate Strategy and Change, Warwick Business School, University of Warwick. Chris holds a BA (Hons) in English from the University of London, an MSc in organization development from Sheffield City Polytechnic, and a PhD from the CNAA. His research interests are in the areas of human resource management, international business and small-medium firms. Chris is the author of *Human Resource Strategies for International Growth* (Routledge 1993) and co-author of a number of major reports including *The Processes of Internationalisation and the Implications for Human Resource Management* (Department of Employment 1992); *The Learning Organisation: A Review of Literature and Practice* (HRDP Partnership 1992); and *Human Resource Development in the Small-to-Medium Size Enterprise* (Department of Employment 1991).

Michael J. Kavanagh is Professor of Management, Organizational Studies, and Psychology at the State University of New York at Albany. Professor Kavanagh received his MS and PhD degrees in industrial psychology from Iowa State University. He is currently Editor of *Group & Organizational Management*. He has published over 100 articles in the fields of personnel/ human resource management and industrial/organizational psychology on a variety of topics. His research interests are performance appraisal, training, implementation of new technology, organizational change, international personnel and human resource management, and human resource information systems.

Paul S. Kirkbride is a Programme/Client Director at Ashridge Management College where he leads the academic team responsible for HRM, change and leadership. He is also a Visiting Professor at the University of Hertfordshire. Prior to joining Ashridge Paul held the British Aerospace Professorship of Organisation Development at the then Hatfield Polytechnic. He obtained both his Master's degree in industrial relations and his PhD in management from the University of Bath. His current research interests include strategic human resource management, international human resource management, international/cross-cultural management, organizational culture and organizational change and development. His research work has been published internationally in journals such as *Asia Pacific Human Resource Management*, *Industrial and Labor Relations Review*, *International Journal of Human Resource Management*, *Journal of Industrial Relations*, and *Organization Studies*. His forthcoming publications include *Cross-Cultural Human Resource Development* (McGraw-Hill).

Marián Kubeš is Director of the Institute of Creativity at the Slovak Academy of Sciences in Bratislava. He obtained his MA in educational psychology from Comenius University, Bratislava and his PhD in psychology from the Institute of Experimental Psychology, Slovak Academy of Sciences. His research interests include individual differences in cognitive styles in problem-solving and creativity, team building, and organizational development. Marián has standardized the Kirton Adaption-Innovation Inventory (KAI) on Slovak and Czech populations. His current research focuses on controversial issues in the field of human creativity. Marián has published in several professional journals and is an active trainer and consultant.

Christopher Leeds is Senior Lecturer in the Département d'Etudes Anglaises et Nord-Américaines at the University of Nancy II. Chris holds a BSc from the London School of Economics and an MA from the University of Southern California. His research interests cover international negotiations, cross-cultural management and French and British management comparisons. His recent publications include 'The French approach to handling conflicts and to negotiating' in P. Fenn and R. Gameson (eds) *Construction Conflict Management and Resolution* (E & F.N. Spon 1992) and 'Conflict theories, government policies and the urban riots of the early 1980s' in T.F. Marshall (ed.) *Community Disorders and Policing: Conflict Management in Action* (Whiting & Birch).

Bianka Lichtenberger is Senior Consultant (International Management Development) with Alusuisse Lonza Ltd in Zurich and a Visiting Professor in HRM at the Rotterdam School of Management. Until recently she was a Research Officer at the Enterprise and Management Development Branch of the International Labour Office (ILO), Geneva. Bianka obtained master's degrees in economics and sociology from the Universität Freiburg and the Economic University of Vienna before completing her PhD in international management at Universität Hamburg. Her research and consulting interests are in the areas of international human resource management, management development and industrial relations. Her recent publications include *Interkultuelle Mitarbeiterfuhrüng* (Intercultural Leadership, Stuttgart 1992) and *Unternehmensführung in Polen* (Management Development in Poland, Munich 1992).

Lesley Mayne is a Research Officer in the Centre for European Human Resource Management at the Cranfield School of Management. She has research interests in international human resource management and is currently working on a major research programme on strategic human resource management assessing developments across Europe.

Gérard Naulleau is an Associate Professor at ESCP (Ecole Supérieure de Commerce de Paris) and EAP (European School of Management, Paris). He graduated from the HEC School of Management, Jouy-en-Josas and obtained his PhD from the Paris Graduate School of Social Sciences (Ecole des Hautes Etudes en Sciences Sociales, Paris). His current research interests include comparative management in Europe and the management of international joint ventures. His publications have appeared in *Management Education and Development* and *Gérer et Comprendre*.

Joseph Prokopenko is Head of the Research and Programme Development Section, Entrepreneurship and Management Development Branch, at the International Labour Office (ILO) in Geneva. His PhD is in the area of international economics and management. He has worked extensively with the ILO and with the Academy of Sciences of the Ukranian SSR. His research interests cover structural adjustment, economic globalization, privatization, productivity improvement and human resource development. His recent publications include *Management Implications of Structural Adjustment* (1989), *Entrepreneurship Development in Public Enterprises* (1991), and *Human Resource Management in Economies in Transition* (1992).

Mike Regan is Group Personnel Director for Electrolux UK. Mike holds a BA in economics from Leeds University and is a Fellow of the Institute of Personnel Management. Mike began his career in the personnel function of

RHP Bearings Ltd. In 1976 he joined the North of England Engineering Employers' Association where he covered all aspects of industrial relations for some 300 member companies. After joining Thorn Lighting as Personnel Manager in 1982, Mike became Personnel Director of Thorn EMI Major Domestic Appliances in 1985. Following the acquisition by Electrolux of the Thorn white goods and commercial food service interests in 1987, he became Group Personnel Director for Electrolux UK in January 1988. Mike is active in executive management development programmes within Electrolux on an international basis.

Christian Scholz is Professor of Business Administration and Director of the Europa Institute at the University of Saarland in Saarbrucken where he teaches organizational behaviour and human resource management and is currently in charge of the MBA programme. Christian received his master's and doctoral degrees at the Regensburg University and has conducted research work at the Harvard Business School. His current research interests focus on corporate culture and international HRM. He has authored several books including *Strategisches Management* (de Gruyter 1987) and *Personal-management* (Vahlen 1993 – 3rd edition).

Hugh Scullion is Senior Lecturer in Human Resource Management and Director of the MA Human Resource Management Programme in the School of Business Management at the University of Newcastle upon Tyne. Hugh obtained a first class honours degree in political economy from Glasgow University and a master's in industrial relations from the University of Warwick. He spent six years researching workplace industrial relations at Warwick University's Industrial Relations Research Unit. His current research interests lie mainly in the field of international business, strategy, and human resource management. He is co-author of a major study on industrial conflict (*The Social Organization of Industrial Conflict*, Blackwell, 1982 – with P.K. Edwards) and has published widely on strikes and management strategy.

Jean Woodall is Reader in Human Resource Management at the Kingston Business School, Kingston University. Jean obtained both her undergraduate degree and PhD from the University of Manchester. Her research interests include management development in different cultures, women's managerial career development, education–industry links, and work-based learning. Jean has researched and published extensively on politics in Eastern Europe. Her most recent publication is *Case Studies in Personnel* (co-authored with D. Winstanley, IPM 1992)

Acknowledgements

The papers collected in this volume were mostly selected from those presented at the Third Conference on International Personnel and Human Resources Management held at Ashridge Management College in the summer of 1992.

The conference was sponsored by Ashridge in conjunction with the Department of Business Administration, University of Illinois, USA and the School of Business, Bond University, Queensland, Australia. The conference was the third in a worldwide series following Singapore in 1987 and Hong Kong in 1989. The Ashridge Conference was attended by over 130 participants from more than fifteen different countries.

The theme of the Conference was 'Human Resources Management in the New Europe of the 1990s' with particular focus on recent developments in both Western and Eastern Europe. This theme was addressed by the majority of the eighty plus papers presented in the Conference and also by invited plenary addresses from Dr Chris Brewster of Cranfield School of Management and Dr Joseph Prokopenko of the International Labour Office, who focused on Western and Eastern European developments respectively, and whose contributions are reproduced in this volume.

The standard of papers at the Conference was such that two volumes have emerged since. In addition to the present volume, a selection of more wide-ranging papers have been included in Shaw, J.B. and Kirkbride, P.S. (eds) *Research in Personnel and Human Resources Management – Supplement 3 – International Human Resources Management* (JAI Press 1993).

As lead organizer of the Conference and Editor of this volume I would like to take this opportunity to thank all those people (presenters, participants, and Ashridge staff) who made both the Conference and volume possible. A special vote of thanks is due to the following key individual contributors:

- Michael Osbaldeston (Chief Executive, Ashridge) and Peter Beddowes (Dean, Ashridge Management College) for institutional support and personal encouragement.
- Professor Kendrith ('Ken') Rowland (University of Illinois), the 'father' of this conference series, together with co-organizer Professor J.B. ('Ben')

Shaw (Bond University) for trusting me to organize the Conference and assisting so ably with the international co-ordination and reviewing of submissions.

- Dr Chris Brewster (Cranfield), Professor Paul Evans (INSEAD), and Dr Joseph Prokopenko (ILO) for excellent plenary addresses.
- Sara Crowe and Catherine Trew for their excellent administrative work and total dedication; Christine Brown and Virginia Merritt for their sterling marketing contributions; and Barbara Gregory for her typing and editorial work on this volume.
- Rosemary Nixon of Routledge for advice and encouragement.
- and, finally, to Judy, Daisy, Holly, and William for their patience with my continual disappearances to my study while working on this project.

Any errors or omissions remain entirely my own responsibility.

Paul Kirkbride, Ashridge 1993

Abbreviations

CEO	Chief executive officer
CIS	Commonwealth of Independent States
CPE	Centrally planned economy
EBA	European Business Analysis
EC	European Community
ECU	European Currency Unit
EMS	European Monetary System
EMU	Economic and Monetary Union
ERM	Exchange Rate Mechanism
EU92	Europe 92
EXEC	International Executive Programme
FE/HE	Further education/higher education
FGJV	Franco-German joint venture
FTE	Full time education
HCN	Host country national
HR	Human resource
HRD	Human resource development
HRIS	Human resource information system
HRM	Human resource management
IBL	International Business Leadership programme
IC	Impulse control
IE	Impulse expression
IJV	International joint venture
ILO	International Labour Organization
IOO	International Industrial Observatory
JV	Joint venture
KHF	Know-How Fund
LBDQ	Leadership Behavior Description Questionnaire
MBA	Master of Business Administration

METD	Management eduction, training and development
MIS	Management information system
MNC	Multinational company
NACE	Nomenclature des Activités dans la CEE
OD	Organization(al) development
ODA	Overseas Development Administration/Agency
PCN	Parent country national
PHARE	Poland and Hungary: Assistance for Economic Restructuring
PHRM	Personnel and human resource management
PWCP	Price Waterhouse Cranfield Project
R&D	Research and Development
RMC	Regional management centre
SEM	Single European Market
SME	Small-medium enterprise
SMS	Strategic management system
TCN	Third country national
TEMPUS	Trans-European Mobility Scheme for University Students
UA	Uncertainty avoidance
UNEDO	United Nations Economic Development Office
UNRRA	United Nations Relief and Rehabilitation Administration
VAT	Value added tax
VET	Vocational education and training
WOS	Wholly owned subsidiary

Introduction

Paul S. Kirkbride

INTRODUCTION

The title of this book, 'Human Resource Management in Europe', and the theme of the conference from which most of the contributions were drawn, 'Human Resources Management in the New Europe of the 1990s', both raise a series of interesting and not entirely semantic questions.

First, the use of the term 'Europe' begs the question as to what really constitutes Europe. There are, of course, a series of potential answers to this inquiry. Increasingly there has been a tendency to loosely use the term Europe to refer to the European Community (EC). This is not surprising in that the 36 years since the Treaty of Rome in 1957 have seen the Community expand from the initial six (Belgium, West Germany, France, Italy, Luxembourg and the Netherlands) via the additions of Denmark, Ireland and the United Kingdom (1973), Greece (1981), and Spain and Portugal (1986), to the current twelve as of 1993. The EC has come to dominate Western Europe in both economic and political terms during this period.

These trends have been reinforced by the EC decision in 1985 to create a Single European Market or a 'Europe without frontiers'. This came into effect on 31 December 1992 and aims to remove almost all physical, technical and fixed barriers to competition and internal trade. Closely associated with this initiative is the concept of the establishment of economic and monetary union (EMU) which would allow a single market to operate more efficiently via the development of a Community central bank and a common currency. Initially progress in this direction involved the establishment of the European Monetary System (EMS) and associated Exchange Rate Mechanism (ERM). The European Commission, under President Jacques Delors, envisaged a series of steps towards full EMU starting with the completion of the Single Market and moving, via a tightening of the ERM, to a system of fixed and locked exchange rates, and the establishment of a single currency. However, events during 1992 such as the near collapse of the ERM, the political furore over the failure of Denmark to ratify the Maastricht Treaty, and the United Kingdom's perceived delaying tactics over progress to EMU must cast some doubts on the suggested timetable for progress to EMU, if not on its final achievement.

A politically important aspect of the EC, particularly relevant to human resource management, is the social dimension represented by the Charter of Fundamental Social Rights and associated draft directives. Together these initiatives represent a move towards a comprehensive system of European employment law. It is therefore clear that the EC raises some pressing and far-reaching issues, problems, and opportunities for human resource practitioners. Some of these are discussed at length in this volume but, as examples, they would include the need for harmonization of employment conditions, the need to meet EC statutory requirements, dealing with increased cross border mobility (transfers and hiring), and the need to develop new 'pan-European' managers for pan-European organizational structures.

However, despite its comparative dominance, Europe should not be conflated with the EC. Several European countries including Norway, Sweden and Switzerland are currently not members of the EC, although some of these are, at the time of writing, considering membership. In addition, and perhaps more important, our conception of Europe has been greatly widened since the collapse of the Iron Curtain by the 'opening up' of what was previously Eastern Europe. Thus a greater Europe would now include countries such as Albania, Bulgaria, the Czech and Slovak Republics, Estonia, Hungary, Latvia, Lithuania, Poland, Romania, and the individual components of the former Yugoslavia. A wider definition would also include the individual components of the former USSR. The opening up of 'poorer' Eastern European countries has created a set of issues, problems and tensions, which have yet to be addressed and resolved, but are currently being perhaps most keenly felt in the new united Germany.

Europe then may be said to currently be in a state of flux. At the same time that Western Europe appears to be slowly, and rather unsurely, moving towards greater economic and political integration another very different integrated bloc has crumbled leaving a legacy of serious economic problems. The key issues for the countries of Eastern Europe to resolve include the transition to a market economy, the privatization of state industries, dealing with rising inflation, creating currency convertibility, maintaining productivity and avoiding hyper-unemployment. The implications and problems for human resource professionals in these countries are both urgent and stark.

A second definitional and semantic issue raised by the title of this volume concerns the use of the term 'human resource management' (HRM). This concept has become the subject of extensive, and often negative, theoretical debate in the academic literature (Blyton and Turnbull 1992) while at the same time spawning two recent journals (*Human Resource Management Journal* and *International Journal of Human Resource Management*). Indeed the debate has become so detailed and dense that one might consider elevating HRM to the level of an 'essentially contested' term (Lukes 1974). In the practitioner sphere, on the other hand, the term has been accepted fairly positively and without critical comment. Part of the debate concerns the applicability of what was originally an American map, model or theory (Noon

1992) to the European context. We are aware of this debate, which is dealt with in detail by Brewster in Chapter 5 of this volume, and would suggest that our use of the term in the title is in the general sense of 'the policies, procedures and processes involved in the management of people in work organizations' (Sisson 1990: 1) rather than in the narrower sense of the specifically American model (Beer *et al*. 1984).

The final semantic issue raised by the title of this volume is to what extent Europe represents a distinct context for the operation of HRM. Obviously we have already alluded to potential specificities in the economic and political spheres, but another major potential differentiator remains the cultural context. Here there are several questions. To what extent can we discern a pan-European culture and thus suggest that a pan-European model of HRM might emerge (Thurley and Wirdenius 1989) which would be distinctive from both American and Japanese models of HRM? Or is it the case that the countries of Europe are so culturally diverse that HRM becomes almost country specific? Or can one identify regions within Europe where sufficient cultural homogeneity exists to suggest that common patterns of HRM practice and approach may occur? These questions will be extensively debated in Part 1 of this volume.

OUTLINE OF THE BOOK

The papers collected in this volume are structured on a thematic basis. Others (cf. Brewster and Tyson 1991; Poole 1986) have taken a comparative approach to the study of human resource management. Such an approach yields pragmatic and managerial information about how different countries manage human resources as well as more academic insights into issues such as the forces for convergence and divergence. However such approaches are beset with a variety of theoretical and methodological problems including levels of analysis, choice of comparative subject matter, choice of countries, the cultural frameworks of the researcher(s), comparability of official statistics and the cultural appropriateness of different methodologies (Brewster and Tyson 1991: 5–9). In addition there are the simple logistic problems involved in liaison with international research partners, language issues, and agreeing appropriate research frameworks.

A recent example of work in a similar genre is provided by two special issues of *Employee Relations* edited by John Berridge and Ingrid Brunstein and dedicated to 'Human resource management in the European Community' (Berridge and Brunstein 1992a, b). Based on an HRM network generated by the 'Strasbourg Network' of thirty-eight management schools, contributors from ten of the countries in the EC (excluding, for a reason not specified, Belgium and Luxembourg) were invited to review HRM in their own countries. Contributors were asked to assess the current state of HRM, discuss the current problems of HRM, and forecast the future challenges facing HRM in their countries. It should be noted that they were not asked to

take an explicitly comparative approach. As the editors argue, the aim
was not:

> to give proof of a preconceived theory, according to which *the* European
> HRM shows certain contours or characteristics, or against which national
> systems could be evaluated for their conformity or divergence. Such a
> predetermined concept, or comparative plan, would have risked overly
> orienting the writers' approach or excessively influencing those ideas being
> read into their national 'story'. (Berridge and Brunstein 1992 a: 4)

Given the origins of this volume in a conference, a detailed comparative
approach was obviously inappropriate and a simple country approach risked
a lack of cohesion and integration. For these reasons a thematic structure was
adopted. Four key themes or sets of issues were identified. First, a crucial
issue, as noted by Brewster and Tyson (1991), is the cultural context against
which HRM operates in Europe. Second, recent developments in the EC have
created a large number of implications for human resource management and
HR managers. Third, the recent massive changes in Eastern Europe have
highlighted a large number of HR issues which are crucial to the development
of the newly liberated economies. Finally, given the spread of companies
across Europe and increasing moves to multinational and transnational status
by European organizations, there is the need to address the creation of a new
breed of 'pan-European' managers.

Part I focuses on the cultural context. Leeds, Kirkbride and Durcan
(Chapter 2) argue that Europe is divided by significant cultural differences
and suggest that the increasing moves towards economic and political
integration within Europe will have to contend with these cultural factors.
They argue that this diversity is compounded by the collapse of the Eastern
bloc and the potential assimilation of these cultures into a more widely
defined Europe. Leeds *et al.* review a number of key cultural dimensions and
locate individual countries at appropriate points. They then build upon this
analysis to produce a 'map' of six distinct 'cultural clusters' which can be
found within Europe (Anglo, Germanic, Latin-Mediterranean, Near Eastern,
Northern-Quasi-Latin, and Scandinavian). Durcan and Kirkbride (Chapter 3)
focus down to one aspect of managerial behaviour, leadership, and suggest
that existing leadership models and theories are largely the creation of the
cultural values of the American society in which they were mostly developed.
These American cultural values are then contrasted with those of two of the
European country cultural clusters; Mediterranean and Scandinavian. Durcan
and Kirkbride then attempt to tease out the outlines of culturally specific
Mediterranean and Scandinavian models of leadership. Lichtenberger and
Naulleau (Chapter 4) note that international joint ventures (IJVs) are a key
strategic form for the 1990s but suffer from a high failure rate which recent
studies have constantly attributed to the role played by human resource and
cultural factors. Their research work focuses on French–German joint ventures
and shows the clear cultural differences in the perceptions each partner has of

the other. Lichtenberger and Naulleau conclude by stressing the potential advantages of cultural diversity and the need for culturally synergistic arrangements within IJVs. Finally in Part I, Brewster (Chapter 5) attempts to address the vexed question of whether 'HRM' is different in Europe. He begins by reviewing the US origins of the concept and argues that it has two key elements: the existence of a considerable degree of independence to take personnel decisions and a close link between corporate strategic orientation and HRM activity. Brewster then draws upon evidence from his Price Waterhouse Cranfield Project on international strategic human resource management to test these elements in a European context. He suggests that organizational autonomy is untypical of most European countries as organizational HRM systems are constrained by a series of factors at national, organizational and HR levels. These factors include national culture, legislative framework, patterns of ownership and bargaining patterns. Brewster also suggests that the 'integration' of business strategy and HRM does occur in Europe but in a very different manner than that expected in the US literature. Finally he attempts to discern the outline of a 'European' approach to HRM which would 'embed' HR strategy more closely in the relevant environmental context.

Part II covers recent developments in the EC, although one chapter does include some data from non-EC European countries. Hendry (Chapter 6) focuses on the implications of the Single European Market (SEM) for HRM. He predicts an overall initial loss in jobs which obscures the fact that the EC will perhaps be divided into 'winners' (Belgium, Denmark, France, Ireland, Italy, Netherlands and Germany) and 'losers' (Greece, Spain and the United Kingdom). He identifies the pressures to adopt a 'high-skill' strategy and traces the failings of the UK in this area. Hendry also discusses the increased internationalization required by firms and the issue of the creation of either European or global firms. He sees UK firms as often being more global than European but generally supports the need for the development of a 'Euromanager' cadre. Hendry concludes pessimistically by arguing that the UK will continue to compete where its current competitive advantage lies: in low wage, labour intensive, low skill and low productivity sectors. Chapter 7 by Brewster, Hegewisch and Mayne uses data from the Price Waterhouse Cranfield database to answer the question: are HR practices converging within Europe? After a detailed review of data on pay, working practices, equal opportunities and training the authors conclude that national culture (defined widely to include economic circumstances, history, legislation and fixed policies) appears to be a better predictor of patterns of HR practice than either industrial sector or size of organization. Thus despite the pressures towards convergence from a developing European labour market, the influence of the EC, and the increasing number of European multinationals, it would appear that cultural factors are extremely resistant. Brewster *et al.* conclude that while there is increasing common understanding of key HR issues ('ends') there is considerable divergence in how different countries (and organizations within them) handle such issues ('means'). In Chapter 8 Kavanagh and Scholz point out that many US firms erroneously believed that the SEM would create a 'United States of Europe' with the implication that the HR policies and practices adopted by a subsidiary in one of the twelve countries could then be 'rolled-out' to the other eleven. As a rejection of this viewpoint Kavanagh and Scholz focus on the implications of the SEM for pan-European human resource information systems (HRIS). They argue that increased EC legislation will lead to an increased need for sophisticated HRIS but that there will be a series of technical difficulties in implementation. The authors agree with Brewster *et al.* (Chapter 7) that while EC directives will be common across Europe, they will be implemented in different ways depending, in part, on the nature of the cultural context. Kavanagh and Scholz identify two contrasting scenarios for the future. The first is where national cultural differences cause serious problems and result in the adoption of only basic HRIS in firms. The second, which the authors lean towards, is where the pressures of the SEM and associated legislation override the cultural problems and lead to the adoption of sophisticated HRIS by European companies.

Part III deals with the developments in the former Eastern European bloc. Prokopenko (Chapter 9) focuses generally on Eastern European restructuring and the implications for HRM. He seeks to differentiate between Eastern Europe and 'the West' in terms of a model of stages of HRM development. Prokopenko sees Eastern Europe as achieving the first stage of 'initiation' and, potentially, the second stage of 'functional growth', while some Western organizations are seen as progressing through the third and fourth steps of 'controlled growth' and 'functional integration' towards the final stage of 'strategic integration'. Prokopenko then seeks to document this judgement by characterizing personnel management in Eastern Europe in terms of activities such as selection, remuneration, performance appraisal and trade unionism. He concludes by arguing that the key problem for Eastern Europe is a lack of managerial competence and therefore the key HR issue is a need for management development. As management development in Eastern Europe is currently seen as didactic, non-strategic, centralized and unsophisticated, Prokopenko identifies the need for Western assistance. Woodall (Chapter 10) picks up this need but questions the simple transfer of Western European (and American) management education, training and development to Eastern Europe. Her chapter focuses in particular on the British Know-How Fund (KHF) and developments in Hungary and Poland. Woodall argues that Western 'best practice' has generally not been transferred because needs have not been identified; programmes focus on importing knowledge; little attention is paid to learning transfer or preferred learning styles; little use is made of Eastern European materials; and too much emphasis is placed on visits to the West. She argues that the conception of management is very different in Eastern Europe and that such an understanding is a prerequisite for designing management education, training and development initiatives in Eastern Europe. In Chapter 11, Kubeš and Benkovič present the view from the recipients of such technology transfer. Their chapter reviews the history of HRM in Czechoslovakia and attempts to predict future trends in the newly-created Czech and Slovak Republics. They note that the paucity of management training has created an influx of HR 'messiahs' from the West offering various 'quick fix' solutions. They echo Woodall's point concerning the need to develop indigenous approaches to training and development as well as suggesting the need to develop a theory of the emerging HRM system in Eastern Europe.

Part IV deals with the creation of a cadre of 'pan-European' managers. Scullion (Chapter 12) reports data from an empirical study of forty-five British and Irish organizations in relation to the recruitment of international managers. He finds a heavy, and increasing, use of expatriates to run foreign operations. Reasons given for this surprising finding include the lack of skilled local managers, the need to control the subsidiary, and the need to maintain international trust and credibility. Scullion also reports that 70 per cent of his sample predict future shortages of international managers. He then reports how this sample have attempted to resolve this shortage including; better identification of potential international managers; attraction of more graduates to international trainee positions; the use of specialist international management development programmes; and the use of language training. Regan (Chapter 13) provides a case example of how Electrolux have attempted to use training and development initiatives to create a global management capability to deliver a corporate globilization strategy. In his discussions Regan notes the common 'lag' between strategic change and the development of required managerial capability. He also notes the need to explicitly identify and address cultural differences which exist within the business. He concludes by stressing the need for the global corporation to maximize the advantages of cultural diversity and create cultural synergy. Finally, Barham and Berthoin Antal (Chapter 14) focus on the competences required by the various types of international managers in multinational and transnational companies. From a quantitative research study in a number of major corporations from around the world, they identify two distinct sets of competences. The first, referred to as 'doing', cover what successful international managers appear to do which is different. Here Barham and Berthoin Antal discuss the activities of championing international strategy; operating as a cross-border coach and coordinator; acting as an intercultural mediator and change agent; and managing personal effectiveness for international business. The second set of competences, referred to as 'being', cover the personal characteristics of successful international managers and consist of cognitive complexity, emotional energy, and psychological maturity. Barham and Berthoin Antal conclude, in line with Scullion (Chapter 12), that the potential shortage of international managers can be resolved by training and development, but only if such development is long term, organizationally focused and involves appropriate experience.

REFERENCES

Beer, M., Spector, B., Lawrence, P., Mills, Q. and Walton, R. (1984) *Managing Human Assets*, New York: Free Press.

Berridge, J. and Brunstein, I. (eds) (1992a) Human resource management in the European Community – Part 1, *Employee Relations* 14:4.

—— (1992b) Human resource management in the European Community – Part 2, *Employee Relations* 14:5.

Blyton, P. and Turnbull, P. (eds) (1992) *Reassessing Human Resource Management*, London: Sage.

Brewster, C. and Tyson, S. (eds) (1991) *International Comparisons in Human Resource Management*, London: Pitman.

Lukes, S. (1974) *Power: A Radical View*, London: Macmillan.

Noon, M. (1992) 'HRM: A map, model or theory?', in Blyton, P. and Turnbull, P. (eds) *Reassessing Human Resource Management*, London: Sage pp. 16–32.

Poole, M. (1986) *Industrial Relations: Origins and Patterns of National Diversity*. London: Routledge.

Sisson, K. (1990) 'Introducing the Human Resource Management Journal', *Human Resource Management Journal* 1(1):1–11.

Thurley, K. and Wirdenius, H. (1989) *Towards European Management*, London: Pitman.

Part I
The cultural context

2 The cultural context of Europe

A tentative mapping

Christopher Leeds
Paul S. Kirkbride
Jim Durcan

INTRODUCTION

The importance of the cultural aspect of European unity is becoming increasingly recognized. Jean Monnet before his death is reputed to have said that if he had known its significance earlier he would have focused initially on the cultural rather than the economic aspects of creating European unity. Unconscious identity with one's own cultural values has been identified as the root cause of most international business problems (Ronen 1986: 31).

In this chapter it is contended that important culture differences divide Europe and that this fact is significant in relation to harnessing the diverse qualities of different parts of both the EC and of the wider Europe in order to create closer economic and business cooperation. Important differences exist
· between the northern and southern components of what is commonly referred to as Western Europe and between the various parts of what was once the Eastern European communist bloc. Unfortunately the difficulties of research access since the Second World War has meant that much more is known about cultural differences in the former as opposed to the latter.

Many of the seminal studies on culture, which are relevant for our purposes, have come from sociologists or anthropologists. The culture of a group has been defined as the rules for interaction in different situations, and additionally as an instrument used for solving universal problems in a special way according to local environment needs (Peabody 1986: 214–15). It has also been expressed as the special 'collective programming of the mind of members of a group, which is reflected in its particular assumptions, perceptions, thought patterns, norms and values' (Hofstede 1991: 8). Values are considered particularly significant in terms of the tendency of individuals (considered collectively as a culture) to prefer certain conditions or state of affairs to others.

Individuals acquire values as part of the general socialization process involved in growing up in a country, region, and family group. Values are associated with the national culture of a country as boundaries encourage interaction and socialization within them. However, the movement of peoples across national boundaries, the periodic changing of frontiers, the preservation by particular groups of a culture different from the mainstream culture, and differences in social and economic experience mean that subcultures exist in all countries. Consequently, whatever are described as the mainstream cultural traits are best considered as a central tendency or average. Individuals will differ in the extent to which they share the values associated with any particular country.

This chapter reviews a number of studies which have sought to identify and describe the key dimensions of cultural difference. Further, it considers the extent to which national cultural values integrate and differentiate European countries one from another. The studies reviewed include those of Hall (1959, 1976); Hall and Hall (1990); Hofstede (1980, 1985, 1991, 1992), Laurent (1983, 1986), Mole (1990) and Trompenaars (1988). Our aim is to increase our understanding of cultural differences and similarities within Europe and to sensitize us to potential cultural pitfalls as well as opportunities for potential cultural synergies.

Context and time

One of the major contributions to our understanding of cultural differences is that made by Hall (1959, 1976) who drew attention to the difference between the nature of low context and high context societies. Context refers to 'the information that surrounds an event; it is inextricably bound up with the meaning of that event' (Hall and Hall 1990: 6). Cultures can be compared on a scale from high to low context.

> A high context (HC) communication or message is one in which *most* of the information is already in the person, while very little is in the coded, explicit, transmitted part of the message. A low context (LC) communication is just the opposite; i.e., the mass of information is vested in the explicit code. Twins who have grown up together can and do communicate more economically (HC) than two lawyers in a courtroom during a trial (LC), a mathematician programming a computer, two politicians drafting legislation, two administrators writing a regulation.
>
> (Hall 1976 quoted in Hall and Hall 1990: 6 – emphasis in original)

Low context peoples, such as Americans, Germans, Swiss, Scandinavians and other Northern Europeans, appreciate explicit, clear, written forms of communication, as provided by computers, books, reports and letters. In contrast, high context peoples, such as the Japanese, Arabs and Southern Europeans, divulge less information officially in written forms, but tend to be better informed than low context people, since they develop extensive informal networks for exchanging information verbally face to face or by telephone. High context people are also more adept in interpreting non-verbal aspects of communication, and seeing the significance of what is implicit or not said, pauses, silence, tone, and other subtle signals. Information is also said to spread unofficially more rapidly in high context countries.

Hall also draws attention to the fact that conceptions of time differ cross-culturally. Low context peoples are generally monochronic in that they are used to doing one activity at a time, and are task based, wanting to complete deadlines and schedules, and disliking interruptions. Punctuality is valued and time economized. For very monochronic peoples such as the North Americans and Germans, lateness for an appointment suggests a deliberate slight to the other party. High context peoples are generally polychronic. They may do many things at the same time and do not mind being interrupted, particularly if family or social problems are involved. High context peoples tend to have a more relaxed view of time and often a non-linear time perspective. As a result punctuality and attention to small increments of time becomes of lesser importance. Low context peoples would define lateness in terms of a small number of minutes whereas high context peoples may define it as a longer period of minutes or even in terms of hours.

Low context peoples tend not to mix work and social topics when in negotiations, and to compartmentalize their work and personal relationships. High context peoples are more flexible or elastic in the management of their work or that of others. Business and pleasure may be mixed, and time spent on rapport-building during meetings. In such circumstances it is argued that deadlocks in business will not be broken nor problems solved unless people allow time to develop correct interpersonal relations. Once these are attained, it becomes easier to solve technical problems. Engagements and agendas at meetings may be modified quickly as circumstances change.

Hall attempted to 'map' various countries on his low-high context dimension and subsequent researchers have tended to accept Hall's original positioning with few modifications. It is noticeable that Northern European countries such as Denmark, Germany and Holland are low context, Southern European countries are high context and Britain and France are in a mid position, being partly low and high context (see Table 2.1).

Misunderstandings can easily arise between high context Southerners and low context Northerners in Europe if allowances are not made for their

Table 2.1 Locating low and high context cultures

Country	High context	Low context
West Germany		xxxx
German Swiss		xxxx
Scandinavian		xxx
North America		xxx
Belgium, Holland, Denmark		x
France	x	
Great Britain	xx	
Southern European	xxx	
Middle East	xxx	
Asia, Africa, Latin America	xxx	
Japan	xxxx	

different approaches to communication. While the Southerner may be more volatile, impatient and talkative than the Northerner, he or she may give less concrete information when involved in business communications, and only short replies to questions, assuming that the Northerner is better informed than they actually are with background information. Northerners may, as a result, feel they have received insufficient answers. In the reverse situation, the Northerner may appear long-winded to the Southerner, giving more facts and figures than the latter considers necessary. If a North European does not receive a fairly quick answer to a business proposal he or she may assume the other party is not interested. In Southern Europe, including France, where people take time to consider projects, it might indicate the reverse. On the other hand a Northern failure to reinforce the proposal by informal contacts might be taken as a signal of lack of interest in the South.

However, in terms of overall communication, Southerners may appear long-winded to the Northerner since they may indulge in indirect, roundabout explanations accompanied by stories and much embellishment. The Northerner, preferring more 'down to earth' communication, may be regarded by the Southerner as too abrupt. Low context peoples are more able to separate criticism or corrective feedback from themselves whereas high context people may take it more personally. Consequently more time is needed in effective discussion to ensure a person is accorded respect and 'face'.

Hofstede's four dimensions

Perhaps the major contribution to the 'mapping' of cultural values on a worldwide scale was that of Hofstede (1980). From a factor analysis of his extensive database of 116,000 IBM respondents over two time periods he was able to delineate four dimensions which seemed to identify key cultural differences. These dimensions were: power distance (low to high); uncertainty avoidance (weak to strong); individualism/collectivism; and masculinity/femininity. His empirical data allowed countries to be scored and located on each of these four dimensions. Table 2.2 shows the scores on all four dimensions for all the Western European countries in his data sample.

The power distance index (low to high) measures 'the extent to which the members of a society accept that power in institutions and organizations is distributed unequally' (Hofstede 1985: 347). In all Northern European EC countries (Denmark, Ireland, Germany, Netherlands, and the UK) as well as other non-EC Northern European countries (Finland, Norway, Sweden), Hofstede's findings were that power distances were relatively small. The consequences for organizations in such societies are that one can expect to find flattish hierarchies; bureaucracy minimized; tasks delegated; a belief that power should be used legitimately; consultative management styles; and a degree of autonomy for subordinates (Hofstede 1991: 27–8).

Table 2.2 Scores of European countries on Hofstede's cultural dimensions

Country	Power distance	Uncertainty avoidance	Individualism/ collectivism	Masculine/ feminine
Denmark	18	23	74	16
Finland	33	59	63	25
France	68	86	71	43
Greece	60	112	35	57
Ireland	28	35	70	68
Italy	50	75	76	70
Norway	31	50	69	8
Portugal	63	104	27	31
Spain	57	86	51	42
Sweden	31	29	71	5
Turkey	66	85	37	45
UK	35	35	89	66
Mean*	51	64	51	51

Source: Hofstede 1980: 315
Note: * These values represent the means of the scores of the 39 countries in Hofstede's original
survey.

Hofstede found that EC countries in Southern Europe (France, Greece, Italy, Portugal, Spain) had large or medium power distances (Hofstede 1991: 141). Characteristics of high power distance organizations include: steep hierarchies; autocratic, directive or paternalist management; special privileges and status symbols for senior staff; and an ambivalent attitude of employees to management. While subordinates tend to have a dependency relationship with superiors, being afraid to disagree with them, they sometimes reject managers they disrespect; a behaviour which Hofstede calls counter-dependence (Hofstede 1991: 27).

Hofstede defines uncertainty avoidance (from strong to weak) as society's fear of the unknown and the extent to which 'a culture programs its members to feel either uncomfortable or comfortable in unstructured and ambiguous situations' (Hofstede 1992: 6). Characteristics of low uncertainty avoidance (UA) societies, which include Denmark, Holland, Ireland and the UK, are: tolerance of differing views; limited influence of experts; informality; few rules; control of one's emotions (Hofstede 1991: 111–12).

These values are expressed in British organizations by a preference for those managers who are outward-going, decisive and practical and geared towards action or taking decisions fairly rapidly. Less store has been placed on intellectual skills, qualifications or specialism. The Danish, like the British, are reputed to be decisive and action-oriented, not taking too long to seek alternatives when discussing problems or making decisions (Schramm-Nielsen 1991: 68–9).

The Germans, in contrast to the British and Danes, tend to be high on uncertainty avoidance, as reflected in the importance given in business to expert advice, qualifications, thoroughness, order, and detailed rules. All Southern European countries (France, Greece, Italy, Portugal, and Spain)

rank high on uncertainty avoidance, indicating a desire for minimizing ambiguity and anxiety and to control the future. Characteristics of high uncertainty avoidance societies include emphasis on laws and rules to cover all eventualities, safety and security measures, desire for long careers in the same business, and focus on formal procedures (Hofstede 1991: 116). Hofstede points out that the need for rules and laws in Latin countries can lead to the growth of nonsensical or dysfunctional rules. People seem less concerned about what happens in reality since some rules are only formally followed having been divested of any practical meaning (Hofstede 1991: 121). Businessmen from weak UA countries may not enjoy coping with numerous rules, petty or rigid, that they may experience in strong UA countries, even if many of them are not actually followed by the indigenous population. This can cause problems in merger or joint venture situations.

Hofstede defines individualism as societies where ties are loose, where everyone is expected to care for himself/herself and immediate family only, and where emphasis is placed on individual achievement, identity and decision-making. Managers prefer to keep a distance from subordinates both professionally and personally. Organizations exert control by inducing 'guilt' feelings in potential violators of rules. Hofstede describes collectivist cultures as associated with strong extended family units, individual dependence on the group which protects members in exchange for loyalty, a strong 'in-group' – 'out-group' dichotomy; and sophisticated networks and alliances (relations, close friends and associates) which bind 'in-groups'. Key values include achieving harmony at work, consensus in meetings, face-saving in work and social situations, and group decision-making. Inducing 'shame' is a means of group control over individuals who may violate group norms. People are high context and polychronic and motivated by involvement in achieving group aims rather by seeking self-advancement. In Hofstede's findings, all of Western Europe is individualist except Portugal and Greece, with the UK being ranked as the second highest individualist country worldwide after the USA (Hofstede 1991: 53).

The masculinity–femininity dimension is the only one for which Hofstede claims a significant difference exists between the scores of men and women. In masculine countries he argues that gender roles tend to be fairly strictly demarcated and that stereotypically male values such as competitiveness, individual advancement, materialism, profit, assertiveness, strength and action-focused activities tend to be appreciated. Masculine countries in his data sample include Germany, Greece, Italy, Spain, and the UK. In feminine countries (Denmark, Finland, Norway, Portugal, and Sweden) more appreciation is given to stereotypically female values such as cooperation, warm relationships, caring and nurturing, the quality of life, while less differentiation exists between male and female roles.

Some commentators have criticized the use of the terms masculinity–femininity, preferring concepts such as 'tough' and 'tender' or 'assertive' and 'nurturing'. Trompenaars has developed a similar dimension called achievement ('doing') versus ascription ('who you are'). His findings regarding this dimension tend to confirm Hofstede's results on Europe regarding masculinity–femininity (Wheatley and Bing 1992).

The systematic–organic dimension

The systematic–organic dimension is based on the extent to which people believe that prescribed relationships or a rational order should be applied regarding human behaviour and organizations. The terms 'systematic'(or 'mechanistic') and 'organic' have appeared intermittently in the management literature since at least the early 1960s (cf. Burns and Stalker 1961) and have been extensively used in organizational analysis (Morgan 1986).

When people react 'systematically' an organization is regarded rather like a machine, and loyalty to the organization prevails over loyalty to members. A close correlation exists between the formal system, stipulated official rules and procedures, and what actually happens. Features include methodical planning, keeping to schedules, following agendas in meetings, and precise job definitions. Competence and professionalism is considered important for managers whose authority or power will derive largely from their particular function or specialism. A manager will not be expected to offer advice outside his particular role or responsibility. People may compete by trying to out-perform others.

When people react 'organically' an organization is seen rather as a social organism which develops according to circumstances and needs of members. Informal rules or unwritten codes are more significant than official practices in determining reality. Features include: vague job definitions, informal communication, fostering of private alliances based on trust and mutual obligation, minimization of 'red tape' opportunism and improvization. Many official rules may exist, often of a detailed nature, but these tend to be applied, avoided or modified in practice according to what is considered best for the organization or its members.

In 'organic' societies order and control tends to be based on personal influence and power, the latter coming less from a person's competence or role, but from his position in the hierarchy. Managers have a high standing in society and it is accepted that they might offer advice outside their particular function. People are status-conscious, use power for personal ends and compete through outmanoeuvring others (Mole 1990: 169).

The systematic/organic distinction has recently surfaced as one key dimension of European cultural difference (Mole 1990: 188). The other dimension utilized by Mole is one of leadership.

The leadership dimension is based on the extent to which it is believed that power is given by groups to individuals. This form of words was carefully chosen to reflect that a leader's authority, at least in a European business organisation, can only be exercised with the consent of the people who are being managed. The values associated with followership are identical to those associated with leadership. The spectrum of belief about leadership ranges from individual to group.

(Mole 1990: 167)

Individual leadership can generally be seen as a directive, authoritarian, top-down and autocratic form of leadership where power is seen as a right to be exercised by superiors over inferiors, while group leadership is seen as a participative, egalitarian, bottom-up, and democratic style where everyone has a right to be heard and to contribute. Using these two dimensions, Mole has constructed a 'map' of the European cultural terrain (see Figure 2.1). According to this 'map' Mediterranean European countries are clustered on the left ('organic') side while Northern European countries are generally clustered towards the right ('systematic') side.

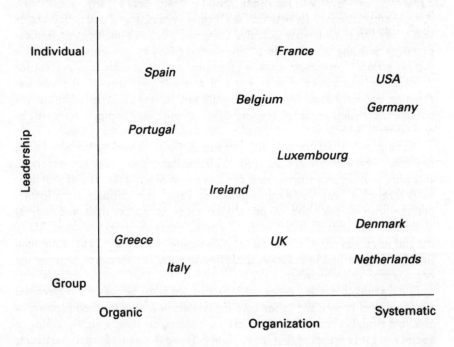

Figure 2.1 The Mole map of Europe

Universalism and particularism

Universalism and particularism are concepts which are fairly well established in the cross-cultural literature (Adler 1986). Universalism (societal obligation) implies that people generally apply the same rules, standards, or act in a similar manner towards other members of society whatever the circumstances. No rigid distinction tends to be made between the public or private domain or between 'in-group' (family and close friends) and 'out-group' relations. In such 'inclusive' cultures everyone is considered a potential friend or enemy to a higher degree than in particularist 'exclusive' cultures. Both the United States and the UK have been cited as good examples of countries where universalistic norms apply (Peabody 1985: 208).

Particularism (personal obligation) implies that people operate different codes depending with whom they are dealing. They operate two codes, one governing behaviour within the private domain (relations, close friends, and associates) and another governing relationships with others. In societies which make important or rigid 'in-group'/'out-group' distinctions such as Greece, Italy and to a lesser extent France, outsiders may be regarded with suspicion or mistrust (Barzini 1968: 205; Fleury 1990: 129; Peabody 1985: 139–40). Within such cultures (universalistic) rules, as created by the State, or any other organization or body, may be modified according to circumstances or situations, by people acting on a particularistic basis. It is this value which illuminates the apparent paradox in high uncertainty avoidance cultures of having a plethora of rules and then ignoring them.

Some interesting data on this dimension are provided by the work of Fons Trompenaars (Trompenaars 1988; Wheatley and Bing 1992). Trompenaars gathered data from plants of the Royal Dutch/Shell Group in five countries, from five hosiery organizations in different countries, and, later, he used the same questions in a survey involving over fifty countries worldwide. One of the questions Trompenaars asked relates to whether a bystander in a car accident should modify or not his testimony to support his friend the car driver or the killed pedestrian. The most and least universalistic countries in this respect in descending order were Germany, UK, Holland, Italy, Belgium, France and Spain (Wheatley and Bing 1992). The total scores for this dimension based on an earlier survey of nine countries were as follows in descending degree of universalism: USA 73 per cent; Holland 65 per cent; Sweden 61 per cent; Austria 63 per cent; Italy 57 per cent; Singapore 50 per cent; Greece 49 per cent; Spain 38 per cent; Venezuela 35 per cent (Trompenaars 1988: 86). These data support an assertion that in general terms Northern European countries tend to universalism while Southern European countries tend towards particularism.

Diffuseness and specificity

The diffuseness–specificity dimension refers to the scope or extent of a person's involvement in a relationship. Diffuse relations occurs when the actors involve various levels of their personality simultaneously. In contrast specific relation patterns describe interaction when only one specific aspect of the actor's personality is involved (Trompenaars 1988: 66). Trompenaars links specificity and diffuseness to Kurt Lewin's U-type and G-type personalities. U-types have only a very small private zone and so interactions between such people are relatively easily established as the private zone is swiftly transcended. Because the U-type personality can easily separate private from non-private matters, he or she is more open to interactions with relatively unknown actors with whom he or she shares specific interests. U-types have expectations of easy open access to others' thoughts and intentions.

Interaction between G-types are more difficult at first because the private zones are large, and so personal layers may be involved early on in a relationship. However, once relationships are established, they are likely to be relatively intimate involving diffuse aspects of the interacting individuals. Establishing these relations require significant investments of time and attention. The findings of Trompenaars on this dimension tend to reinforce broadly the North–South Europe distinction with the Dutch and British operating a specific orientation and Latin countries such as Italy, France, and Belgium (plus Germany) preferring diffuse relationships (Wheatley and Bing 1992).

Numerous publications have testified to a difference between Northern Europeans and Southern Europeans in business dealings, such as meetings and negotiations. For businessmen from Southern European and Mediterranean countries the personal side of relationships, establishing a degree of rapport, intimacy or friendliness before deals or contracts are concluded, is more important than for their Northern counterparts. The latter may be concerned merely with the technical or legal aspects. The Scandinavian countries with their low 'masculinity' scores and egalitarian cultures might be said to show aspects of both styles.

The neutrality–affectivity dimension

The neutrality–affectivity dimension as defined by Trompenaars assesses the degree of emotional involvement in face to face contacts. At work do you want people around who are friendly or trustworthy or those you can count on to help you do your job and who can be relied upon to do theirs? His results showed that those respondents who preferred 'task-focused' colleagues were first Germans, and in descending order France, UK, Holland, Spain and Italy (Wheatley and Bing 1992).

The neutrality–affectivity dimension overlaps partially with the dimension impulse control–impulse expression. Northern Europeans have been described as having 'impulse control' (IC) cultures where people control their sentiments, feelings or emotions, especially in public. Southern Europeans, generally more expressive and volatile, have been described as 'impulsive expression' (IE) cultures. The Germans, who have few inhibitions about expressing their sentiments, are also IE while the French, influenced by Cartesian standards, are described as a controlled IE culture (Peabody 1985: 211). The findings of Peabody may not conflict with those of Trompenaars. They may merely reflect another aspect of the neutrality–affectivity dimension not covered in the latter's research. Similarity of values does not necessarily produce similarity of behaviour. Numerous observers of Anglo–French business relations have remarked that the control of emotion and hostility is partly exercised by the British through smiling or being humorous in public, and by the French and Italians through a code of formal politeness.

Other cultural differentiators

Many other authors have sought to explore inter-European cultural differences, but empirical studies are relatively rare. Laurent (1986) conducted research based on questionnaires completed by middle and senior level managers following courses at INSEAD, Versailles, France. His research focused more on behaviours and attitudes than values. A question concerning the need for a superior to have precise answers to questions subordinates might ask produced the levels of agreement shown in Table 2.3. The high scores in agreement amongst French and Italian managers may reflect their reputation for being more directive and less willing to delegate than Danish or British managers, or for a preference to create dependency or paternalist relationships.

Table 2.3 Should a superior have precise answers for the questions subordinates might ask?

Country	% agreement
Japan	77
France	59
Italy	59
Belgium	59
West Germany	40
United Kingdom	30
Denmark	27
Holland	18
Sweden	13
USA	13

Source: Laurent 1986

Another of Laurent's findings showed Italian and French managers expressing numerically greater disagreement than German, Danish or British managers with the statement regarding the need to bypass the hierarchy often to achieve work efficiency (Laurent 1983: 82). This has been interpreted that the French and Italians appear more conformist or inflexible than their Northern counterparts (Adler 1986). In reality the replies of the French and Italians may reflect conflict-avoiding strategies of managers used to higher power distance bureaucracies and reluctance to admit the widespread prevalence of informal or unofficial practices. While the French feel the need for directions, rules, dependence within a formal system, a characteristic of high conflict avoidance countries, they are also noted for counterdependence, ability to bend the rules, modify plans, autonomy, and non-conformism within the informal system (Gauthey and Xardel 1990: 75; Hofstede 1991: 27).

Laurent's conclusions as a result of the findings of a series of questions was that French and Italians saw their role and relation to the hierarchy more in a social and personal sense, and they believed building up power was important and networking within the informal system. The British and Danes took a more functional interpretation of their role (Laurent 1983: 82–3). This latter interpretation would be supported by the universalist–particularist values described earlier.

EUROPEAN COUNTRY CLUSTERS

Our analysis of dimensions of cultural difference has perhaps demonstrated that on most dimensions countries are not spaced equally, but instead form clusters. This has been noted by several of the leading commentators on culture and comparative management (Hofstede 1980, 1991; Ronen 1986). We would suggest that it is perhaps at the level of the country cluster that cultural differences have their greatest explanatory power.

Some writers, however, have over-generalized, for example in grouping all Western countries as individualist (Koopman 1991: 10). Yet one blunt but informative distinction is the difference, noted by many commentators, between a Northern European cluster and a Southern European cluster (Madariaga 1952: 61). Fleury (1990: 128), for example, divides up Europe with a line which crosses France around Paris, cuts south down the eastern border of France, through northern Italy and up north across what was northern Yugoslavia. Thus the northern part of France is seen as more similar to the Northern Europe cluster while the bulk of France is seen as Southern European. Fleury observes that it is easier for marketing staff based in Paris, culturally speaking, to adjust to Cologne, London or Brussels than to Marseilles or Bordeaux.

Some form of intermediate zone has been suggested between the Nordic countries and the Latin/Mediterranean countries. The intermediate zone would include, for certain purposes, UK, Germany, parts of France, Italy, while for other purposes UK and Germany are in the North, Italy in the South with France straddling all three (Usunier 1992: 203).

Thus we can argue that one can distinguish some key differentiators between Northern and Southern Europe based on the cultural dimensions that we have already discussed (see Table 2.4). Naturally there are exceptions to this overall pattern which would include the fact that Germany tends to be high on uncertainty avoidance, impulse expression, and diffuseness in relationships; that Italy is seen as both individualist and collectivist by different commentators; the fact that France and the UK are both intermediate in terms of low–high context, and the fact that the Scandinavian countries are all high on femininity and relationship building.

If we go beyond the crude North–South dichotomy we can distinguish a

Table 2.4 Differences between Northern and Southern Europe

Researchers	The North	The South
E.T. Hall	Low context/monochronic	High context/polychronic
	Task-focused	People-focused
Trompenaars	Achievement	Ascriptive
Hofstede	Individualism	Collectivism
Hofstede	Low uncertainty avoidance	High uncertainty avoidance
Hofstede	Low power distance	High power distance
Mole	Systematic	Organic
Trompenaars	Specific relationships	Diffuse relationships
Trompenaars	Neutral relationships	Affective relationships
	Low contact	High contact
Peabody	Impulse control	Impulse expression
Trompenaars	Universalism	Particularism
	Inclusive societies	Exclusive societies

number of reasonably clear country clusters (see Fig. 2.2) which parallel the work of other commentators (Ronen 1986). These would include:

1 Scandinavian: Denmark, Finland, Norway, and Sweden.
2 Anglo: Ireland and the UK in Europe but also other English-speaking countries such as Australia, New Zealand and Canada (excluding Quebec), and the United States.
3 Germanic: Austria, Germany, and Switzerland.
4 Latin and Mediterranean: Italy, Portugal, and Spain.
5 Near Eastern: Greece and Turkey. The Turks and Greeks are close culturally, and both are proud of their European and Oriental associations. However the Greeks have also been considered very close to the Italians culturally.
6 Northern (quasi) Latin: France and Belgium have frequently been placed in a separate cluster of two. However, France, is often also put in the Latin and Mediterranean group.
7 Miscellaneous. Regions such as Alsace (France), the Flemish and German-speaking Belgium and countries such as Luxembourg are difficult to categorize. They possess their own special identity as well as cultural traits based on national identity, and are also influenced by values from neighbouring countries such as Holland and Germany. Holland, not included in many cluster studies, has been placed in the Nordic group (Ronen 1986: 257), yet also shares many of the traits associated with the Anglo group.

Naturally no one country or cluster group possesses cultural traits which are unique since traits found in one area of the world may be found, to a lesser or greater extent, elsewhere. No country or group is mutually exclusive in this respect, but is linked, regarding values and behavioural patterns, as in a series of concentric circles, with other parts of Europe or elsewhere.

The origins or reasons for the cluster groupings can be speculatively

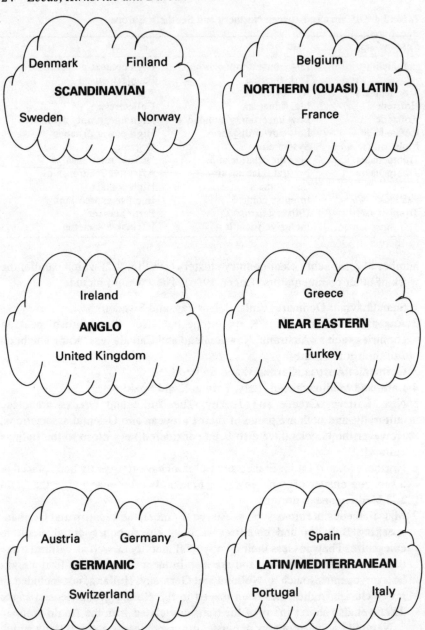

Figure 2.2 Cultural clusters in Europe

explained by a range of factors or influences sometimes reaching back into the distant past, including history, religion, topography, language, colonization and immigration patterns. The Near Eastern cluster can be explained by the similar colonizing experiences of Iran, Turkey and Greece, which shared in different degrees, the effects of the Empires built by ancient Persia, Alexander the Great and the Turks. The use of national units for clustering purposes is considered logical because national borders delineate legal, political and social environments within which organizations and workers function (Ronen 1986: 255).

General labels associated with large parts of Northern Europe are: Protestantism and puritanism; harsh or cool climates linked to ideas of struggle and activity; patriarchal attitudes; centrifugal tendencies; autonomy and voluntarism; producing things and commercial activities. The 'small power distance' cultural feature of much of Northern Europe may be due to the influence of German tribes noted for organizational patterns associated with flat hierarchies and closeness, and contact with small groupings.

Southern Europe, in contrast, is associated with: Catholicism (except in Greece); a warm climate; with emphasis placed on artistic activities; enjoyment or the 'quality of life' or on 'being' or consuming rather than 'doing' or producing. Less individualism prevails since people depend more on each other as a result of centripetal forces and matriarchal attitudes. Extended families are more important and also private networks of friends and associates. Islam was an important influence in parts of Southern Europe until the fifteenth century, and earlier the impact of the Roman Empire there was far greater than in Northern Europe. The latter influence was no doubt the origin of 'large power distance' as a cultural feature in Southern Europe, associated with the vast hierarchies and structure of the ancient Romans.

CONCLUSION

Researchers involved in cross-cultural investigations, including those mentioned in this chapter, have considerably advanced our understanding in this area since the early pioneering studies. Existing research findings provide a useful guide or map which, combined with other elements such as sensitivity and power of observation, will help businessmen and managers cope more effectively internationally in developing the effective functioning of culturally diverse joint ventures, boards of directors, teams and workforces.

The problem is that in certain areas cross-cultural researchers are by no means agreed as to what are the significant cultural concepts and dimensions. The subject is still in its infancy, and such a complex one that Hofstede has rightly observed we will probably never be able fully to understand different cultures. Cultures are also constantly in the process of change. Numerous criticisms have been made of cross-cultural research, some unfounded. One viewpoint is that their findings suffer from 'the tendency to over simplify national culture and make comparisons based on exaggerated cultural stereotypes' (Thurley and Wirdenius 1990: 33). Although we do not share that interpretation, neither do we think that the available research findings should be accepted unthinkingly and without question. There are merits and weaknesses in both empirical and 'observational' research and much to be said for vigorously comparing the findings of the different types of cultural investigations.

There are already clear models and an established body of theory relating to both American and Japanese management. However, it has been aptly observed that 'there is as yet no generally accepted ideology or model of European management' (Thurley and Wirdenius 1990: 11). In some respects Europe may be in an intermediate position between American and Japanese values and practices respectively. In other respects Europe may evolve into quite a different form. It might also be a more modern and effective form if the various diverse talents can be harnessed constructively.

REFERENCES

Adler, N.J. (1986) *International Dimensions of Organizational Behavior*, Boston: PWS Kent.
Barzini, L.C. (1968) *The Italians*, Harmondsworth: Penguin Books.
Burns, T. and Stalker, G.M. (1961) *The Management of Innovation*, London: Tavistock.
Fleury, P. (1990) 'Au-dela des particularismes ... Quels fonds commun universel?' *Intercultures* 8 (December 1989–January 1990): 119–30.
Gauthey, F. and Xardel, D. (1990) *Management Interculturel: Mythes et Realities*, Paris: Economica.
Hall, E.T. (1959) *The Silent Language*, New York: Anchor Press/Doubleday.
—— (1976) *Beyond Culture*, New York: Anchor Press/Doubleday.
Hall, E.T. and Hall, M.R. (1990) *Understanding Cultural Differences*, Yarmouth, Mass.: Intercultural Press.
Hofstede, G. (1980) *Culture's Consequences: International Differences in Work-Related Values*. Beverly Hills, California.: Sage.
—— (1985) 'The interaction between national and organizational value systems', *Journal of Management Studies* 22 (4): 347–57.
—— (1991) *Cultures and Organizations*, Maidenhead: McGraw-Hill.
—— (1992) 'The reintegration of Eastern Europe in the family of nations', Plenary speech at SIETAR International's XVIII Annual Congress, Montego Bay, Jamaica, 8–13 May 1992.
Koopman, A. (1991) *Transcultural Management*, Oxford: Basil Blackwell.
Laurent, A. (1983) 'The cultural diversity of Western conceptions of management', *International Studies of Management and Organisation* XIII (1–2): 75–96.
—— (1986) 'The cross-cultural puzzle of international human resource management', *Human Resource Management* 25 (1): 91–102.
Madariaga, S. de (1952) *Portrait de l'Europe*, Paris: Claman Levy.
Mole, J. (1990) *Mind your Manners: Managing Culture Clash in the Single European Market*, London: Industrial Society.
Morgan, G. (1986) *Images of Organizations*, Beverly Hills, California.: Sage.
Peabody, D. (1985) *National Character*, Cambridge: Cambridge University Press.
Ronen, S. (1986) *Comparative and Multinational Management*, New York: John Wiley.

Schramm-Nielsen, I. (1991) 'Relations de travail entre Danois et Francais dans les entreprises privées', In Gauthey, F. and Xardel, D. (eds) *Management Interculturel: Modes et Modèles*, Paris: Economica.

Thurley, K. and Wirdenius, H. (1990) *Towards European Management*, London: Pitman.

Trompenaars, F. (1988) *The Organization of Meaning and the Meaning of Organization*, modified printed version of doctorate dissertation, University of Pennsylvania.

Usunier, J-C. (1992) *Commerce Entre Cultures: Vol.1*, Paris: Presses Universitaires de France.

Wheatley, D.F. and Bing, J.W. (1992) 'Managing cultural differences using the Trompenaars model/database', Presentation made at SIETAR International's XVIII Annual Congress, Montego Bay, Jamaica, 8–13 May 1992.

3   Leadership in the European context
Some queries

Jim Durcan
Paul S. Kirkbride

INTRODUCTION

The last decade has seen the rapid development of a leadership literature concerned with leaders as transformers or visionaries (Bass 1985; Bennis and Nanus 1985; Burns 1978; Kouzes and Posner 1987; Tichy and Devanna 1986). This literature contrasts with that of the preceding three decades which emphasized the importance of leader behaviour, particularly behaviours concerned with initiating structure and consideration (Fleishman 1953; Stogdill and Coons 1957). Both of these major theoretical developments, transformational and transactional leadership respectively, have been the creation of American academics working within US cultural perspectives. Indeed leadership research can be taken as the exemplar of American academic hegemony over a topic area in the social sciences.

The purpose of this chapter is to re-examine both of these models of leadership paying particular attention to the fundamental assumptions implicit in them. Those fundamental assumptions are then compared with US cultural values identified in cross-cultural studies. These cultural values are then contrasted with those of groups of European countries. This contrast indicates that the US models do not necessarily travel well. Europe, with its more evident diverse cultural paradigms, seems to require different models of leadership. Some preliminary models of leadership in the European context are derived. These alternative models suggest a research agenda which offers the opportunity to examine different models of leadership rather than merely looking for supporting data for the American models.

MODELS OF LEADERSHIP: TRANSACTIONAL

Transactional models are grounded in a belief in the importance of the leader in achieving higher performance. In the simplest forms of this theory followers are regarded as 'potential productives' to be energized and brought to their full capacity by appropriate forms of leader behaviour. In 'situational leadership', one of the most used theories of leadership in a training context, different productive capacities and stages of development among followers are recognized (Hersey and Blanchard 1977). These differences require flexibility of leadership style if the leader is to develop fully his or her followers through his or her interventions.

Implicit in this range of models is a belief that full utilization of followers' productive capacity cannot be achieved through the exercise of whatever power and authority is invested by the organization in the leader. On the contrary, it is held that optimal productivity and performance levels require not only the consent of the followers but their wholehearted commitment. Those beliefs in the limitations of leader power and the need to win follower commitment are crucial underpinnings to the theory of transactional leadership.

Insofar as situational leadership focuses on the followers it regards followers as capable of developing to the point where they achieve psychological and job maturity at which stage they are able and willing to perform productively while receiving relatively little initiating or consideration behaviour from their leader. This final stage of development for followers implies that they achieve a state where they are fulfilled by exercising their discretion in their tasks within the guidelines established by the leader. The model assumes that the natural goal of followers is to achieve as much independence as possible from the leader by taking responsibility for themselves and their tasks and exercising their own judgement in discretionary situations rather than relying on the judgement of their leader. (It also serves to reinforce the conception of the leader as someone who is time pressured and thereby benefits by being able to delegate freely to followers. That assumed concern with time and the need to 'free it up' is a further example of a fundamental assumption.)

Although one commonly refers to a singular leader and followers in the plural, a more accurate depiction would be that of a singular follower. Transactional theory, based on contingent models of leadership such as path-goal theory (House 1973; House and Mitchell 1974) and situational leadership (Hersey and Blanchard 1977) emphasizes the individuality of each follower and the need for flexibility of behaviour on the part of the leader to respond to each individual. This approach is summed up in the dictum 'different strokes for different folks' (cf. Harris 1973). Leader behaviour is not directed immediately towards groups but rather to the individual personalities which comprise those groups. This model implies that the relationship between the follower and the leader is more significant to the follower than the relationship between the leader and the group or between follower and follower. In the workplace followers are assumed to be individualistic, needing personalized attention and a one to one relationship with the leader. The importance of the group or team with which the leader must interact is seen as secondary, compared with the individual follower-leader relationship.[1]

Finally, the transactional model presumes a trade or an exchange. Leaders' contribution to the exchange is to provide those behaviours which they perceive are wanted and needed by their followers. The followers' contribution is that they provide the productive performance which the leader seeks. If the leader is perceptive about his or her followers and skilful in his or her deployment of behaviours each follower is expected to respond accordingly. It is not assumed in this model that leaders want any reciprocating behaviours from their followers. The objective of leaders in this transaction is materialistic in terms of the achievement of performance targets. As Fiedler and Chemers argue:

> The leadership role or function involves the motivation, direction, supervision, guidance, and evaluation of others for the purpose of accomplishing a task. . . . The effectiveness of a leader is usually measured on the basis of ratings given by immediate supervisors or, whenever possible, by measuring the performance of the leader's group'.
>
> (Fiedler and Chemers 1984: 4)

Effective leaders are those who achieve higher levels of performance. Different versions of transactional leadership place different emphasis on the appropriate mixes of initiating and consideration behaviours. These emphases vary from the prescriptive early models of Blake and Mouton (1964) to more complex contingent models of the kind proposed by Fiedler (Fiedler 1967; Fiedler and Chemers 1984). These differences do not alter the assumed objective of the leader. The objective remains that of maximizing productive performance. The appropriate sets of behaviours are simply means to an end.

The underlying assumption then is that of the importance of materialism, of productive achievement. Effective leadership is to be judged by its impact on performance. The quality of the leader–follower relationship is only an issue in relation to its impact on performance. Any impact is confined to the follower. The quality of the relationship is not seen as having value to the leader.

MODELS OF LEADERSHIP: TRANSFORMATIONAL

Transformational leadership shares some but not all of the above underlying assumptions. The mechanism for achieving performance has now become the leader's skill in creating and communicating a vision which links leader and followers to behaviours which enhance organizational effectiveness. The leader's skill in choosing and deploying behaviours which enhance follower performance has now been replaced by the leader's skill in securing 'buy-in' to his or her vision. The assumption that leader power and authority on its own is insufficient to secure wholehearted follower commitment and performance remains.

Followers are assumed to contribute most strongly when the vision touches more than their simple self-interest. Instrumental calculative behaviour and its attendant reward systems is overlaid but not replaced by the engagement of values and emotions. Followers respond most strongly when transformational leadership is linked to empowerment. In these circumstances the follower's discretionary capacity in relation to performance and judgement is given maximum scope subject only to the guidance provided by the vision. Again the underlying assumption is that of an individual follower whose full productive potential can only be utilized when the follower is placed in situations requiring analysis, evaluation and decision. It is assumed that, prior to the espousal of transformational leadership and empowerment, the individual had been inhibited from optimal performance by organizational pressures including leadership style.

Transactional and transformational leadership diverge most sharply on the issue of whether the leader interacts with the individual or the group of followers. Transformational leadership emphasizes the role of the vision as a means of uniting the collective, followers and leader, in a team devoted to the vision's achievement. Indeed it may be suggested that when the vision has been communicated successfully the followers will continue to strive to achieve it even after the leader's departure. It may be further argued that leaders who are adjudged by the group as having deviated from the vision risk expulsion from the team. This emphasis on the collective role in achieving and, in some circumstances, shaping the vision and on the leader's relationship with the whole group distinguishes transformational from transactional leadership.

The underlying assumptions reflect a stronger belief in the importance of group norms and dynamics including that of pressure and support from colleagues in pursuit of a common end. It also implies that the personal relationship between leader and follower is less important than the common identification with and commitment to the vision.

The final point of comparison between the two models concerns the leader's objectives in establishing a relationship with his or her followers. Again it seems that the objective is that of improving the organization's competitive performance by raising follower performance. We appreciate that some leaders, in embarking on this quest, see themselves as empowering their followers and attach positive values to that process. None the less, the two models seem to be quite close. Leadership is valued as a means of achieving greater productivity rather than as a means of enhancing the relationship between leaders and followers or between followers and followers.

AMERICAN CULTURAL VALUES AND THEORIES OF LEADERSHIP

To what extent are the underlying assumptions of the largely American transactional and transformational leadership models a cultural artefact? In order to address this question we need to be able to identify the key facets of American (US) culture and then to distinguish these American cultural values from those more typical of various European countries. In order to do this we will utilize the well established model of four key cultural dimensions proposed by Hofstede (1980) after an extensive empirical study. In doing so we are cognizant of the criticisms which have been levelled against his work (Westwood and Everett 1987), but believe it offers a robust framework for some initial investigations.

From his large database of 116,000 IBM respondents over two time periods Hofstede derived four key dimensions of cultural difference from a factor analysis: power distance; uncertainty avoidance; individualism–collectivism; and masculinity–femininity. His data allowed the individual country scores for 40 countries to be located on each of the four dimensions. Table 3.1 displays the scores for the USA together with the maximum, minimum, and mean scores for each dimension.

Table 3.1 The scores of the USA on Hofstede's dimensions of cultural difference

	USA	Maximum	Minimum	Mean
Power distance	40	94	11	51
Uncertainty avoidance	46	112	8	64
Individual/collectivism	91	91	12	51
Tough/tender minded	62	95	5	51

Source: (Hofstede 1980: 315)

The power distance index measures 'the extent to which the members of a society accept that power in institutions and organizations is distributed unequally' (Hofstede 1985: 347). The USA emerges as a country in which the inequalities are restricted and where the inequalities are subject to a degree of challenge and questioning. This is consistent with a situation where the exercise of power and authority by leaders will have limited effectiveness, because the power itself is limited and because followers may question its exercise. That questioning is likely to be greater the greater the power that it is attempted to exercise.

The uncertainty avoidance index reflects 'the degree to which the members of a society feel uncomfortable with uncertainty and ambiguity, which [then] leads them to support beliefs promising certainty and to maintain institutions protecting conformity' (Hofstede 1985: 347–8). High uncertainty avoidance could manifest itself in close rule observance, high preference of employment stability and avoidance of stress. Followers in such a society might be expected to prefer highly structured, stable work environments in which discretion was exercised elsewhere. The USA emerges as significantly more tolerant of uncertainty than average, i.e. as one where individuals may prefer less structured situations in which they can exercise their discretion.

Individualism stands for 'a preference for a loosely knit social framework in society in which individuals are supposed to take care of themselves and their immediate families only' in contrast to collectivism which stands for 'a preference for a tightly knit social framework in which individuals can expect their relatives, clan, or other in-group to look after them, in exchange for unquestioning loyalty' (Hofstede 1985: 348). Of the 40 countries covered in Hofstede's original research the USA emerged as the most individualistic. In the work setting this high level of individualism is associated with a strong calculative approach to employment and a lack of identity with the organization. In the USA context it might be associated with a willingness to switch employment to obtain better rewards and a sense of the importance of the individual, even in the setting of the total organization.

The masculine–feminine dimension distinguishes those cultures which emphasize 'achievement, heroism, assertiveness, and material success' (masculine) from those (feminine) which emphasize 'relationships, modesty, caring for the weak, and the quality of life' (Hofstede 1985: 348). The USA is above average on the masculine side of the dimension.

These individual cultural values could be aligned with the underlying assumptions of transactional and transformational leadership. The level of correspondence seems high. The relatively low power distance scores are consistent with the assumption that the leader lacks sufficient power or respect to obtain wholehearted assent by simply commanding it. The US data suggest that leaders are not accorded sufficiently high degrees of support or respect to make that a viable course of action in most instances.

The relatively low score for uncertainty avoidance is consistent with the assumption that employees desire discretion over their work without too close supervision. It is also consistent with the view that leaders expect and support such desire because it matches their own cultural expectations.

The individualism/collectivism index with its very high individualism score seems to support the notion that leaders and followers have a one to one relationship rather than a one to group relationship. This degree of match seems closer for transactional rather than transformational leadership. The latter models offers vision as a means of providing direction to each individual in the organization so that he or she can use his or her discretion while striving towards the organization's objectives. Again it may be regarded as significant that each individual is assumed to need a sense of direction. By implication that sense of direction will not be given by interaction with the group.

Finally, the assumed objective of both models of leadership is that of greater performance. Such an objective is consistent with the masculinity score recorded for the USA. It is also consistent with the suggestion that the leader–follower relationship is not valued in its own right but only as a means to an end.

Although these levels of correspondence are individually intuitively persuasive they should not be viewed in isolation. To understand the significance of cultural values it is necessary to do more than examine the individual components, attention must be paid to the whole picture.

A more holistic approach would recognize the overall direction given the high level of individualism, the lower levels of uncertainty avoidance and power distance, and the higher masculinity score. Altogether these values emphasize the importance of the individual in charge of their own destinies, responsible for themselves and their actions, determined to produce outcomes favourable to themselves, a country where 'a man's gotta do what a man's gotta do'. Presented in such stark fashion values may be regarded as little more than cultural stereotypes. Certainly most US citizens would differ from the average picture presented here.

Yet the overall impact is that of a society which will emphasize the role and significance of the individual within the organization and the wider community. From this it is not fanciful to suggest that the society will invest the leader role with greater importance, greater responsibility than would a less individualistic society. Indeed US society may 'romanticize' the role of leaders precisely because such individuals are seen as personifying society's values rather than because of the 'real' contribution which the leader makes (Meindl *et al.* 1985; Meindl and Ehrlich 1987).

EUROPEAN CULTURAL VALUES

The second part of our argument is to examine different sets of cultural values within Europe and to consider their possible impact on societal perceptions of and approaches to leadership. If transactional and transformational models of leadership are representations of American culture, might different models be required in other cultures?

In examining European cultural values one cannot regard Europe as a homogeneous unit. Europe is very diverse in its cultural values between different countries and, in some instances, within the same countries. Some of the tensions implicit in these differences are reflected in the current breaking up of larger states in Eastern Europe into their component parts. For the purposes of this analysis three small clusters of European countries have been identified and analysed. The clusters reflect similarities in their cultural values (Table 3.2). These clusters are Anglo (United Kingdom, Ireland); Scandinavian (Denmark, Finland, Norway, Sweden) and Mediterranean (France, Greece, Italy, Portugal, Spain, Turkey) and are shown in Figure 3.1.

Anglo cultural values: their implications for leadership

The Anglo cluster, which could be extended beyond Europe to include Canada, Australia, and New Zealand, contains countries which resemble the cultural characteristics of the USA. These countries score low on the power distance and the uncertainty avoidance index, very high on individualism and high on masculinity. In these circumstances it is not unreasonable to suppose that transactional and transformational models of leadership would have greater application and acceptance in these countries. The underlying assumptions of the models 'fit' the cultural values of the societies.

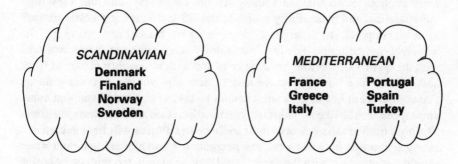

Figure 3.1 Selected country clusters in Europe

Table 3.2 Scores of selected countries on Hofstede's cultural dimensions

Country	Power distance	Uncertainty avoidance	Individualism/ collectivism	Masculine/ feminine
Anglo				
UK	35	35	89	66
Ireland	28	35	70	68
Scandinavian				
Denmark	18	23	74	16
Finland	33	59	63	25
Norway	31	50	69	8
Sweden	31	29	71	5
Latin/Mediterranean				
France	68	86	71	43
Greece	60	112	35	57
Italy	50	75	76	70
Portugal	63	104	27	31
Spain	57	86	51	42
Turkey	66	85	37	45
USA	40	46	91	62

Source: Hofstede 1980: 315

Scandinavian cultural values: their implications for leadership

The Scandinavian cluster have power distance scores which range from very low to low, uncertainty avoidance scores which are low to moderate, individualism scores which are high and masculinity scores which are very low. In relation to uncertainty avoidance these scores do not seem significantly different to those of the 'Anglos'. The power distance scores, on average, are lower as are the individualism scores although the differences are not great. The greatest difference between the Anglos and the Scandinavians is on the masculinity/femininity dimension with the Scandinavians vastly more feminine.

The difference on this dimension is so marked that it shifts the whole orientation of Scandinavian society. In the same way that the very high individualism and masculinity scores in the USA affects the whole approach to leadership so, it is argued, does the low masculinity score of the Scandinavian cultures. The low masculinity score suggests major concerns with the quality of working relationships and with the quality of life, at work and outside. The power distance and uncertainty avoidance scores indicate that commitment has to be won, it cannot be taken for granted and that many employees would like to exercise greater discretion in their working lives. The high individualism scores in Scandinavian cultures will be reflected in a strong separation between work and personal life and a belief that the former should not interfere with the latter. It will not be associated with competitive behaviours in the way it is in Anglo cultures because of the different orientations to materialism and achievement.

In Scandinavian societies the development of semi-autonomous work teams might seem a logical extension of organizational structures in the scope it provides to improve the quality of working life and of relationships in the workplace. It would also be consistent with moves towards greater forms of industrial democracy and worker participation. Such involvement would be regarded as valuable in its own right. Leaders are more likely to be seen to be effective in their ability to foster good working relationships and to encourage harmony and cooperation in their workplace.

The contrasts with Anglo cultures are very stark. In Anglo cultures proposals for greater industrial democracy are much more likely to be debated in terms of their potential contribution to greater performance rather than as being important in themselves. Anglo experience with joint consultation and employee involvement has been mixed. Part of the explanation for this may be that Anglos, when consulted or involved, expect, because of their high masculinity scores, to shape the final outcomes. If views differ about appropriate final outcomes the result is conflict. In Scandinavian cultures the purpose of consultation is to provide involvement, not necessarily to shape the decision. Involvement is valued in its own right and not simply as a means to an end (i.e. determining the final decision). In Anglo cultures effective leaders are those 'who can make it happen' where 'it' is performance. If, in making it happen, relationships are damaged that may be accepted as the necessary price to pay. Social consensus and harmony are much less valued. Consequently their non-achievement is more easily accepted. In contrast, in Scandinavian cultures a leader who simply emphasized greater materialism and productivity would be operating outside the cultural norms and would risk the rejection that that implies.

Mediterranean cultural values: their implications for leadership

The Mediterranean cluster presents a much sharper contrast with each of the other two clusters although there are also some significant differences within the cluster. The power distance scores are moderate to high. All the countries in the Mediterranean cluster have much higher power distance scores than in either of the other clusters. These moderate to high scores suggest societies in which inequalities of power and influence are greater and in which these differences are accepted. In such societies leaders are more likely to be able to influence their followers because of their position. There will be less necessity for leaders to seek follower commitment through providing appropriate behaviours and rewards or via the creation of a shared vision.

The uncertainty avoidance index provides another key differentiator. The Mediterranean cluster share scores which range from high to very high. This indicates a much lower tolerance of uncertainty and ambiguity, a strong preference for operating within structured environments. A critical part of the role of the leader in such cultures may be to act as a buffer or an insulator; absorbing the shocks and uncertainties of the environment and replacing them by structure and order.

As the business environment becomes more internationalized, as the pace of change grows more rapid and the forces of international competition develop further the degree of uncertainty and ambiguity affecting societies is increasing dramatically, perhaps even exponentially. In such circumstances either the underlying cultural values must change to enable the burden of adjustment to be more widely shared among members of the society or the role of the leader is going to assume more and more importance. This growing importance may be manifested in an insulating replacement of complexity and ambiguity by simplicity and certainty so that the leaders undertake the task of determining the nature and scale of the changes required to respond to the external pressures.

Alternatively the growing importance of leadership may be evident in more subtle processes in which the leader interprets and explains the external changes and their consequent internal effects to their followers. The role of the leader is that of providing meaning and perception so that the new developments may be integrated into the existing culture to form a new synthesis. This role would be consistent with Schein's observation that 'the unique and essential function of leadership is the manipulation of culture' (Schein 1985: 317).

In relation to individualism/collectivism the Mediterranean cluster seems to contain two sub-groups. France and Italy have high individualism scores similar to those of the other two clusters. Greece, Portugal and Turkey have high collectivism scores. Spain falls between these two sub-clusters.[2] In the French and Italian cases the individualism may reflect itself in a greater sense of individual choice, a stronger feeling of calculative involvement with organizations so that loyalty has its bounds. Its impact on leaders may be that followers feel free to switch loyalties in the event of leaders' failing to meet follower expectations. In the Italian case the analysis may be complicated by marked regional differences within the state.

In the case of Greece, Turkey and Portugal the high collectivism scores are likely to produce quite different patterns. The relationship of the individual with the group including the leader is much stronger. There is less scope for the individual to decide to opt in or out. Employing organizations may be family-owned concerns employing significant numbers of family members and others who closely associated with the family. The involvement with the organization and its leaders will carry an emotional or moral overtone which in turn reinforces the high power distance score but extends to include the concept of reciprocal obligation. The leader is not free to leave the relationship. Nor may the leader decide not to offer leadership. The relationships would not permit such an opt out. It would not be acceptable within such a culture for the leader to share or delegate the burden of decision-making to his followers. Such an act is likely to be seen as negation of leadership rather than a positive step towards empowerment. Employment patterns of this kind may also exist in France and Italy where family-run concerns are supportive of collectivist values.

With the clear exception of Italy the Mediterranean cluster have moderate femininity scores. Italy ranks as moderate to high on masculinity. This preference for femininity is not as marked as in the Scandinavian case but it is quite different from the Anglo cultures. If the masculine/feminine dimension can be taken as an indicator of the kinds of outcomes valued by societies it suggests that successful leaders in the Mediterranean cluster will be those who maintain cohesion and take care of all members of the group, not just the successful ones. The high power distance and high uncertainty avoidance scores do not admit an option of achieving these goals through teamwork and devolved responsibility. It will be seen as the leader's responsibility to achieve the desired state of affairs. Using the same logic in the case of Italy would suggest Italian leaders may be judged more heavily on their capacity to meet the materialistic needs of their followers.

Overall the Mediterranean cluster of cultures shares a higher power distance and uncertainty avoidance index but differ in regard to individualism/collectivism and masculinity/femininity. The shared characteristics suggest a greater role for leadership and greater demands on that leadership. Where those features are also associated with moderate collectivism and femininity the effect is to emphasize the importance of the quality of relations, the significance of reciprocal obligation, and the need to maintain cohesion. In those instances where the scores indicate more individualistic and masculine cultures it would suggest a more calculative materialistic emphasis to the evaluation of leadership.

CONCLUSIONS AND PROPOSALS

In this chapter we have sought to argue that different cultures will conceptualize leadership quite differently according to the values of that culture. One consequence of this proposition is that models of leadership are culturally specific. Transposed to incompatible cultures the models will either be seen as irrelevant because they ignore locally significant processes and values or, if adopted, will be understood and manipulated in ways different to those of their native culture.

Among the significant cultural differentiators in respect of leadership are the measures by which leader success is adjudged. At its most stark that may reveal itself as a division whereby in masculine cultures leader success is a function of material improvement while in feminine cultures leader success may be judged by the quality of relations and the maintenance of harmony and cohesion. One research area would be to investigate the ways in which different cultures measure leader effectiveness.

Another issue concerns the perceived power and authority of leaders and the extent to which follower attitudes are related to perceptions of that power and authority. Recent theoretical developments in regard to leadership have underplayed the significance of power and authority almost to the extent of regarding leadership through the exercise of power as illegitimate. Such value judgements are typical of low power distance cultures. Such judgements may also obscure a real appreciation of the processes and forces at work in high power distance cultures. Possible avenues of research could include the degree of congruency between leaders and followers in regard to the former's power and authority, the processes by which power and authority may be enhanced or diminished, and the relationship between perceptions of leader power and employee attitudes of commitment, identification and compliance.

It is axiomatic of much current management literature that employees must be empowered (Block 1987) if organizations are to compete effectively in what Tom Peters alliteratively and evocatively describes as the 'nanosecond nineties' (Peters 1992). Such empowerment is pragmatically adjudged a necessary condition of success, it is seen as 'right', in accord with society's values, and it is seen as being desired by employees. The latter group, it is recognized, may take some persuading to exercise their new discretion in the light of previous organizational practice but, once they trust the new policy, their cooperation and engagement will be forthcoming. It is possible, probable that the whole empowerment doctrine is the product of low power distance, low uncertainty avoidance, individualistic, and masculine cultures which see it as a means of gaining a competitive advantage. In such cultures it may yield a competitive advantage, appealing as it does to the society's core values. It is also possible that such proposals would be less enthusiastically received in cultures with different cultural values. One is tempted to draw parallels with the generally disappointing performance of quality circles when they were adopted wholesale in US and UK firms. Again, some interesting lines of research and investigation offer themselves. How tolerant are organizational members of uncertainty and ambiguity? To what extent is leadership welcomed and looked for? How comfortable are individuals acting on their own initiative?

Much of Anglo management interest of the last decade in organizational cultures has been concerned with ways of providing direction without management, with gaining employee loyalty and commitment and performance, with achieving a competitive edge. Strong organizational cultures may be seen as attempts to reverse the calculative self-interest of an individualistic society, to create a new sense of identity, to establish a new set of norms, to forge a new set of self-controls to replace the organizationally inspired controls which were failing to provide the desired level of competitive performance. Such concerns are real and strong appropriate organizational cultures may meet them within certain societies. One of the implications of this chapter is to cast doubt on their appropriateness to other different cultures.

Finally, some caveats are probably in order. We have chosen to focus our analysis on the level of country clusters rather than on the level of individual countries. Partly this is the result of space limitations, but more seriously because we believe that culture is not neatly coterminous with the existing geographical, political and legal boundaries of countries within Europe. We would argue that while there may be differences between countries within clusters it is the larger differences in core value orientations *between* clusters which are likely significantly to impact leader and follower behaviours. This is not to deny, however, the existence of cultural differences between countries in our clusters or, indeed, to ignore the cultural heterogeneity *within* many of the countries discussed.

We have also used the four-dimensional framework from Hofstede as a convenient heuristic device, both to identify key differences in cultural values between our country clusters and to begin to hypothesize about potential differences in leadership. Our usage does not imply uncritical acceptance of his analysis or imply that there are not other key cultural dimensions or differentiators.

We also realize that much more research needs to be done to support our tentative analysis. Our initial literature review has, as yet, revealed little written on leadership in specific European cultures and what does exist is often nothing more than the testing of American models with European data. We have also failed to find 'indigenous' theories of European leadership. This may be partly due to the hegemony of American models, but may also be because 'leadership' is not seen as such a salient concept in Europe; or is seen as salient but in another guise and under another label; or because it is not 'romanticized' in the same way as it is in American culture.

We have already noted during this chapter areas in which further research could develop and here would simply reiterate the necessity of further research work which focuses on leadership in a European context, on European interpretations of leadership functions, on the relations between leaders and followers in different cultural contexts, and on the symbolic aspects of leadership as a social construction.

NOTES

1 It should be noted, however, that this was not always the case with earlier theories of leadership. Bryman (1992) notes that one of the major characteristics of the Ohio approach was that subordinates' rankings of their leaders using instruments such as the LBDQ (Leadership Behavior Description Questionnaire) were aggregated and averaged to produce group-level descriptions of the leader. In redressing the criticism of the absence of situational specificity, one may suggest that the more recent contingency theories have increasingly focused attention on individual followers, environmental conditions and task characteristics at the expense of group dynamics.
2 One possible explanation of these differences might be the extent of industrialization. High collectivism scores in Europe tend to be correlated with larger agricultural sectors.

REFERENCES

Bass, B.M. (1985) *Leadership and Performance beyond Expectations*, New York: Free Press.

Bennis, W.G. and Nanus, B. (1985) *Leaders: The Strategies for Taking Charge*, New York: Harper & Row.

Blake, R.R. and Mouton, J.S. (1964) *The Managerial Grid*, Houston, Texas: Gulf Publishing.

Block, P. (1987) *The Empowered Manager: Positive Political Skills at Work*, San Francisco: Jossey-Bass.

Bryman, A. (1992) *Charisma and Leadership in Organizations*, London: Sage.

Burns, J.M. (1978) *Leadership*, New York: Harper & Row.

Fiedler, F.E. (1967) *A Theory of Leadership Effectiveness*, New York: McGraw Hill.

Fiedler, F.E. and Chemers, M.M. (1984) *Improving Leadership Effectiveness: The Leader Match Concept*, 2nd edn, New York: John Wiley.

Fleishman, E.A. (1953) 'The description of supervisory behavior', *Journal of Applied Psychology* 37: 1–6.

Harris, T.A. (1973) *I'm OK – You're OK*, London: Pan.

Hersey, P. and Blanchard, K.H. (1977) *Management of Organizational Behavior*, 3rd edn, Englewood Cliffs, New Jersey: Prentice Hall.

Hofstede, G. (1980) *Culture's Consequences: International Differences in Work-related Values*, Beverly Hills, California: Sage.

——— (1985) 'The interaction between national and organizational value systems', *Journal of Management Studies* 22 (4): 347–57.

House, R.J. (1973) 'A path–goal theory of leadership effectiveness', in Fleishman,

E.A. and Hunt, J.G. (eds) *Current Developments in the Study of Leadership*, Carbondale, Illinois: Southern Illinois University Press.

House, R.J. and Mitchell, T.R. (1974) 'Path-goal theory of leadership', *Journal of Contemporary Business*, 3: 81–97.

Kouzes, J.M. and Posner, B.Z. (1987) *The Leadership Challenge: How to Get Extraordinary Things Done in Organizations*, San Francisco: Jossey-Bass.

Meindl, J.R. and Ehrlich, S.B. (1987) 'The romance of leadership and the evaluation of organizational performance', *Academy of Management Journal*, 30: 91–109.

Meindl, J.R., Ehrlich, S.B. and Dukerich, J.M. (1985) 'The romance of leadership', *Administrative Science Quarterly* 30: 78–102.

Peters, T. (1992) *Liberation Management: Necessary Disorganization for the Nanosecond Nineties*, London: Macmillan

Schein, E.H. (1985) *Organization Culture and Leadership*, San Francisco: Jossey-Bass.

Stogdill, R.M. and Coons, A.E. (eds) (1957) *Leader Behavior: Its Description and Measurement*, Columbus, Ohio: Bureau of Business Research.

Tichy, N.M. and Devanna, M.A. (1986) *The Transformational Leader*, New York: John Wiley.

Westwood, R.I. and Everett, J. (1987) 'Culture's consequences: a methodology for comparative management studies in Southeast Asia?' *Asia-Pacific Journal of Management* 5 (3): 187–202.

4 Cultural conflicts and synergies in the management of French–German joint ventures

Bianka Lichtenberger
Gérard Naulleau

INTRODUCTION

In the face of newly opening markets, intensified competition, and the need for increasing scale, many companies have put the formation of international joint ventures (IJVs) on their agendas for the 1990s. For international companies, the strategic benefits are compelling: IJVs are an expedient way to crack new markets, to gain skills, technology, or products and to share fixed costs and investments (Bleeke and Ernst 1991).

This form of organizational growth may even become more attractive in the future even though many mergers in the past ten years have not succeeded (Olie 1990). It has also been argued that the barrier around the EC, as a whole, acts as an incentive for European companies to develop contacts with partners in the United States, Japan and elsewhere.

However, the evidence of IJVs – with intra- or inter-EC cooperation – appears strongest in sectors where development of a competitive new product requires immense investment. At the same time, IJVs are also being considered as an instrument of organizational learning (Kogut 1988) which offers excellent alternatives to mergers and acquisitions, contracts and internal development for transferring or gaining 'organizational embedded knowledge'.

Yet a number of analyses on IJVs suggest that these organizational entities are difficult to manage and are doomed to instability and failure. According to a recent study on 49 partnerships, 67 per cent of the alliances ran into serious managerial trouble in the first two years (Bleeke and Ernst 1991). Typically, most research on IJVs has been focused on designing models to describe decision criteria or strategic determinants for would-be partners. Only a few studies have been devoted to the analysis of the reasons for the managerial difficulties of the IJV, and in particular to the field of HRM as compared to other areas (Shenkar and Zeira 1987). This chapter focuses on cultural issues that are prevalent in this form of international cooperation and seeks to apply them to French–German JVs.

CRITICAL ISSUES IN MANAGING IJVs

An analysis of the literature on international management, business law, political science and accounting indicates that there is no precise definition of the IJV. At times they are defined very broadly, encompassing all types of cooperation between companies. However, most definitions (Young and Bradford 1977; Shenkar and Zeira 1987) describe the IJV as a separate legal and organizational entity built from the partial holdings of two or more parent firms, in which the headquarters of at least one is located outside the country of operation of the IJV. Equity distribution between the parent firms may be unequal but without absolute dominance by one party. By construction, IJVs are unstable organizational forms with some of the following critical issues.

Strategy of partners and control of IJVs

One important issue is the consequence of strategic contributions of the partners on the evolution of their relative balance in the IJV. When establishing an IJV, each firm makes a contribution to combine mutual advantages. Partners then closely monitor their collaboration in order to fit the IJV into the rest of their operations with the wish of maintaining their global competitive position (Blodgett 1991). Their ability to take advantage of the IJV may well depend on the nature of the contributions brought in by each partner. Studies have identified fifteen different categories of strategic contributions desired by partners when establishing an IJV (Geringer 1991). Research evidence suggests that most unstable IJVs are those built around two categories of contributions: technology know-how/local environment and marketing knowledge (Blodgett 1991). Being a supplier of technology know-how is correlated with the trend for a partner to increase equity in the IJV, whatever his initial equity share might have been. On the contrary, being the supplier of local environment and marketing knowledge is correlated with a trend to decrease the equity of this partner in the JV.

This is related to the fact that 'competitive learning' may be the main reason for 'dynamic parents' (many Japanese firms are known for this) to establish IJVs although no formal reporting can account for this issue. Ownership dominance in an IJV structure does not mean absolute control of the IJV. Organizational games are more complex than in a subsidiary: strategic issues, and particularly those related to organizational learning – and thus to HRM – have to be closely monitored by parents.

Management under 'multiple parenting'

At the daily level, operational issues can be strongly affected by the 'double parenting' phenomenon. How are the powers divided between partners? Just how really autonomous is the IJV? An IJV depends on cooperation among at least three different entitities – the two parents and the IJV itself – each having its own organization set (Evan 1978). If one or more of the parents is assuming operational control, the IJV may quickly lose flexibility and its ability to adapt to environmental turbulences.

Even if a high level of autonomy is given to the IJV, 'double parenting' always affects decision-making procedures. IJV executives may or must report to their own parents' hierarchies in regard to planning and control systems, decision implementation, and human resources issues. In most cases, IJV policies on human resources and management procedures (financial and management reporting) are negotiated between parents so that they fit with their own systems, procedures and policies. However, this is seldom sufficient to prevent competition within the IJV between systems and policies giving managers a strong feeling of incoherence and paralysis. The outcome of this competition largely depends on the authority of the general manager of the IJV and his/her ability to deal with the problems effectively.

Hybrid culture and identity

With their multiple ownership structure, IJVs bring together individuals who differ in national origin, cultural values, and social norms. IJVs are usually hybrids of the multinational organization (one dominant home culture active in all countries where the organization is active) and of the international organization (organizations without a home national culture, in which the key decision-makers may come from any member country), according to the definitions given by Hofstede (1980).

As it has been suggested by this author, multinational organizations are easier to run than international ones because the dominant home culture implies shared value patterns and a common frame of reference. Usually, such dominance does not occur in IJVs and these organizations are therefore bound for head-on conflicts with two or more cultural systems struggling for dominance. This characteristic may promote personnel processes unique to that type of enterprise, as compared, for example, with the wholly-owned subsidiaries (WOS) of the multinational company.

LOW ASSESSMENT OF CULTURAL INFLUENCES IN IJV DIFFICULTIES

These critical issues – non-exhaustive – give some insights into the management challenges the IJV must overcome in order to survive and develop. When focusing on HRM issues, cultural differences between partners may well appear as playing an important role in the difficult games of the IJV. In an assessment of Dutch mergers and acquisitions it appeared that financial issues may dominate the pre-merger phase, but personnel and culture problems are the prominent problems during the implementation (Olie 1990). After a short smoothly completed period, 'we' vs. 'they' stereotypes begin to permeate much of the interaction between the employee groups.

However, these cultural differences are not easily recognized as such by many executives. Table 4.1 summarizes categories which have been considered as 'unlearning' or 'mistakes' by executives of two American and two European IJVs with at least 20 years of IJV experience (Lyles 1987).

Table 4.1 Categories of unlearning and mistakes as mentioned by executives of long-established IJV (Lyles 1987)

Types of unlearning/ mistakes	Firm 1	Firm 2	Firm 3	Firm 4
Building in future conflicts	X		X	X
Partner rapport issues	X	X		X
Technology transfer issues		X	X	
Cultural issues				
Futuristic issues	X	X		
Human resources			X	
Equity issues				X
Partner choice				X

Cultural issues, discussed in the literature as a problem in the IJVs because of country and firm differences, were not mentioned by any of the companies as a major mistake or failure. However, it was mentioned in interviews at the same time as the important category of getting along with the partner. This item, 'partner rapport issues', was rated as unsatisfactory by executives in three of the IJVs.

One explanation can be interpreted as a certain blindness to cultural diversity in which foreigners become mere projections of ourselves. Adler (1986) notes that cultural blindness is both perceptual and conceptual: we neither see nor want to see differences. In fact, research has documented that frequently similarity is being assumed even when differences exist. In a study involving fourteen countries, managers described their foreign colleagues as more similar to themselves than they actually were (Burger and Bass 1979).

In fact, many of the misunderstandings and problems in IJVs do have their roots in cultural differences (Datta 1988), but they are difficult for managers to identify. It seems that cultural differences are implicit factors of difficulties leading to conflicts which are not related to these factors. This lack of awareness, conscious or not, permanently defers possible improvement of partners' relationships and reinforces the typical pathologies of the IJV: double line of decisions, heavy structure, reduced autonomy, high executive turnover and, finally, poor performance (Graham *et al.* 1988).

Yet, a look at Harrigan's list of reasons for IJV failures shows that five of the seven problem areas she identified are centred around people issues (Harrigan 1985):

- Partners could not get along.
- Managers from disparate partners within the venture could not work together.
- Managers within the venture could not work with the owner's managers.
- Owners could not get their personnel down the line to deliver the information and the resources promised.
- Partners simply reneged on their promises.
- Markets disappeared.
- Technology did not prove to be as good as expected.

Intercultural issues may be active in most of the above reasons although they are difficult to recognize. Differences in decision-making and in managerial style have been frequently cited as an important reason for conflicts in IJVs. One party may favour a participative managerial style while the other values a more autocratic or paternalist style of management.

Understanding a management culture is also related to the identification of the stereotypes that representatives of one culture may have about the other. A recent survey on German expatriates and their counterparts in Chinese/German and Brazilian/German JVs come to the conclusion that part of the cultural differences pertain to stereotypes of the other culture (Lichtenberger 1992). Leadership attitudes indicated that the West German expatriates' perceptions about their subordinates' qualifications and attitudes are an important variable influencing managerial success.

Another study on French/Egyptian JVs (Naulleau 1990) also assessed the differences in managerial styles between French and Egyptian managers. In the sample analysed, these differences were cited as a prominent reason for letting one of the partners assume full control of the IJV. Managerial partnership may well be an illusion in many IJVs located in developing countries.

IJVs constitute a specific context where cultural interactions play a major role. However, most comparative management studies have compared work and organizational related cultures as systems, but seldom in a dynamic perspective, when these systems interact as in the IJV context.

WORK AND ORGANIZATIONAL CONFLICTS ON FRENCH–GERMAN JVs (FGJVs)

When focusing our research on France and Germany, we were struck by the remarkably small number of JVs between French and German companies in comparison to local subsidiaries established in the other country by national companies. Compared to the 3,000 German affiliates in France and to the 2,200 French affiliates in Germany, only about 100 firms registered some sort of cooperation with firms of the other country (Boehmer 1991), only a small majority of which were IJVs.

There are several indications that differences between French and German management styles make it more difficult to establish and run an IJV than other alternatives like acquisitions or creations of WOS. Some authors even consider that nowhere else in Europe is the difference between managerial cultures so marked as it is in French and German companies (von Gaertingen 1992).

A more detailed indication of these cultural differences between executives of both countries is provided in a recent trend analysis (Breuer and de Bartha 1990). Two hundred and sixteen companies, including seventy-eight German subsidiaries in France, forty-seven French subsidiaries in Germany, forty-four French headquarters with subsidiaries in Germany and forty-seven German headquarters with subsidiaries in France, answered a questionnaire on differences in work relationships between executives of both countries. Partial results are shown in Table 4.2.

This study concludes that technical questions lead less often to conflictual situations than interrelationship problems. Work and organizational behaviour related issues including relation to time, way of argumentation, information needs, relation to authority as well as organization commitment had been the reasons mentioned for tensions between French and German managers. In Tables 4.3 and 4.4, these differences as perceived by German and French managers working within JVs, are illustrated in three different contexts: the strategic level (important decision-making for the future of the JV), the operational level (strategy implementation, project management) and the external relationships (management of client/supplier relationships). Being asked to characterize their French colleagues, German executives confirmed already known stereotypes of 'French management'. French managers have been described as status and position oriented. Authority is demonstrated through power and distinction. Management in France is considered rather as a 'state of mind' than as a set of techniques. Managerial status is not part of a graded continuum, but rather a change of legal status as well as subtle changes in outlook and self-perception. This might explain different attitudes towards management skills. For example, the design of French organizations reflects and reinforces the cerebral manager. France has a long tradition of centralization, of hierarchical rigidity, and of individual respect for authority.

Table 4.2 Differences in work relationships mentioned by French and German executives (percentage of the surveyed executives mentioning these differences as important or very important)

Items	French HQs	German HQs	French subsidiary	German subsidiary
Cultural differences are causing tension	56	60	55	55
Differences in work methods	63	56	67	75
Differences in hierarchical relationships	26	54	53	44
Differences in relation to time	47	43	76	56
Lack of efficiency in meetings	14	43	54	35
High level of difficulties in team work	–	–	27	32
High level of difficulties in implementing decisions	26	36	–	–
Difficulties in convincing HQs of cultural differences	–	–	60	74

Table 4.3 French managers as perceived by German managers (summary of first round of interviews)

	Relation to time	Argumentation	Information needs	Relation to authority	Organizational commitment
Strategy	Polychronic	Formal (ideas valued)	Various sources	Power Prestige	Political
Operations	Irregular	Iterative	Key points	Insecure	Status oriented
External Relationships	Deadlines negotiable	Emotional	Informal	Personal	Loose

German managers are being perceived by French colleagues as functional, pragmatic and consensus oriented on a strategic level, as time efficient and systematic on the operational level, and rigid in their way of argumentation in external relations.

Table 4.4 German managers as perceived by French managers (summary of first round of interviews)

	Relation to time	Argumentation	Information needs	Relation to authority	Organizational commitment
Strategy	Monochronic	Pragmatic	Factual	Consensus Oriented	Functional
Operations	Regular	Causal	Exhaustive	Conservative	Functional
External Relationships	No negotiations over deadlines	Rigid	Formal	Contractual	Strong

Preliminary survey

From a first round of interviews with consultants and executives working in Franco-German joint ventures (FGJVs), data have been collected on the type of personnel and organizational conflicts in the daily life of FGJV and on the context of their occurrence. These data have been used to identify sensitive questions in the organization and management of the JVs. From the preliminary data collected, the JV life-cycle seems to play a role on the type of conflicts occurring between French and German managers. From the interviews conducted, it was regularly stressed that conflicts evolved with the development of the JV. The life-cycle can be split into three phases:

1 *The start-up phase* which includes feasibility studies, negotiations, partners' agreements, division of responsibilities, choice of management procedures and initial staffing.
2 *The maturity phase* which includes strategy implementation, performance monitoring, organizational structuring, decisions on strategic development.
3 *The end phase* with either termination of the JV or transformation into a WOS by one of the partners.

Conflicts in the start-up phase

Compared to the French approach, the German approach to the agreement decision is said to be characterized by a higher degree of systemization in planning all the steps leading to the JV start-up: business plan, budgets and division of responsibilities. This higher degree of systemization has been reported as a source of tension and conflict between German and French executives. This difference in level of planning systemization is said to raise some feelings of suspicion among French managers, who do not understand why 'so many details should be worked out before any decision has been taken'. In some cases, French executives saw it as a way to postpone the agreement decision by bringing in 'endless details' into the discussion.

The French approach to the agreement decision is said to be characterized by a global appraisal of the opportunity of deciding to start the JV. General figures are used to assess the agreement opportunity. Planning span is reported to be shorter than the German one and the sequencing to be wider. In many cases, this decision-making process of French executives seems to have been interpreted by the German interlocutors as a superficial way of reaching a decision.

In view of these differences, it would be interesting to measure the different perceptions of time needed to sign a JV agreement according to the nationalities of the descision-makers. It would also be interesting to get data on the perception of each side of the most sensitive and difficult questions dealt with during this negotiation and start-up phase. A final undertaking would assess data on the various authority levels of managers associated in the decision-making process. This issue has been regularly raised in the literature on comparative management assuming German managers to be more participative (hierarchically but also horizontally) in the decision-making process than their French counterparts (Lane 1989).

Conflicts in the maturity phase of the JV

According to our preliminary survey, we identified two main conflict areas at this stage:

1 Plan follow-up.
2 Job descriptions and management styles.

First, the German approach to strategy implementation is reported to follow more strictly the operational plan. Performance monitoring is said to have a shorter time span than the French approach. Conflicts arise around the appreciation of actual versus planned between executives and supervisors of the two countries. Criteria for performance appraisal seem to differ, at least, in two directions:

1 More tolerance by the French managers of variance between planned and actual.
2 More direct monitoring of the performance by floor supervisors in the German approach.

In this area, we found that conflicts, mainly about deadlines, seemed to be frequent between managers of the two countries.

The second area of conflict is related to job descriptions and management styles. When designed by the German partner, job descriptions are said to be more complete and precise than when designed by the French partner. As a consequence, hierarchical bypassing practices seem more frequent with French managers than with their German counterparts. Appreciation of working with managers (including supervisors and executives) of the other nationality seems to differ according to the following two criteria:

1   The hierarchical level.
2   The nationality of the manager.

At the lower hierarchical levels, French employees seem to prefer German management, but this trend seems reversed at the higher hierarchical levels. We do not yet have information about German preferences.

In this perspective, data on perceptions of different management styles (participative versus paternalistic or autocratic) in these particular interactive situations would enable us to improve conflictual situations. According to the literature on comparative management, data on perceptions of managers' and employees' commitment (on task, on department, on organization) would also be of great interest. In JVs, the analysis should also include perceptions of the managers' commitment to the JV as compared to commitment to the initial 'mother' company.

Conflicts in the end phase of the FGJV

IJVs are unstable organizations that are bound to evolve, in many cases, towards full control by one of the partners. This should not necessarily be considered as a failure. IJVs can be used, for instance, to negotiate a favourable strategic retreat from a market or as a transitional structure in some difficult environment as such the former East Germany.

At this stage, perceptions of the organizational and structural changes following full control by one of the partners appear to differ between managers and employees of the two nationalities. The French are reported to be more anxious about changes in ownership than their German counterparts. To assess this difference, two discriminating criteria should be considered as a minimum:

1   Nationality of the partner taking over the IJV.
2   Level of previous performance of the IJV.

We may assume that good performance by the IJV before the takeover would give an unequal degree of fear of change by the managers and employees of the two nationalities.

In this phase of the FGJV life-cycle, it would be of interest to gather and assess data on staffing practices after the takeover of the JV by one of the partners. This issue must not be considered as secondary in the research since some French takeovers of JVs have been reported to fail because of a bad handling of staffing practices.

Cultural synergies in French–German joint ventures

Culture in FGJVs generally remains invisible but when visible, it causes problems. Most executives rarely think that cultural diversity benefits the organization. For example, international executives attending management seminars in France listed the advantages and disadvantages of cultural diversity to their organizations. While every executive could list disadvantages, less than a third could list an advantage (Laurent 1983). Hence, most of the research is focusing either on the impact of culture as:

• Nonexistent.
• As only ranging from negative to neutral (being more or less negative).
• As only ranging from negative to positive (being either negative or positive, but not both).

We think that this is an unnecessary limitation in the field of cross-cultural research. Our assumption is that diversity becomes most advantageous when the organization wants to expand. Diversity is an advantage in repositioning the organization starting a new project like a JV. Reviewing the international literature on multicultural organizations we found that cultural diversity most frequently occur as problematic in convergent processes with strong requirements for similarity of the employees. Whereas the same diversity may lead, in divergent processes, to the most advantages (Adler 1986).

Whereas the assessment and categorization of cultural factors influencing conflict occurrence in the organization and management of FGJVs is a necessary first step in this research project, we consider the need to give responsible managers a model showing cultural diversity as leading to both organizational advantages and disadvantages as even more important for a next step in the discussion on cross-cultural management.The extent to which managers recognize cultural differences and its potential advantages and disadvantages defines the organizations approach to managing that diversity. The approach to diversity, and not the diversity itself, may determine the actual positive and negative outcomes to a JV.

Cultural synergy, as an approach to managing the impact of cultural diversity, involves a process in which managers form organizational policies, strategies, structures and practices based on, but not limited to, the cultural pattern of individual organization members and clients. This approach recognizes both the similarities and differences among the nationalities that compose a multicultural diversity.

SUMMARY AND CONCLUSION

While the risks associated with IJVs will always be substantial, systematic and comprehensive pre-venture planning can certainly help to minimize the attendant risks. Much of the current disenchantment with IJVs stems from inadequate planning and frustrations arising out of conflicts over critical cross-cultural diversity which were ignored in the process of setting up the venture.

Cultural synergy is an approach to managing the impact of cultural diversity in cross-cultural groups by recognizing potentially positive and negative impacts. Unlike the more common cultural dominance and compromise approaches in the subsidiaries/headquarters relationships, cultural synergy emphasizes managing the impacts of diversity, rather than attempting to eliminate the diversity itself. As such, it may apply to contexts of both IJVs and mergers.

In introducing culturally synergistic problem-solving to a JV for the first time, line managers and human resource professionals must realize that they are fundamentally involved. IJV plans should, therefore, incorporate the establishment of an HRM function within the IJV, which works closely with each parent in addressing cross-cultural issues that might arise. More research has yet to be conducted in this field to build such an expertise. The diversity of the French and German managerial cultures provide an interesting context in this perspective.

REFERENCES

Adler N. J. (1986) *International Dimensions of Organizational Behavior*, Boston: PWS Kent.

Bleeke, J.and Ernst, D. (1991) 'The way to win in cross-border alliances', *Harvard Business Review* November, 127–35.

Blodgett, L. (1991) 'Partner contributions as predictors of equity share in international joint ventures', *Journal of International Business Studies* 22 (1): 63–78.

Boehmer H. von (ed.) (1991) *Deutsche Unternehmen in Frankreich*, Stuttgart: ICC/ Deutsche Gruppe, Schäffer Verlag.

Breuer, J.P. and de Bartha, P. (1990) 'Etude sur le management franco-allemand': unpublished study.

Burger, P. and Bass, B.M. (1979) *Assessment of Managers: An International Comparison*, New York: Free Press.

Datta, D.K. (1988) 'International joint-ventures: a framework for analysis', *Journal of General Management* 14 (2): 78–91.

Evan, W. M. (ed.) (1978) *Inter-organizational Relations*, Philadelphia: University of Pennsylvania Press.

Gaertringen, J. von (1992) 'Patrons français, apprenez à seduire vos partenaires allemands', *Le Courrier International* 64: 28–9.

Geringer, J.M. (1991) 'Strategic determinants of partner selection criteria in international joint ventures', *Journal of International Business Studies* 22 (1): 41–62.

Graham, J.L. Campbell, N. and Meissner, H.G. (1988) 'Culture, negotiations, and international cooperation ventures', unpublished paper.

Harrigan, K.R. (1985) *Strategies for Joint Venture Success*. Lexington, Mass.: Lexington Books.

Hofstede, G. (1980) *Culture's Consequences: International Differences in Work-Related Values*. Beverly Hills, California: Sage.

Kogut, B. (1988) 'Joint ventures: theoretical and empirical perspectives', *Strategic Management Journal* 9: 319–32.

Lane, C. (1989) *Management and Labour in Europe*. Aldershot: Edward Elgar.

Laurent, A. (1983) 'The cultural diversity of Western conceptions of management', *International Studies of Management and Organization* 13 (1–2): 75–96.

Lichtenberger, B. (1992) *Interkulturelle Mitarbeiterführung: Überlegungen und Konsequenzen für das internationale Personalmanagement*, Stuttgart: M&P Verlag für Wissenschaft und Forschung.

Lorange, P. and Probst, G.J. (1987) 'Joint venture as self-organizing systems: a key to successful joint venture design and implementation', *Columbia Journal of World Business*, Summer: 71–7.

Lyles, M.A. (1987) 'Common mistakes of joint venture experienced firms', *Columbia Journal of World Business*, Summer: 79–85.

Naulleau, G.H. (1990) 'Le management des entreprises conjointes franco-égyptiennes: analyse de la confrontation des codes socio-culturels, unpublished doctoral dissertation, Paris, Ecole des Hautes Etudes en Sciences Sociales.

Olie, R.L. (1990) 'Culture and integration problems in international mergers and acquisitions', *European Management Journal* 8 (2): 206–15.

Shenkar, O. and Zeira, Y. (1987) 'Human resources management in international joint ventures: directions for research', *Academy of Management Review* 12 (3): 546–57.

Young, R.G. and Bradford, S. Jr. (1977) *Joint Ventures Planning and Action*, New York: Arthur D. Little.

5 European HRM
Reflection of, or challenge to, the American concept?

Chris Brewster

THE HRM CONCEPT IN THE LITERATURE

The concept of HRM, and the associated concept of strategic HRM, is being debated increasingly in the literature and used increasingly within employing organizations. The history of the notion of HRM has been summarized elsewhere (Hendry and Pettigrew 1990; Springer and Springer 1990; Beaumont 1991). It developed initially from work in the USA in the 1960s and 1970s and emerged as two distinct, though perhaps not fully formed, strands in the mid-1980s. Since then the concept has been an ever more visible feature of the academic literature, of consultancy services and of organizational terminology. This use of the terminology spread from the USA first into the developed English-speaking world and recently – but less extensively – into Europe.

The meaning of HRM is far from clearly established in the literature: different authorities imply or state different definitions and draw on different evidence. This fluidity in the concept is both instructive, in terms of indicating its potential power as an explanatory theory; and frustrating, in that it becomes impossible to test a theory that can subsume such a range of, often contradictory, propositions (Popper 1945; Guest 1987). Many have attempted to classify the various areas which HRM covers: seeing, in one of the classic texts, a fourfold typology; employee influence, human resource flow (into, through, and out of the organization), reward systems and work systems (Beer *et al.* 1985); or four rather different areas: the acquisition, maintenance, motivation and development of human resources (e.g. DeCenzo and Robbins 1988); or a five-step HRM cycle: selection, performance, appraisal, rewards and development (Storey 1989).

This lack of clarity is one of the criticisms that the concept has faced in Europe. In the UK, for example, HRM has had a mixed reception. In the practitioners' literature, management teaching and among consultancies, it has been promoted as a new orthodoxy and necessary route to corporate, and personnel policy, success. The reception in the academic literature has been more sceptical. This scepticism revolves around several recurring themes apart from the lack of precision; the prescriptive, normative nature of HRM theories; the lack of empirical evidence in support of HRM; the lack of distinction from traditional personnel management theories; the inappropriateness (and undesirability) of human resource management prescriptions with regard to the European industrial relations history and practice. Without going into too much detail and repeating work that has been done elsewhere (see Legge 1989 for example), this section of the chapter outlines the major approaches to the term HRM and details the level of discussion used.

'Hard' and 'soft' views of HRM have always been implicit in the concept but were emphasized most clearly in the mid-1980s by two competing texts. The first was published in 1984, edited by Fombrun *et al.* The second, by Beer *et al.* was published in the following year, and stands, in essence, as a manifesto for the then newly developed HRM element of Harvard's MBA. The difference between the two approaches has been explored elsewhere (Legge 1989; Beaumont 1991, Hendry and Pettigrew 1990). Here it is only necessary to point out the key distinctive features of each approach.

The 'hard' approach focuses on the 'resource' side of the phrase 'human resource management'. It argues that people are organizational resources and should be managed like any other resource: that is, they should be obtained as cheaply and used as sparingly as possible, consistent with other requirements such as those for quality and efficiency; and they should be developed and exploited as fully and profitably as possible. The word 'people' is used rather than 'employees' because techniques such as outsourcing, subcontracting and franchising would in certain circumstances be seen as entirely appropriate to a hard view of HRM. The approach tends to have a much closer relationship to corporate strategy, with HRM often seen to follow such strategies. It is most typically linked to contingent analyses of corporate strategy, or product life-cyle theories or organizational growth theories (see, for example, Lengnick-Hall and Lengnick-Hall 1988).

By contrast the 'soft' approach to HRM concentrates upon the 'human' side of 'human resource management'. It argues that people are a resource unlike any other; for most organizations far more costly than other resources, but for all organizations the one resource which can create value from the other resources. This is the resource whose creativity, commitment and skill can generate real competitive advantage. This most precious resource therefore requires careful selection, extensive nurturing and development, proper rewards and integration into the organization. As such this approach will tend to concentrate on 'employees' and stands clearly in the long tradition of human relations and developmental studies. In this approach human resource management is more symbiotically related to corporate strategy: the presence or absence of certain skills may push the organization into or out of certain markets or products, for example.

Initially the main concern of writers in the UK such as Hendry and Pettigrew (1986) and Guest (1987) was to develop a unified working definition of the concept out of the parallel schools that were developing in the United States. Related concerns were (and are) to separate the concept from its strongly normative and prescriptive use, which, as Hendry and Pettigrew (1990) note, has been inherent from the outset; and to identify its theoretical parameters so that it can be integrated into research agendas. However the concept is defined the subject can of course be addressed at a variety of different levels. This chapter, adopting the terminology proposed by Schuler (1992), is concerned with human resource management at what has been termed the 'programmes' level and is not concerned with the amorphous issues of culture and ethos raised at the philosophical level, nor with the day-to-day administration of practice and process. HR programmes have been defined, somewhat tautologically, as the effect of HR efforts on organizational structure. It is argued that:

> These efforts have in common the fact they they are generated by strategic intentions and directions the firm is taking and that they involve human resource management issues, i.e. that they are major people-related business issues that require a major organizational effort to address. They also share the reality of having strategic goals that are used to target and measure the effectiveness of the HR programme.
>
> (Schuler 1992: 1)

At this level therefore our focus is on the way that organizations equip themselves to handle HR issues and the correlation of activities in this area with the overall strategic directions that the organization is taking.

The core elements of human resource management

If the concept of HRM cannot be comfortably defined to the agreement of most commentators, there should nonetheless be basic core elements that can be said to underlie most views of the topic if its validity is to be testable. Teasing out the core elements that make up HRM is complicated and controversial. Many of the specific areas or actions have been examined by Guest who emphasizes the more 'human' resources aspects of the American theories and their roots in occupational psychology. He conceives of HRM not as an alternative to personnel management but as a particular form of personnel management, which stresses 'the goal of integration, the goal of employee commitment, the goal of flexibility/adaptability, the goal of quality' (Guest 1987). A later paper by the same author discusses a range of 'innovative techniques of the sort typically associated with HRM' including such issues as flexible working practices, quality circles, training in partici-pative skills and job enrichment (Guest 1990: 385).

Legge (1989), in her review of British and American writing on HRM, sees the distinctiveness of HRM as an activity in the following three areas: it gives greater emphasis to the development of the management team than personnel management; it differs from personnel management as an activity for line managers because it is more firmly integrated in the general coordinating activity of line managers, including a greater 'bottom-line' emphasis; it emphasizes the management of corporate culture as a senior management activity (Legge 1989: 27–8).

Hendry and Pettigrew (1986) focus more on the 'hard' side: the elements of strategic integration:.

1 The use of planning.
2 A coherent approach to the design and management of personnel systems based on an employment policy and manpower strategy, and often under-pinned by a 'philosophy'.
3 Matching HRM activities and policies to some explicit business strategy.
4 Seeing the people of the organization as a 'strategic resource' for achieving 'competitive advantage' (Hendry and Pettigrew 1986: 4).

Since then, Hendry and Pettigrew, if anything, appear to have moved further away from a clearly defined policy content of HRM, defining it 'as a range of things affecting the employment and contribution of people, against the criteria of coherence and appropriateness' (Hendry and Pettigrew 1990: 24), though they continue to emphasize the issue of strategic integration as the key distinguishing element of HRM: 'We see HRM as a perspective on employment systems, characterized by their closer alignment with business strategy' (Hendry and Pettigrew 1990: 36). Other texts have also attempted to pull together some of these approaches to identify a limited number of core elements of HRM. Storey (1992) identifies fifteen differences between personnel management and HRM under the four headings of beliefs and assumptions; strategic aspects; line management; and key levers. Mahoney and Deckop (1986) also examined the differences between 'personnel' and 'HRM'. They argue that, overall, HRM involves a wider and broader view in six specific areas:

1 Employment planning: from a narrow technical focus to closer links with business strategy.
2 Communication with employees: from a collective, negotiating focus to a more general approach to more direct communication with employees.
3 Employee feelings: from job satisfaction to concern with the total organ-izational culture.
4 Employment terms: from selection, training, compensation policies focused on individuals to a concern with group working and group effectiveness.
5 Employment cost-benefits: from a concern with cost-reduction through such strategies as reducing turnover, controlling absenteeism to a focus on organizational effectiveness and the 'bottom line'.
6 Employee development: from individual skills to longer-term employment capabilities.

(Mahoney and Deckop 1986: 229–34)

In a similar, but slightly different way, Beaumont identifies five 'major items typically mentioned' in the US literature as part of HRM:

1 Relatively well-developed internal labour market arrangements; in such areas, for example, as promotion, training, individual career planning.
2 Flexible work organization systems.
3 Contingent compensation practices and/or skills or knowledge based pay structures.
4 High levels of individual participation in task-related decisions.
5 Extensive internal communications arrangements.

(Beaumont 1991: 27)

Together, these attempts to synthesize the elements of HRM show some areas of consistency (wider communication for example); some areas of greater or less detail (presumably, for example, flexible work organization is intended to be a contribution to the bottom line; training for the longer term is an aspect of developing an internal labour market); and some areas of uncertainty (not only are the elements of compensation which are seen to be evidence of HRM different but even within Beaumont's synopsis he finds two different elements).

While there can be no certainties here, it is possible to analyse these texts and other academic and even prescriptive texts to identify common elements in most views of HRM. Two elements in particular, one which is only infrequently stated explicitly and one which is highly visible, seem to underlie most discussions of the topic (see Brewster and Bournois 1991).

1 An employing organization with a considerable degree of independence to take personnel decisions, including, *inter alia*:
  • An independence of remuneration policy, allowing for a 'bottom line' focused contingent pay policy.
  • An absence of, or at least a minimal influence from, trade unions.
  • A preference for a carefully controlled, or in some conceptions internal, labour market.
2 A close involvement of HRM and corporate strategy.

EVIDENCE FROM EUROPE

Much of the rest of this chapter addresses these two fundamental, core elements of the HRM concept. Evidence is presented from a variety of sources; but drawing particularly on a major cross-national survey of human resource management in Europe, conducted by the Price Waterhouse Cranfield Project, and referred to here as PWCP (see, for example, Brewster *et al.* 1991; Gunnigle *et al.* forthcoming). The survey was based on a postal questionnaire. This concentrated on hard data in terms of factual information about policies and practices rather than attitudes. It covers the following subject areas:

• HR departments and HR strategy.
• Recruitment policies.

- Pay and benefits policies.
- Training policies and evaluation.
- Contract and working hours flexibility.
- Industrial relations and employee communication.

In the interest of long-term comparability of trends an (as far as possible) identical questionnaire would be used in all countries.

Problems in ensuring that the selection and interpretation of topic areas was not biased by one country's approach, and in the translation of concepts and questions, were to some extent overcome by detailed collaboration between business schools located in each country. Comparability of industrial classifications was made possible by adopting the NACE system used by the EC.

In 1990–91 the questionnaire was tested, translated and distributed to a broad sample of personnel directors in ten countries. Six thousand three hundred organizations responded across all ten countries. A number of these fell below the cut-off level of at least 200 employees. In broad terms the 5,449 usable responses are representative of the employment size, country of origin and sectoral distribution of the economy of each participating country making this the largest and most representative survey of HRM policies and practices in Europe. (For full details of the methodology and the attempts to overcome the problems created by international research see Brewster *et al.* 1991.) The tables in this chapter use the following standard abbreviations in referring to countries: Switzerland (CH), Germany (D),[1] Denmark (DK), Spain (E), France (F), Greece (GR), Italy (I), Ireland (IRL), Luxembourg (L), Norway (N), Netherlands (NL), Portugal (P), Sweden (S), United Kingdom (UK).

Emphasis will be placed, in the analysis presented below, on a contrast between the situation in the USA and in Europe which, it will be argued, have led to different approaches to the notion of human resource management and, hence, to the need for a theory of HRM which encompasses these variations. By its nature, the argument will involve a considerable degree of generalization: conflating differences within the USA and, more tendentiously, within Europe. The analysis is built on the assumption, identified by another commentator on 'the conditions and circumstances within Western Europe', that although there are differences in HRM in each country, taken as a whole 'they stand out as being distinct from other economic areas like the USA, USSR or Japan' (Remer 1986: 363). The argument is also strained by a lack of hard data giving representative information about practice in the USA. Finally, in this brief list of caveats, it is worth repeating that the core elements abstracted from the 'American' texts are, precisely, an abstraction. No conception of HRM in the USA or among its adherents in Europe mirrors this version exactly and many have other perspectives. Nevertheless, it is clear that the two fundamental core elements noted here underlie nearly all the leading texts.

ORGANIZATIONAL AUTONOMY

Central to the notion of HRM as currently propounded is the notion of organizational independence and autonomy. Defining and prescribing HRM strategies only makes sense if the organizations concerned are free to develop their own strategies. Guest (1990) has argued that this view of freedom and autonomy in HRM is peculiarly American, related to the American view of their country as the land of opportunity in which any individual, through hard work or self-improvement, can be a success, with the ideal model of the 'rugged individualist' or self-reliant small businessman, and a vision of the 'frontier mentality'. We can see these ideals reflected in the comparatively low levels of support, subsidy and control provided, or at least commonly understood to be acceptable, from the state. We can see them in the 'private enterprise' culture of the United States. We can see them in the concept of 'the right to manage' and in the antagonism of management towards trade unions.

These factors are untypical of most European countries. Certainly they have some limited acceptability in Great Britain: but each point remains the focus of considerable controversy in Britain. In countries such as Germany and Sweden, by contrast, these assumptions would be held by only a small minority of the population. In the European system organizations are less autonomous. Their autonomy is constrained at a national level, by culture and legislation, at the organizational level, by patterns of ownership, and at the HRM level, by trade union involvement, bargaining patterns and consultative arrangements and the labour market.

Culture and legislation

At the most general level the empirical data on national cultural differences, though limited, points clearly to the uniqueness of the United States. The USA, one of the leading researchers in this field writes, 'is quite untypical of the world as a whole' (Trompenaars 1985). The US culture is more individualistic and more achievement-orientated than most other countries (Hofstede 1980).

These national cultural differences are reflected in legislation. One German authority, Pieper, points out that 'the major difference between HRM in the US and in Western Europe is the degree to which [HRM] is influenced and determined by state regulations. Companies have a narrower scope of choice in regard to personnel management than in the US' (Pieper 1990: 82). Expanding on this, Pieper includes the greater regulation of recruitment and dismissal, the formalization of educational certification, and the quasi-legal characteristics of the industrial relations framework in comparison to the United States. This catalogue clearly shows its origins in the German system. Including other European countries it is possible to add legislative requirements on pay, on health and safety, on the working environment and hours of work; and to supplement those with legislation on forms of employment contract, rights to trade union representation, requirements to establish and operate consultation or co-determination arrangements, and a plethora of other legal requirements.

Furthermore, Europe is unique in the world in having 12 of its countries at present (and more soon) committed to a supra-national level of legislation on a considerable range of aspects of the employer–employee relationship. The EC particularly through the steps associated with its Social Action Programme is having an increasing legislative influence on HRM (Brewster and Lockhart 1992).

Patterns of ownership

State involvement in HRM is not limited to the legislative role. In broad terms in Europe, as compared to the USA, the state has a higher involvement in underlying social security provision, a more directly interventionist role in the economy, provides far more personnel and industrial relations services and is a more extensive employer in its own right by virtue of a more extensive government-owned sector.

Patterns of ownership in the private sector also vary from one side of the Atlantic to the other. Although public ownership has decreased to some extent in many European countries in recent years it is still far more widespread than in the USA. Nor should it be assumed that ownership in the private sector implies the same thing. In Germany, for example, most major companies are owned largely by a tight network of a small number of substantial banks. Their interlocking shareholdings and close involvement in the management of these corporations mean less pressure to produce short-term profits and a positive disincentive to drive competitors out of the market-place (Randlesome 1990).

Trade unions and workforce communication

Europe is a heavily unionized continent. To the surprise of some, the most notable feature of trade unionism over the last few years has been the lack of change. Unions have lost members in most European countries, but in most countries recognition by employers remains high. More significantly union influence is still important (Gunnigle *et al.* forthcoming). In general the unions, 'the social partners' as they are called, instructively, in the EC jargon, tend to be more involved and to have more positive and less antagonistic relations with employers.

Trade union membership in Europe (Table 5.1) ranges from a low of 12 per cent of the working population in France to over 70 per cent in Denmark and higher in the non-EC countries of Scandinavia (OECD 1991). This level of membership is sharply lower in smaller organizations but our data show that in most countries it does not vary significantly with size above 200 employees.

Across Europe, membership tends to be highest in the public sector and lowest in the service sector.

The trade unions can only undertake their primary functions once they are recognized for bargaining purposes by the employing organization. Table 5.2 indicates the proportion of organizations in a range of countries who recognize trade unions. (The question was not asked in some countries where recognition is legally determined and where recognition is widespread.)

Table 5.1 Union membership in EC countries

Country	Percentage of working population
Denmark	73.2
Belgium	53.0
Ireland	52.4
Luxembourg	49.7
UK	41.5
Italy	39.6
Germany	33.8
Portugal	30.0
Netherlands	25.0
Greece	25.0
Spain	16.0
France	12.0

Source: OECD 1991

Table 5.2 Trade union recognition: percentage of organizations which recognize trade unions for the purpose of collective bargaining (1991)

CH	D	DK	E	F	I	N	NL	S	UK
n/a*	n/a*	91	73	n/a*	91	96	43	n/a*	72

Source: PWCP
Note: * Topic not included.

The findings here reflect, to some degree, membership statistics. Of central importance, however, is the overall proportion of employers recognizing trade unions: in most countries more than 7 out of 10 of all employers, and considerably higher in many. Thus, to take one instance, while our research shows the highest union membership figures are found in only a quarter of Spanish organizations, nevertheless 75 per cent of Spanish organizations deal with trade unions. Nine out of ten German organizations belong to employers federations, where membership requires them to recognize trade unions. Even in a country such as the UK, where union membership has decreased drastically in the last decade, and with an employer-supported Government committed to reducing union power, still 7 out of 10 employers negotiate with trade unions.

Trade union recognition varies across sectors, but the variation is less marked than the variation in union membership. Across Europe the public sector was consistently found to have a slightly higher frequency of trade union recognition than that of other sectors. There is a positive relationship between trade union recognition and the size of organization (by number of people employed) in Denmark, Spain and the UK. No such relationship was found to exist in any of the other countries surveyed. Part of the explanation for this slightly unexpected conclusion must lie in the legal requirements for recognition which apply in many European countries (see Brewster *et al.* 1992).

Overall, these are remarkably high figures, particularly compared to other areas of the world. The evidence from these data suggests that the much vaunted predictions of the terminal decline, or even death of the trade union movement seem, to say the least, much exaggerated.

The unions may be well established within most employing organizations with more than 200 employees in Europe, but this leaves unresolved the question of their influence. Assessing influence is problematical. There are no absolute measures, partly because influence is a perceptual matter: if the employers and the unions both believe the union to be influential, then the evidence will show that it is, even if an objective, outside observer might question the basis of that assessment. In our research, therefore, senior HR specialists were asked whether they thought the influence of trade unions within their organizations had increased, decreased, or remained the same over the last three years. Table 5.3 presents the findings.

Table 5.3 Trade union influence: percentage of organizations where trade union influence has increased or decreased (1991)

	Increased	*Decreased*
Switzerland	18	13
Germany	25	10
Denmark	18	12
Spain	44	12
France	7	46
Italy	8	38
Norway	38	6
Netherlands	34	9
Sweden	20	21
UK	4	52

Source: PWCP

Given the decline in union membership and the fact that politically the unions are 'out in the cold' in, for example, the Netherlands and the UK (though not in the countries with socialist or social democratic governments nor even with the conservative governments in Germany and Italy) these figures are significant. They show that, although there is an overall average decline in union influence it tends to be concentrated in some countries, and even in those countries there are always some organizations reporting increases in union influence. Some countries (Germany, Spain, Norway, the Netherlands) have more organizations reporting an increase in union influence than report a decrease. In most countries the majority of organizations report no change. At the very least, any 'withering away of the unions' thesis would find only partial support here. This issue of influence in particular is much more strongly differentiated by nationality than size or sector. It would, of course, be fascinating to know whether trade union officials or activists would have identified similar patterns of influence, but our data leave this question unresolved.

These issues of the trade union position are closely linked to the issue of communication with employees. This is a central strand in many theories of HRM, as well as being a live issue for trade unions, employers, governments and the EC (Brewster and Bournois 1991). Are employing organizations replacing representative channels with direct communication?

This is not a matter of organizational choice in many European countries. Germany and the Netherlands have legislation which covers most organizations above a certain size requiring them to establish works councils. These councils of employee representatives have considerable power to constrain managerial action. Similar, though less powerful works councils operate in countries such as France, and some states such as Sweden give considerable, legal, co-determination powers to trade unions. Some of our major findings on increases in the use of alternative channels of communication are presented in Table 5.4. Decreases have been left out as they are in nearly all cases negligible.

The figure shows a significant increase in all forms of communication: through representative bodies (trade unions or works councils), by direct verbal communication and direct written communication. The latter two in particular have expanded considerably. To a degree, increases in direct

Table 5.4 Channels of employee communications: percentage of organizations which have increased or decreased their use of trade unions/collective bodies, verbal or written direct communications, 1991

	Trade unions/ collective staff bodies	*Verbally, direct to employees*	*Written, direct to employees*
Switzerland	30	43	57
Germany	29	43	43
Denmark	45	55	50
Spain	44	43	43
France	23	55	62
Italy	21	51	44
Norway	55	46	29
Netherlands	47	49	55
Sweden	21	65	61
UK	14	60	58

Source: PWCP

communication to employees can be explained by the development of technology: word processors and mail-merge systems have opened up the possibility of sending 'individual' letters to all employees. However, possibility is one thing: the desire to take advantage of it is another. Clearly there is a widespread move across Europe to increase the amount of communication to employees.

The fact that this communication continues to utilize staff representative bodies as well as going directly to employees indicates that the objective is passing information. The assumption appears to be that passing a message through several channels increases its chances of being received. This inevitably reduces the importance of the union channel. The evidence here, however, suggests that employers in Europe are not using individual communication to replace trade union channels; rather, they are using both forms of communication.

In sum, then, the evidence on the trade unions is that they continue to be a significant feature of the European scene and that, while their influence may be declining currently in certain countries there is little evidence of a concerted move against them by employers. However national differences in extent, style and trends remain.

The controlled labour market

Internal and external labour markets are used to some extent by all organizations. It is the balance between the two that is critical. Key to the organization's focus on internal or external labour markets is the question of control. An internal market is more straightforward to control: external markets more complex. In its simplest conception, an internal labour market exists where organizations tend to recruit at the bottom, with people expected to remain with one organization for their whole working lives, rather than the organization recruiting widely with people expecting to have to move employment between organizations.

The internal labour market is almost an assumption in much of the HRM literature. Thus Beer *et al.* (1984: 16) map out the territory of HRM in a way which allows for 'inflow' and 'outflow' but concentrate on 'internal flow' (Walker 1980). There are variations here as elsewhere throughout Europe. However internal labour markets are important across Europe. Some examples help to make the point: two-thirds of organizations recruit less than 30 per cent of their senior managers externally; in Denmark and Germany, well over half the organizations recruit into clerical work at least partially through apprenticeships; private recruitment agencies for clerical and manual staff are unlawful in Germany and Sweden. Reporting on our data on recruitment in the ten countries covered here across the different levels of employees, one authority concluded 'in all countries recruitment from among their own employees is used most consistently across all categories' (Filella 1991: 18). There is, therefore, a general reliance on internal labour markets, especially at the senior level. This is supported by the extensive training which is undertaken at company level.

The data in Chapter 7 (Brewster, Hegewisch and Mayne) show that training provision is widespread in Europe. Few commentators would go so far as two Dutch commentators on Sweden, who, having pointed out that 'training is seen as the top priority by all enterprises, government programmes, employers' organizations' went on to claim that 'internal . . . flexibility has replaced external . . . flexibility' (Delsen and van Veen 1992: 95-6). Nevertheless, there is clear evidence of the widespread use of internal labour markets in Europe. However, far more than in the USA, the external environment in Europe shapes and supports the internal market. Not only are the employers restricted, in some cases, in their advertising and recruiting methods; they are also strongly supported by educational systems in many countries that provide high levels of educational and vocational training.

Thus, the high levels of in-company training need to be read alongside the national data on educational standards and particularly, vocational training within the educational (or at least outside the employing organizational) context. The way that governments collect statistics means that detailed comparisons need to be treated with caution. Tables 5.5 and 5.6 give the figures for the EC countries collected by the EC's Directorate General for Employment, Industrial Relations and Social Affairs. They show the percentage of over-18s in higher education and government support for vocational training. Here too, the external environment impinges upon (or perhaps is part of) human resource management.

This is followed through into the vocational training level. Taking the most widely discussed example, Germany, the picture is clear: 'the system of vocational training supplies companies with well-trained labour, especially the so-called *Facharbeiter*. Since this system is run in joint co-operation with state agencies, companies enjoy the advantage of not being solely responsible for financing such training' (Pieper 1990: 10).

Nor is training the only example of national support for the external labour

Table 5.5 Share of 18–24 age group in higher education (EC, 1986–87, %)

Spain	22
France	21
Belgium	21
Germany	21
Denmark	21
Greece	19
Netherlands	18
Italy	17
Ireland	14
Portugal	11
UK	9

Source: Abstracted from *Employment in Europe* (1991)

Table 5.6 Public expenditure on labour market training as a percentage of GDP in the member states 1988–89

Ireland	0.59
Denmark	0.53
France	0.32
Germany	0.29
UK	0.25
Greece	0.23
Netherlands	0.22
Portugal	0.22
Belgium	0.14
Spain	0.12
Italy	0.03
Luxembourg	0.02

Source: Abstracted from *Employment in Europe* (1991)

Table 5.7 Public expenditure on labour market programmes (1988, %GDP)

Belgium	4.21
France (1987)	3.07
West Germany	2.41
Italy	1.61
Netherlands	3.82
Norway	0.93
Sweden	2.59
Spain	3.14
UK	2.50
USA	0.69

Source: OECD (1989)

market. Table 5.7 outlines the percentage of GDP devoted to public expenditure on labour market programmes. The figures include training, retraining and job transition support, job creation schemes and programmes to help younger people and the long-term unemployed get into the labour market.

These levels of educational and vocational training and of Governmental labour market support mean that European organizations are more free to develop external market strategies with a comparatively low degree of risk. This is, in fact, what has happened. The data presented in Chapter 7 (Brewster, Hegewisch and Mayne) shows unequivocally that European organizations are increasingly using the high levels of education and training and the high levels of government support for employment measures to develop more flexible employment patterns. Thus, they are able to draw upon both internal and external labour markets.

Restricted organizational autonomy

In sum, then, this section has shown that organizations in Europe have restricted autonomy (or from another angle, higher levels of support) in their handling of the relationship with employees. The culture of Europe has little in common with the 'frontiersman' approach of and to business leaders in the USA; patterns of ownership are different; legal regulation of the employment relationship is much more extensive; and trade unions are more firmly embedded. Furthermore, the higher levels of state support in the external labour market open up the possibility of a lower risk dual option in the choice of labour markets. On organizational autonomy, then, the first underlying element of HRM, it is possible to argue that the European experience is manifestly different from that of the USA. The next section examines the second element: the integration of HRM with business strategy.

HRM AND BUSINESS STRATEGY

One of the most widely discussed distinctions between HRM and old fashioned personnel management is the closer linking of the former to business strategy. This is largely a feature of the more prescriptive writing; there is little compelling evidence, despite exhortation from an early stage, (Walker 1978; Craft 1981) that such linkage is taking place in reality, even in the USA (Guest 1990). This section of the chapter considers this element under the short-hand expression 'integration'.

By *integration* is meant the degree to which the HRM issues are considered as part of the formulation of business strategies (see for example, Schreyögg 1987; Butler 1988; Wohlegemuth 1988; Guest 1989a; Brewster and Holt Larsen 1992). There is, in research as well as in the business community, an increasing awareness of the relationship between business strategy and HRM (Storey 1989; Freedman 1991). Indeed, in Germany particularly, the debates about HRM have tended to focus on the issue of 'strategy' (see Conrad and Pieper 1990 for a full review of the German debate on HRM). The more organizations become knowledge, service or hi-tech oriented, the more human behaviour becomes a competitive factor, closely linked to the strategic direction of the organization.

It has been argued that such an integration of business strategy and HRM has several advantages:

> First, integration provides a broader range of solutions for solving complex organizational problems. Second, integration ensures that human, financial, and technological resources are given consideration in setting goals and assessing implementation capabilities. Third, through integration organizations must explicitly consider the individuals who comprise them and must implement policies. Finally, reciprocity in integrating human resources and strategic concerns limits the subordination of strategic considerations to human resource preferences and the neglect of human resources as a vital source of organizational competence and competitive advantage.
>
> (Lengnick-Hall and Lengnick-Hall 1988: 459-560)

Nevertheless, much is still unknown about the dialectic relationship between strategy and HRM. As proxies of integration we can take findings in three areas: HR specialist involvement in the main policy-making forum of the organization (board of directors or equivalent); HR specialist involvement in the development of corporate strategy; and whether or not such strategies are linked with HR policies which are translated into targets and evaluated (see Brewster and Holt Larsen 1992). The first two items require little explanation. In European countries personnel or HR specialists rarely reach the very highest positions in employing organizations (Coulson-Thomas 1990; Coulson-Thomas and Wakeham 1991). Of course, this varies by country: HR specialists at the top would appear to be more common in Scandinavia. It is also true that there are numerous Chief Executive Officers who may not have come from the personnel function but exhibit a particular interest in HRM. However, these are still exceptions. In practice an informed HR input to top-level debates is most likely only where there is an organizational structure which provides for the head of the HR functions to be present at the key policy-making forum. Our third proxy item, targeted and evaluated HR policies, requires more explanation. It is argued that a full integration of HR into business strategy can only occur where this function, like production, marketing, finance, has set targets against which it is measured. The assumption here is that aspects of business strategy which are seen as important by an organization's top team are monitored against set objectives.

Tables 5.8 and 5.9 indicate the proportion of companies with an HR presence at the level of the board (or equivalent); and the role that such board-level HR specialists play in the development of corporate strategy. These show significant differences across Europe, but in most countries a clear majority of organizations have an HR presence at the top strategic level: as many as four out of five organizations in Sweden, France and Spain. However in some countries, notably Germany and Italy, the HR function is only rarely represented at board level.

Table 5.8 Head of Personnel or Human Resources function on the main board of directors or equivalent (%) (1991)

Switzerland	58
Germany	19*
Denmark	53
Spain	80
France	83
Italy	18
Norway	67
Netherlands	44
Sweden	87
UK	47

Source: PWCP
Note: * 1990 data

The data underestimate this factor of integration. In Germany, for example, the Codetermination Act of 1952, as amended in 1976, requires the executive boards of large companies to have a labour director with responsibility for staff and welfare matters. Furthermore, the executive board is overseen by a supervisory board on which, depending on size and sector, legislation provides for a third or a half of the seats to be reserved for employee representatives (Gaugler and Wiltz 1992). These state-determined requirements are in addition to, or perhaps supplement, having the head of the function on the main board. Inevitably they mean that human resource issues are an integral part of corporate decision-making. The Netherlands and Denmark also have two-tier boards with union representation on the supervisory board. Other legal requirements for consultation and disclosure also have the effect of raising awareness of HR issues at the top level.

When we examine personnel department involvement in the development of corporate strategy the picture changes somewhat. In Germany and Italy our respondents tell us that human resource issues are taken into account from the outset in the development of corporate strategy by more organizations than the number who have board level responsibility for the HR function: supporting the point made in the previous paragraph. In the Netherlands and the UK, HR influence from the outset approximately mirrors board level involvement. In the other six countries there are considerable numbers of HR specialists with a place on the board who, nevertheless, are not involved in the development of corporate strategy until a later stage. Furthermore, there are marked differences in the proportion of organizations going on from there to develop formal HR strategies, particularly written strategies (see Table 5.10).

Table 5.9 Stages at which personnel specialists are involved in the development of corporate strategy (percentage of organizations in each country) (1991)

	From the outset	Consultative	Implementation	Not consulted	Don't know/ missing
Switzerland	48	20	6	14	12
Germany	55	19	6	8	13
Denmark	42	30	9	4	15
Spain	46	21	8	2	23
France	50	22	12	2	13
Italy	32	23	17	3	25
Norway	54	24	6	4	11
Netherlands	48	31	8	3	13
Sweden	59	28	4	5	6
UK	43	27	8	7	15

Source: PWCP

Table 5.10 Percentage of organizations with personnel/HR management strategy (1991)

	Written	Unwritten	No strategy	Don't know/ missing
Switzerland	58	32	9	1
Germany	20	43	32	5
Denmark	61	22	14	3
Spain	40	40	15	4
France	29	46	17	8
Italy	33	40	11	16
Norway	74	16	6	3
Netherlands	54	30	12	4
Sweden	68	23	10	0
UK	45	27	22	6

Source: PWCP

The ten countries differ in the degree to which they are likely to translate their HR strategies into work programmes and plans. Nearly all the German organizations with written HR strategies go on to put them into operation; only half the Danish organizations do so. However, there is little change in the general order of integration (see Table 5.11).

Table 5.11 Organizations with written HR strategy translated into work programmes and deadlines (%) (1991)

Switzerland	42
Germany	18
Denmark	36
Spain	36
France	25
Italy	32
Norway	46
Netherlands	34
Sweden	45
UK	38

Source: PWCP

There is considerably greater variation when this translation of strategies into programmes and deadlines is taken one step further, to identify what proportion of these organizations evaluates the performance of the personnel department (Table 5.12). On this measure both the UK and Italy move up the order quite sharply; Norway moves down a considerable way. It appears that though personnel departments in UK and Italian organizations are less likely to be integrated into the business, they are considerably more likely, where they are integrated, to have their performance monitored.

This raises the issue of the rationale for such monitoring. The assumption made earlier was that organizations tend to measure what is important to them: hence the evaluation of the personnel or HR department would indicate

Table 5.12 Organizations with written HR strategy translated into work programmes and deadlines where performance or personnel department is systematically evaluated (%) (1991)

Switzerland	24
Germany	8
Denmark	18
Spain	23
France	16
Italy	27
Norway	19
Sweden	27
UK	27

Source: PWCP

a degree of seriousness being accorded to the function. An alternative explanation is that these departments are having to prove their value, whereas in countries where they are less commonly measured their value is taken for granted. Thus in Germany, where the extensive legal and quasi-legal requirements of employment mean a substantial administrative role at least, less than one in ten organizations with written HR strategies evaluate the performance of the personnel department.

Comparing the countries on these criteria some other anomalies, besides those on evaluation, stand out. Spain appears to be one of the least consistent countries, being near the top of the scale on board membership, much further down in terms of written HR strategies and their translation into work programmes and otherwise in central positions. This volatility is understandable given the dramatic and comparatively recent change from fascism to democracy in Spain, rapid economic growth following accession to the EC, and the subsequent attempts of the personnel function to clarify its new role.

Other anomalies concern France's high rating on board membership and early involvement in the creation of corporate strategy compared to its much lower rating on the HR strategy issues. It is arguable that this fits in with stereotypes (supported by some evidence, see Laurent 1983 and Hofstede 1980) of France as a rigidly hierarchical country: the influential senior HR specialists do not want their autonomy restricted by written policies.

A final point to make about the linkage of human resource management and corporate strategy concerns the nature of the link. In the USA there is a widespread belief that HRM is the dependent variable and business strategy the independent variable in this relationship (see, for example, Galbraith and Nathanson 1978; Tichy *et al.* 1982). 'The critical managerial task is to align the formal structure and the HR systems so that they drive the strategic objectives of the organization' (Fombrun, Tichy and Devanna 1984: 37). The assumption is that human resource management is in some sense 'strategic' when it follows closely the corporate strategy of the organization. This conception is open to three kinds of criticism.

First, it shows a considerable misunderstanding of the process of strategy formulation. The concept of strategy needs to be treated with some caution (Crow 1989; Morgan 1989). It has been pointed out that a search for clear examples of coherent overarching strategies which lead directly to implementation would be extremely limiting; in practice the line from formulation to implementation is subject to much variability and a perspective which takes account of this, and the effect of actors, processes and contextual conditions is required (Child 1985). Mintzberg (1978: 935) indeed argues that 'formulation' of strategy does not take place – it it much less explicit, conscious or planned. He suggests using the term 'formation' instead. The development of strategy is in fact a complex, iterative and incremental process, so that is is difficult to define a point at which the corporate strategy can be 'finalized' sufficiently to allow the 'HRM strategy' to be created. (For a brief, clear view of this issue see Hendry and Pettigrew 1990: 34.)

Second, there is considerable evidence from the States (Springer and Springer 1990; Devanna, Fombrun *et al.* 1984; Quinn Mills and Balkaby 1985; Burack 1986; Butler 1988; Commerce Clearing House 1989) that the integration of HRM with business strategy is in practice rare even among large corporations (see Guest 1990, Kochan and Dyer 1992). British authors have gone so far as to suggest that, like previous theories of management, American texts on HRM 'need to be read, therefore, as indictments of what American industry largely was not' (Hendry and Pettigrew 1990: 19).

Third, the process described in the USA is built on different assumptions from those which operate in much of Europe. The rational/logical view that is widespread in America leads to a view that HRM strategies should be determined by experts closely following the business strategy. Indeed it is a direct importation of this approach that informs the research reported above. The data indicate that HRM is more closely integrated into the strategic level in Europe. However, this view of the implication of such integration is built on a particular set of assumptions. Thus, for example, discussing how what he calls 'modern personnel management' could be more closely integrated with the organization's functioning, a German author draws the conclusion that 'this could perhaps mean that staff participation in the organisational process . . . might be more feasible now than was the case in the past' (Remer 1986: 361). American texts tend not to make the assumption that employees will be involved in the process of strategy formation.

Authors such as Pieper have argued that, in Germany, HRM 'seems to be more a theoretical construct than an applied reality' (Pieper 1990: 18). These authors are looking for an American-style HRM in Germany, and not finding it. However, in general the evidence presented here for Europe as a whole is supported by case study evidence in the UK which argues 'that there has indeed been a remarkable take-up by large British companies of initiatives which are in the style of the "human resource management model"' (Storey

1992: 28). Overall it appears that in Europe there may be a higher degree of integration of HRM at the top levels of organizations than there is in the USA: especially when the extra-organizational cultural and legislative influences are included.

ALTERNATIVE APPROACHES TO HRM

This chapter has argued that the concept (or perhaps bundle of concepts) of HRM that has come to Europeans from the USA has two key components: organizational autonomy and strategic integration. It has also argued that these components look very different from the other side of the Atlantic. This final section of the chapter attempts to pull together these differing threads; to argue that despite differences within Europe, a European approach to HRM is discernible; and to use that to build on available theories to propose a more internationally applicable model of HRM.

Such an ambitious programme would be more daunting if much of the groundwork had not already been laid. Europeans are increasingly critical of the American model. Looking at the UK, Guest sees 'signs that . . . the American model is losing its appeal as attention focuses to a greater extent on developments in Europe' (Guest 1990: 377) and the same author is elsewhere sceptical of the feasibility of transferring the American model to Britain. However, the elements of a model that could serve as the basis for comparative international research are not made explicit.

The inapplicability of American models in Europe has also been noted in Germany. Gaugler does so implicitly; he returns to the first principles of personnel management in developed economies, those that have to be fulfilled by any company anywhere such as: the procurement of the right number of staff with the right qualifications at the right time and the right costs; the management of compensation; company leadership and response to employee expectations of fair treatment, acceptable working conditions and opportunities to do fulfilling work. However, Gaugler concludes that the different legal, institutional and economic context show that there is no uniform model of personnel management: 'An international comparison of HR practices clearly indicates that the basic functions of HR management are given different weights in different countries and that they are carried out differently' (Gaugler 1988: 26). Another German, Pieper, surveying European personnel management similarly concludes that 'a single universal model of HRM does not exist' (1990: 11). Critiques of any simplistic attempts to 'universalize' the American models have also come from France (see, for example, Bournois 1991a, b).

It is valuable to point out weaknesses in theory, but it is not sufficient. There is a need to move beyond that to, at least tentatively, proposing improvements to the models. This is more important in the light of two very different developments: the increasing interest in the linkage between HRM and economic success; and the drive towards Europeanization.

The HRM–economic success equation

It is frequently argued that there is a direct correlation between strategic HRM and economic success. Porter (1980, 1985) believed that HRM can help a firm obtain competitive advantage. Schuler and Macmillan (1984: 242) make a similar point, that 'effectively managing human resources' gives benefits which 'include greater profitability'. Other authors make the point explicitly that 'firms that engage in a strategy formulation process that systematically and reciprocally considers human resources and competitive strategy will perform better . . . over the long term' (Lengnick-Hall and Lengnick-Hall 1988: 468); HRM has even been propounded as 'the only truly important determinant of success' (Beyer 1991: 1). Salaman (1992) comments 'this is an obvious but important point'. Pieper builds on this to argue that 'since HRM is seen as a strategic factor strongly influencing the economic success of a single company one can argue that it is also a strategic factor for the success of an entire nation' (1990: 4).

The problem both with the obvious point and the logical extension to national success is that there is a marked dearth of evidence to support them. Indeed at the most visible level, the national level, there is some evidence that on the most generalized assumptions taken here the evidence points in the opposite direction.

Thus, those nations who allow least autonomy to their managements (with most legal regulation and trade union influence), tend to have been most successful in recent years. Those successful nations, in Europe, include some where organizations tend to have an HR function closely integrated with business strategy and some where it is only rarely represented at board level. Many successful European states have moved in the direction of external labour markets. National differences in human resource management and in practices linked frequently with views of 'good HRM practice' have no correlation with national differences in economic performance.

Part of the answer to this problem is undoubtedly methodological, based around the impossibility of finding nations (or organizations) which are equal in all substantial areas except HRM strategies. It seems unlikely however that better methodology would resolve the issue. This raises two possibilities: the first is that the link with economic success, despite its obvious logic, is a fallacy. The second, more promisingly, is that current conceptions of HRM are inadequate. This would go some way towards explaining the lack of correlation of a narrowly conceived view of organizational strategies with economic success.

It has been recognized from the earliest discussions of personnel administration and management that practice here has to be related to directly impinging environmental factors – such as labour markets and state legislation. Literature, perhaps, lagged rather behind practice. A paper at the end of the 1960s on the then dominant 'human relations' approach argued that the human relations literature of the immediate post-war years and the succeeding organization development and change literature ignored all external, economic variables (Strauss 1968). The same critique could well be applied to much of the more prescriptive HRM literature. This could be shown as in Figure 5.1.

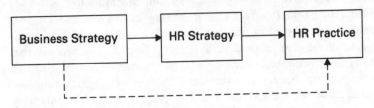

Figure 5.1 Popular prescriptive model of HRM
Source Brewster *et al.* (1983)

From the early 1980s this debate has been widened. Several authors in that period (see for example, Fombrun 1982, 1984; Nkomo 1980; Tichy et al 1982), argued that human resource management needed to follow the corporate strategy literature in acknowledging, and positioning itself in line with, environmental influences. Indeed, Beaumont recently commented that, whatever the other failings of the latest writing on HRM, it 'no longer ignores external, economic variables' (Beaumont 1991: 22). This was, for example, included in the 'perspective' proposed by Lengnick-Hall and Lengnick-Hall where 'competitive strategy' and 'HR strategy' are still in separate boxes (but boxes which are connected or, in their terms, 'mesh') and which are both impacted by external issues: for HR these issues are labour market; skills and values; culture and economic conditions. Only the last overlaps with issues for competitive strategy (Lengnick-Hall and Lengnick-Hall 1988: 467). This, and similar suggestions from other American authors, are simplified into the position represented in Figure 5.2. The environment is conceived of as including different things. For example, Lengnick-Hall and Lengnick-Hall include economic conditions, industry structure, distinct competence, product market/scope, competitive advantage; Beer et al (1984) include in their 'situational factors' some of these HR characteristics (work force characteristics, management philosophy, task technology) and some external ones (business strategy and conditions, labour market, unions, laws and societal values). For ease of representation these are left out of the diagram.

These approaches have been criticized in the USA. In his article mentioned earlier on human relations, Strauss also attacked contemporary approaches as ignoring (or being anti-) trade union and being based on a unitary view of organizations (Strauss 1968). The same criticisms have been made about theories of HRM. It is in response to this that Beer *et al.* supplemented the Figure 5.2 diagram with the notion of a plurality of interests by including (potentially conflicting) 'stakeholder interests' in their classic 'map of the HRM territory' (Beer *et al.* 1984: 16). Interestingly, however, much of their

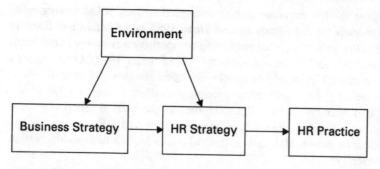

Figure 5.2 American environmental models of HRM

succeeding discussion reflects a unitarist concept of the organization; and in fact moves into a clearly normative and prescriptive path.

These models have been subject to significant criticism in Europe. Poole (1990) wishes to add to the Beer *et al.* map 'globalization' – the practice of multinational corporations including, centrally, the transfer of executives between countries (Brewster 1991) – power and strategic choice. Hendry and Pettigrew (1990) similarly start from the Beer *et al.* model and wish to amplify it to categorize the factors influencing strategic decision-making in HRM, under the headings of 'economic' 'technical' and 'socio-political'. Under 'economic' they include ownership and control, organizational size and structure, the growth rate of an organization, industry structure and markets; under 'technical' they refer to skill, work organization and labour force requirements of technologies; 'socio-political' encompasses the institutional framework, particularly the national education and training system.

The environmental factors have been central to discussions of this issue in other European countries (see, for example, Bournois 1990 in France). A more explicit instance can be taken from Remer (1986), discussing personnel management in the more administrative German context: he does so in terms of 'external characteristics' (economy, technology, society, employers, politics, law, science, culture).

Pieper categorizes the environmental factors affecting HRM similarly to Harvard, or to Hendry and Pettigrew. However, he feels that this approach does not overcome the problem of presenting 'lists' of things and, in the last instance, is atheoretical and forced to rely once again on the black box of culture to explain international differences (1990: 22).

Whether these lists of environmental issues are contextual or are an intrinsic aspect of the HRM concept may be more than a matter of semantics. It is noteworthy that it is in general the American authors who have seen it as contextual and the European authors who have wanted to include these areas *within* the concept. Going down the route of seeing these issues as contextual has led to the often very detailed, case-study based, and sophisticated, attempts to create a 'contingency' approach to HRM. Thus Schuler (1989), a leading figure in this movement, has attempted to link HRM strategies to life-cycle models (as did Fombrun and Tichy 1983 and Kochan and Barocci 1985) and to Porter's models for achieving competitive advantage in different industry conditions (Schuler and Jackson 1987; Schuler 1989). Other authors have argued that HRM should be contingent upon markets (Baird *et al.* 1983; Dertouzos *et al.* 1989) and upon groupings within organizational levels (Lorange and Murphy 1984). The examples could be multiplied (see also Macmillan and Schuler 1985 where the reciprocity of HR and strategy is clearly stated; Lengnick-Hall and Lengnick Hall 1988; Schuler and Macmillan 1984; Schuler 1991).

This contingent determinism has been adopted by some authors in Europe (Ackermann 1986; Besseyre des Horts 1987, 1988). However contingency theory has come under attack in the corporate strategy literature (originated by Child 1976 and followed through by such authorities as Porter 1980, 1985 – and in the recent debate on 'organizational economics' led by Donaldson in the *Academy of Management Review* 1990). A major critique is that it allows little role for managerial action other than that of identifying the current position and matching strategy to it. Many of the 'contingency' school of HRM writers fall into a form of strategic determinism in which management's task is essentially no more than to establish the 'fit' of HRM to a given, usually corporate strategy driven, scenario. Such attempts have been sharply criticized by Conrad and Pieper (1990); by Staehle (1988), who criticizes the American literature accessible in Germany for its derivative approach to personnel management which is seen as dependent upon corporate strategy, rather than contributory to it; and by Poole: 'strategic choices imply discretion over decision-making (i.e. no situational or environmental determinism)' (Poole 1990: 5).

The Europeanization of theory

There is a general trend in theorizing in Europe towards arguing that an over-ready acceptance of American models has gone beyond its provable value: and that the time is now ripe for distinguishing specifically European approaches. It is surely no coincidence that this coincides with the revitalization of the EC and Europe's economic success compared to the USA.

This, it seems to me, is a precise description of the position of European human resource management theory. There has been general criticism of the importation of American theory (Cox and Cooper 1985). In the context of HRM specifically, European authors have argued that 'we are in culturally different contexts' and, 'rather than copy solutions which result from other cultural traditions, we should consider the state of mind that presided in the search for responses adapted to the culture' (Albert 1989: 75, translation in Brewster and Bournois 1991).

Thurley and Wirdenius were concerned with the development of a functional model of management, particularly in the context of international business activities, rather than with HRM in particular or the comparative analysis of different national models of HRM. But they are relevant here because they try to distil what is particular to 'Europe' rather than the US or Japan. They focus on the cultural context of management, and, in the face of the predominance of American and Japanese conceptions of management, the need 'now to distinguish "European Management" as a possible alternative approach' (Thurley and Wirdenius 1991: 128). They see this as necessary to reflect the different cultural values and legal–institutional practices that are dominant in Europe. Such a European approach has the following characteristics:

European Management:

- Is emerging, and cannot be said to exist except in limited circumstances
- Is broadly linked to the idea of European integration, which is continuously expanding further into different countries (i.e. the 12)
- Reflects key values such as pluralism, tolerance, etc., but is not consciously developed from these values
- Is associated with a balanced stakeholder philosophy and the concept of Social Partners.

(Thurley and Wirdenius 1991: 128)

A 'European Model'?

Our evidence here suggests that two paradoxical trends run through HRM in Europe. First, there are clear country differences which can be understood and explained in the context of each national culture and its manifestations in history, law, institutions and trade union and employing organization structures; or in terms of regional clusters within Europe (Filella 1991). Second, there is an identifiable difference as outlined above between the way in which HRM is conducted in Europe and the situation in the USA; a difference which allows us to speak of a European form of HRM and to question the appropriateness of the American concept of HRM in this other continent. (I would add that intuitively I believe that there may also be questions about the relevance of the US form of the concept in other continents too.)

What is needed is a model of HRM that re-emphasizes the influence of such factors as culture, ownership structures, the role of the state and trade union organization. Clearly the European evidence suggests that managements can see the unions, for example, as social partners with a positive role to play in human resource management: and the manifest success of many European firms which adopt that approach shows the, explicit or implicit, anti-unionism of many American views to be culture-bound.

Attempting to encompass these areas within a concept of HRM takes it back towards the industrial relations system approach first outlined by Dunlop (1958) in which the state and its agencies, employers and their associations and employees and their representative bodies formed the constituent elements. Until recently a call to re-establish the primacy of the wider industrial relations concept may have been seen as a nostalgic attempt to deny the replacement of an older theory by a new one. However, the publication by Kochan *et al.* (1986) has breathed new life into the older theory. A major weakness of an otherwise very important book is its lack of a comparative, international framework. The evidence presented here is that one element of the Kochan *et al.* argument – that governmental, market and labour-management relations are interwoven – would have been all the stronger if they had drawn international comparisons. It is our contention that HRM theory needs to adopt the wider perspective of the model proposed by Kochan *et al.*, and a more comprehensive view of the actors in the system, if it is to become a theory that stands the test of international application.

This chapter proposes a model of HRM (outlined in Figure 5.3) which places HR strategies firmly within, though not entirely absorbed by, the business strategy. The two-dimensional presentation does not show, but must be taken to include, an interaction between the two rather than one following from the other. The model also shows, in a simplistic form, that the business strategy, HR strategy and HR practice are located within an external environment of national culture, power systems, legislation, education, employee representation and all the other issues discussed above. The organization and its human resource strategies and practices in turn interact with and are part of that environment. The model places HR strategies in close interaction with the relevant organizational strategy and external environment in a way that is not unforeshadowed in much of the literature but is indicated simply and clearly here.

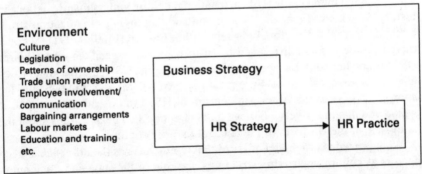

Figure 5.3 International model of HRM

This different presentation of the HRM concept points towards a model which places HRM firmly within the national context: thus allowing fuller understanding of situations which differ from that existing in the USA. The advantages of this approach include a better fit of the model to the European scene and experience. This changes the debates in Europe from two angles. From the normative side, where commentators and consultants have criticized employing organizations for not adopting the 'American' model, this approach allows a change. Rather than searching for, and not finding, traditional HRM, and then criticizing employing organizations and their personnel specialists for not adopting these 'modern' approaches, the model enables the consultants to be more modest and employers to be less defensive. From the analytical side, where academics have found little evidence of HRM in practice and significant shortcomings in the concept as it has come across to us from the USA, the model enables analysts to move beyond discussions of whether HRM should be 'accepted' or 'rejected' to a more positive debate about the forms and styles of HRM.

By allowing for a greater input into HRM from the environment in which the organization is located, this approach also enables the analysts to link HRM more clearly with some of the advantages in international competition which leading strategic theorists claim will accrue to certain sorts of organizations: specifically, those which take greater account of personnel requirements, are more tolerant of ambiguity and challenge, are in a position to take greater risks and are more accepting of variability (Bartlett and Ghoshal 1989; Hedlund and Rolander 1990). Perhaps based partly on this reasoning the model provides a closer fit between HRM and national success. The fact that personnel aspects are brought into corporate strategy by culture, legislation, union involvement can be encompassed here: thus going a considerable way towards explaining why some countries, even including those with limited natural resources, that do not meet the traditional criteria of HRM, are nonetheless among the most successful in the world. The link between positive HRM and economic success is restored.

A final note (not a conclusion)

This chapter has focused upon presenting data on HRM practices in Europe and outlining the challenge that the European perspective provides to at least many of the 'American' notions of HRM. Developing the concept to take account of the more limited autonomy (or greater support) of organizational managers which is evidenced in Europe, and including the external factors within a different presentation of the concept of HRM, has a value beyond the presentation of simple diagrams. Clearly, it needs refinement, but it does present a way forward. Without some adaptation to take account of the European (and perhaps other?) non-American situations, the HRM concept will continue to attract fundamental critiques, even in its most sophisticated form, for its failure to accept different degrees of managerial independence, different approaches to working with employee representatives and governmental involvement and, most damagingly, its inability to link HRM to economic performance. This chapter, by attempting to clarify some of these fundamental bases of the concept, suggests one way forward.

The conceptual limitations of this chapter will be apparent. One in particular is the conflating of Europe into a single entity. There is some rationale for this – the EC provides a unifying political theme even for countries which at present only aspire to join it; and in many areas the similarities between countries in Europe as distinct from those in other continents are more obvious than differences within Europe. Nevertheless differences within Europe are important and are touched on in this chapter – and addressed in more detail in Brewster and Bournois 1991, Filella 1991, Brewster and Holt Larsen 1992 and particularly in Chapters 2, 3 and 7 of this book.

A second over-simplifiction in the model, and one where it needs development, is in its relation to MNCs. Clearly it shows the need for international organizations, and particularly international managers to be aware of, and to adapt to, local environments – as in practice they frequently do (Brewster 1992). However a more complicated, perhaps three-dimensional, model would be required to provide a full picture of the world environment within which many international organizations operate.

The methodological limitations are in one sense at least less important as the chapter has drawn on a range of data and other research. Nevertheless a continual frustration is the lack of directly comparable data from the USA. In at least some respects the focus on case-study evidence in the United States has led to a theoretical debate which, it has been argued, is 'data-poor' (Kochan and Dyer 1992). There is a real need for a substantial survey of organizations in the USA to establish hard data on the extent of particular practices in human resource management.

NOTE

1   Our data are collected from what was West Germany and our analysis refers to that part of the state. Comparable data are currently being collected for the eastern Länder (a project funded by the Anglo-German Foundation) and will prove a fascinating comparison.

REFERENCES

Ackermann, K.F. (1986) 'A contingency model of HRM strategy – empirical research findings reconsidered', *Management Forum* 6: 65–83.

Albert, F.J. (1989) 'Les ressources humaines, atout stratégique', *Editions L'harmattan* 75.

Baird, L., Meshoulam, I., and Degive, G. (1983) 'Meshing human resources planning with strategic business planning: a model approach', *Personnel* 60 (5): 14–25.

Bartlett, C.A. and Ghoshal, S. (1989) *Managing Across Borders: The Transnational Solution*, Cambridge, Mass.: Harvard Business School Press.

Beaumont, P.B. (1991a) 'The US human resource management literature: a review', in Salaman, G. (ed.) *Human Resource Strategies*, Milton Keynes: Open University, pp. 20–37.

Beer, M., Spector, B., Lawrence, P.R., Mills, Q.N. and Walton, R.E. (1984) *Managing Human Assets*, New York: Free Press.

Beer M., Lawrence P. R., Mills Q. N. and Walton R. E. (1985) *Human Resource Management*, New York: Free Press.

Besseyre des Horts, C.H. (1987) 'Typologies des pratiques de gestion des ressources humaines', *Revue Française de Gestion* Sept–Oct 149–55.

—— (1988), 'Vers une gestion stratégique des ressources humaines', *Editions d'Organization* Sept–Oct 69–84.

Bettis, R.A. and Donaldson, L. (1990) *Academy of Management Review*, (special issue) 15 (3): 367–8.

Beyer, H.T. (1991) 'Personalarbeit als integrierter Bestandteil der Unternehmensstrategie', paper presented to the 1991 DGFP Annual Congress, Wiesbaden.

Bournois, F. (1990) 'La place de la fonction ressources humaines en Europe: similitudes et différences', *Actes du 1er Congrès de L'Association Française de Gestion de Ressources Humaines*, Bordeaux, Nov pp. 107–22.

—— (1991a) 'Gestion des RH en Europe: données comparées', *Revue Française de Gestion*, Mar. April–May 68–83.

—— (1991b) *La Gestion des Cadres en Europe*, Paris: Editions Eyrolles.

Brewster, C. (1991) *The Management of Expatriates*, London: Kogan Page.

—— (1992) 'Choosing to adjust: UK and Swedish expatriates in Sweden and the UK', Proceedings of the First International Conference on Expatriate Management, Hong Kong: FICEM, pp. 59–65.

Brewster, C. and Bournois, F. (1991) 'A European perspective on human resource management', *Personnel Review* 20 (6): 4–13.

Brewster, C. and Holt Larsen, H. (1992) 'Human resource management in Europe: evidence from ten countries', *International Journal of Human Resource Management*, 3 (3): 409–34.

Brewster, C. and Lockhart, T. (1992) *The EC*, in Brewster *et al.* (eds) *The European Human Resource Management Guide*, London: Academic Press.

Brewster, C. and Tyson, S. (eds) (1991) *International Comparisons in Human Resource Management*, London: Pitman.

Brewster, C., Richbell, S. and Gill, C. (1983) 'Industrial relations policy: a framework for analysis', in Thurley, K.E. and Wood, S. (eds) *Management Strategy and Industrial Relations*, Cambridge: Cambridge University Press.

Brewster, C., Hegewisch, A. and Lockhart, T. (1991) 'Researching human resource management: the methodology of the Price Waterhouse Cranfield Project on European trends', *Personnel Review* 20 (6): 36–40.

Brewster, C., Hegewisch, A., Holden, L. and Lockhart, T. (eds) (1992) *The European Human Resource Management Guide*, London: Academic Press.

Brewster, C., Hegewisch, A., Lockhart, T. and Mayne, L. (1993) *Flexible Working Patterns in Europe*, London: Institute of Personnel Management.

Burack, E.H. (1986) 'Corporate business and human resource planning practices, strategic issues and concerns', *Organisational Dynamics* 15: 73–87

Butler, J.E. (1988) 'Human resource management as a driving force in business strategy', *Journal of General Management* 13 (4): 88–102.

Chaffee, E.E. (1985) 'Three models of strategy', *Academy of Management Review* 10: 89–98.

Child, J. (1976) 'Organizational structure, environment and performance: the role of strategic choice', *Sociology* 6: 1–22.

—— (1985) 'Managerial strategies, new technology and the labour practice', *Job Redesign: Critical Perceptives of the Labour Process*, D. Knights *et al.* (eds), Aldershot: Gower.

Commerce Clearing House (1989) *The 1989 ASPA/CCH Survey: Corporate Restructuring*, Chicago: CCH.

Conrad, P. and Pieper, R. (1990) 'HRM in the Federal Republic of Germany', in Pieper R. (ed.) *Human Resource Management: An International Comparison*, Berlin: Walter de Gruyter.

Coulson-Thomas, C. (1990) *Professional Development of and for the Board*, London: Institute of Directors.

Coulson-Thomas, C. and Wakeham, A. (1991) *The Effective Board: Current Practice Myths and Realities*, London: Institute of Directors.

Cox, C.J. and Cooper, C. (1985), 'The irrelevance of American organisational sciences to the UK and Europe', *Journal of General Management* 11 (2): 27–34.

Craft, J.A. (1981), 'A critical perspective on human resource planning', *Human Resource Planning* 3: 39–52.

Crow, G. (1989) 'The use of the concept of "strategy" in recent sociological literature', *Sociology*, 23 (1): 1–24.

DeCenzo, D.A. and Robbins, S.P. (1988) *Personnel/Human Resource Management*, 3rd edn, Englewood Cliffs, New Jersey: Prentice Hall.

Delsen, L. and van Veen, T. (1992) 'The Swedish model: relevant for other European countries?', *British Journal of Industrial Relations* 30 (1): 82–105.

Dertouzos, M.L., Lester, R.K. and Solow, R.M. (1989) *Made in America: Regaining the Productive Edge*, Cambridge, Mass.: MIT Press.

Devanna, M.A., Fombrun C.J., Tichy, N.M., and Warren, L. (1982) 'Strategic planning and human resource management', *Human Resource Management* 21: 1–17.

Donaldson, L. (1990) 'The ethereal hand: organizational economics and management theory', *Academy of Management Review* 15 (3): 369–81.

Drucker, P. (1990) *Managing the Non Profit Organization*, Oxford: Butterworth Heinemann.

Dunlop, J.T. (1958) *Industrial Relations Systems*, New York: Henry Holt.

Dyer, L. (1985) Strategic human resources management and planning, in Rowland, K.M. and Ferris, G.R. (eds) *Research in Personnel and Human Resources Management* 3, Greenwich, Connecticut: JAI Press.

Employment in Europe (1991) Luxembourg: Office of Official Publications of the EC.

Filella, J. (1991) 'Is there a Latin model in the management of human resources', *Personnel Review* 20 (6): 15–24.

Fombrun, C. (1982) 'Environmental trends create new pressures on human resources' *Journal of Business Strategy* 3 (1): 61–9.

—— (1983) 'Strategic management: integrating the human resource systems into strategic planning', *Advances in Strategic Management*, 2, Greenwich, Connecticut: JAI Press.

—— (1984) 'The external context of human resource management', in Fombrun, C. Tichy, N. and Devanna, H. (eds) *Strategic Human Resource Management*, New York: John Wiley, pp. 3–18.

Fombrun, C. and Tichy, N.M. (1983) 'Strategic planning and human resources management: at rainbow's end', in Lamb, R. (ed.), *Recent Advances in Strategic Planning*, New York: McGraw-Hill.

Fombrun, C., Tichy, N. and Devanna, M. (eds) (1984) *Strategic Human Resource Management*, New York: John Wiley.

Freedman, A. (1991) *The Changing Human Resources Function*, New York: Conference Board.

Galbraith, J.R. and Nathanson, D.A. (1978) *Strategy Implementation: The Role of Structure and Process*, St Paul, Minnesota: West Publishing.

Gaugler, E. (1988) 'HR management: an international comparison', *Personnel* 65 (8): 24–30.

Gaugler, E. and Wiltz, S. (1992) 'Germany', in Brewster C., Hegewisch A., Holden L., Lockhart T. (eds) *The European Guide to Human Resource Management*, London: Academic Press.

Guest, D. (1987) 'Human resource management and industrial relations', *Journal of Management Studies* 24 (5): 503–22.

—— (1989a) 'HRM: implications for industrial relations', in Storey, J. (ed.) *New Perspectives on Human Resource Management*, London: Routledge.

—— (1989b) 'Personnel and HRM: can you tell the difference?', *Personnel Management*, January: 48–51.

—— (1990), 'Human resource management and the American dream', *Journal of Management Studies* 27 (4): 377–97.

—— (1991) 'Personnel management: the end of orthodoxy?', *British Journal of Industrial Relations*, 29 (2): 149–76.

Gunnigle, P., Brewster, C. and Morley, M. 'Evaluating change in industrial relations: evidence from the Price Waterhouse Cranfield Project', *P+: Journal of the European Foundation for the Improvement of Working and Living Conditions*, forthcoming.

Hedlund, G. and Rolander, D. (1990) 'Action in heterarchies – new approaches to managing the MNC', in Bartlett, C.A., Doz, Y. and Hedlund, G. (eds), *Managing the Global Firm*, London: Routledge, pp. 15–46.

Hendry, C. and Pettigrew, A., (1986) ''The practice of strategic human resource management', *Personnel Review* 15 (5): 3–8.

—— (1990) 'Human resource management: an agenda for the 1990s,' *International Journal of Human Resource Management* 1 (1): 17–43.

Hinterhuber, H.H. and Holleis, W. (1988) 'Gewinner im Verdrangungswettbewerb – Wie man durch Verbindung von Unternehmensstrategie und Unternehmenskultur zu einem führenden Wettbewerber werden kann', *Journal für Betriebswirtschaft* 38 (1): 2–18.

Hofstede, G. (1980) *Culture's Consequences: International Differences in Work-Related Values*, Beverly Hills, California: Sage.

—— (1983) 'The cultural relativity of organizational practices and theories', *Journal of International Business Studies* 13 (3): 75–90.

—— (1991) *Cultures and Organizations: Software of the Mind*, Maidenhead: McGraw-Hill.

Kochan, T.A. and Barocci, T.A. (1985) *Human Resource Management and Industrial Relations*, Boston: Little, Brown.

Kochan, T.A. and Dyer. L. (1992) 'Managing transformational change: the role of human resource professionals', Sloan Working Paper 3420-92-BPS, MIT, Mass.

Kochan, T.A., McKersie, R.B. and Capelli, P. (1984) 'Strategic choice and industrial relations theory', *Industrial Relations* 23: 16–39.

Kochan, T.A., Katz, H.C. and McKersie, R.B. (1986) *The Transformation of American Industrial Relations*, New York: Basic Books.

Laurent, A. (1983) 'The cultural diversity of Western conceptions of management', *International Studies of Management and Organization* 13 (1–2): 75–96.

Legge, K. (1989) 'Human resource management: a critical analysis', in Storey, J. (ed.) *New Perspectives on Human Resource Management*, London: Routledge.

Lengnick-Hall, C.A. and Lengnick-Hall, M.L. (1988) 'Strategic human resources management: a review of the literature and a proposed typology', *Academy of Management Review* 13 (3): 454–70.

Lorange, P. and Murphy, D. (1984) 'Bringing human resources into strategic planning: systems design considerations', in Fombrun, C., Tichy, N. and Devanna, M. (eds.), *Strategic Human Resource Management*, New York: John Wiley.

Macmillan, I.C. and Schuler, R.S. (1985) 'Gaining a competitive edge through human resources', *Personnel* 62 (4): 24–9.

Mahoney, T. and Deckop, J.R. (1986) 'Evolution of concept and practice in personnel administration/human resource management', *Journal of Management* 12 (2): 223–41.

Miller, E.L. and Burack, E.H. (1981) 'A status report on human resource planning from the perspective of human resource planners', *Human Resource Planning* 4: 33–40.

Mintzberg, H. (1978) 'Patterns in strategy formation', *Management Science* 24 (9): 934–48.

Morgan, D. (1989) 'Strategies and sociologists: a comment on Crow', *Sociology* 23 (1): 25–9.

Nkomo, S.M. (1980) 'Stage three in personnel administration: strategic human resource management', *Personnel* 57: 189–202.

—— (1987) 'Human resource planning and organisation performance: an exploratory analysis', *Strategic Management Journal* 8: 387–92.

OECD (1989) *Employment Outlook*, Paris: OECD.

—— (1991) *Employment Outlook*, Paris: OECD.

Pieper, R. (ed.) (1990) *Human Resource Management: An International Comparison*, Berlin: Walter de Gruyter.

Poole, M. (1990) 'Human resource management in an international perspective', *International Journal of Human Resource Management* 1 (1): 1–15.

Popper, K.R. (1945) *The Open Society and its Enemies*, London: Routledge and Kegan Paul.

Porter, M. (1980) *Competitive Strategies*, New York: Free Press.

—— (1985) *Competitive Advantage*, New York: Free Press.

Quinn Mill, D. and Balbaky, M. (1985) 'Planning for morale and culture', in Walton R. and Lawrence P. (eds) *Human Resource Management – Trends and Challenges*, Boston, Mass.: Harvard Business School Press.

Randlesome, C. (1990) *Business Cultures in Europe*, Oxford: Heinemann.

Remer, A. (1986) 'Personnel management in Western Europe – development, situation and concepts', in Macharzina, K. and Staehle, W.H. (eds) *European Approaches to International Management*, Berlin: Walter de Gruyter.

Salaman, G. (ed.) (1992) *Human Resource Strategies*, London: Sage.

Schein, E. (1977) 'Increasing organizational effectiveness through better human resource planning and development', in Schein, E. (ed.) *The Art of Managing Human Resources*, New York: Oxford University Press, pp. 25–45.

—— (1987) 'Increasing organizational effectiveness through better human resource planning and development', *Sloan Management Review* 19 (1): 1–20.

Schreyögg, G. (1987) 'Verschlüsselte botschaften neue perspektiven einer strategischen personalführung', *Zeitschrift Führung und Organisation* 56 (3): 151–8.

Schuler, R.S. (1991) 'Strategic HRM: linking people with the strategic needs of the business', unpublished paper, New York University.

—— (1992) 'Strategic human resource management: linking the people with the strategic needs of the business', *Organizational Dynamics* 21 (1): 18–32.

Schuler, R.S. and Jackson, S.E. (1987) 'Linking competitive strategies with human resource management practices', *Academy of Management Executive* 1 (3): 209–13.

Schuler, R. and Macmillan, S. (1984), 'Gaining competitive advantage through human resource management practices', *Human Resource Management* 23 (3): 241–55.

Springer, B and Springer, S. (1990) 'Human resource management in the UK – celebration of its centenary', in Pieper, R. (ed.) *Human Resource Management: An International Comparison*, Berlin: Walter de Gruyter.

Staehle, W.H. (1988), 'Human resource management', *Zeitschrift für Betriebswirtschaft*, 5/6: 26–37.

—— (1990) 'Human resource management and corporate strategy', in Pieper, R. (ed.) *Human Resource Management: An International Comparison*, Berlin: Walter de Gruyter.

Staffelbach, B. (1986) *Strategisches Personalmanagement*, Bern-Stuttgart.

Storey, J. (ed.) (1989) *New Perspectives on Human Resource Management*, London: Routledge.

—— (1992) 'HRM in action: the truth is out at last', *Personnel Management*, April: 28–31.

Storey, J. and Sisson, K. (1989) 'Limits to transformation: HRM in the British context', *Industrial Relations Journal* 20: 60–5.

Strauss, G. (1968) 'Human relations – 1968 style', *Industrial Relations* 7: 262–76.
Thurley, K. and Wirdenius, H. (1991) 'Will management become "European"?: strategic choices for organizations', *European Management Journal* 9 (2): 127–34.
Tichy, N.M., Fombrun, C.J., and Devanna, M.A. (1982) 'Strategic human resource management', *Sloan Management Review* 24: 47–61.
Trompenaars, A. (1985) 'Organization of meaning and the meaning of organization: a comparative study on the conception of organizational structure in different cultures', unpublished PhD thesis, University of Pennsylvania (DA 8515460).
—— (1991), quoted in Hampden-Turner C., 'Towards a multi-cultural approach to creating wealth and value', paper presented to the Fifteenth EAPM Conference, Istanbul, June 1991.
Walker, J.W. (1978) 'Linking human resource planning and strategic planning', *Human Resource Planning* 1: 1–18.
—— (1980) *Human Resource Planning*, New York: McGraw-Hill.
—— (1989) 'Human resource roles for the '90s', *Human Resource Planning* 12 (1): 55–61.
Walsh, K. (1985) *Trade Union Membership, Methods and Measurement in the European Community*, Luxembourg: Eurostat.
Walton, R.E. (1987) *Innovating to Compete: Lessons for Diffusing and Managing Change in the Workplace*, San Francisco: Josey-Bass.
Weiss, D. (1988), *La Fonction Ressources Humaines*, Paris: Editions d'Organization.
Wohlgemuth, A.C. (1988) 'Human resources management und die wirkungsvolle vermaschung mit der unternehmungspolitik', *Management-Zeitschrift Industrielle Organization* 56 (2): 115–18.

Part II

Developments in the European Community

6 The Single European Market and the HRM response

Chris Hendry

THE SINGLE EUROPEAN MARKET AND INDUSTRIAL RESTRUCTURING

The completion of the SEM as of 1 January 1993 had two objectives: (1) to stimulate trade within the EC through the removal of 'artificial' barriers, and (2) by means of the restructuring and internationalization of European firms that resulted, to improve their ability to compete in world markets. The Single European Act of 1986 which set this process in motion aimed to remove barriers to the movement of goods and resources across the frontiers of the twelve member states in three ways: (1) eliminating direct, obstacles to trade (i.e. customs controls); (2) lowering non-tariff constraints (i.e. differing technical standards and regulations governing goods and services); and (3) equalizing prices resulting from the varying rates of indirect taxes (VAT) and excise duties. The common European Exchange Rate Mechanism (ERM) was also intended to contribute to a level playing field by reducing the scope of member countries to vary the value of their currencies. All of these directly impact upon intra-European trade by companies domiciled within the Community.

The removal of these barriers was expected to produce a once-and-for-all boost to trade and efficiency at the time of completing the SEM. However, in the longer term, realizing the benefits of the SEM requires the exploitation of scale benefits – by companies rationalizing facilities and standardizing products, and by external restructuring through mergers and acquisitions. At the same time, European firms would need to engage in closer cooperation and pool their research and development expertise and funds through various forms of joint venture and alliance in order to develop their technological competitiveness and market strength *vis-à-vis* the USA and Japan.

With fewer, larger firms increasingly dominating the world economy (Bower 1988), the significance of the scale issue can be gauged from various sectoral comparisons between Europe and the USA. For example, the EC has (or had at the last count) fifty tractor manufacturers, the USA has four; the EC has 300 domestic appliance manufacturers, the USA has four; the EC has eleven manufacturers of railway stock, the USA has two; the EC has eleven manufacturers of telephone exchanges, the USA has four; and so on.

The Sectoral Impacts of the Single European Market

While standardization, rationalization, and forms of alliance are part of the normal competitive process, and would continue to happen anyway without the SEM and supporting intiatives, the SEM is expected to impact especially on some forty manufacturing sectors where there are significant non-tariff barriers to intra-Community trade. These forty sectors represent about 50 per cent of industrial value-added in the Community out of a total of 120 such sectors (Directorate-General for Economic and Financial Affairs 1988). At the same time, industrial goods as a whole account for around 70 per cent of trade both within the Community and with the outside world. Thus, although the forty manufacturing sectors are not of absolute significance to the European economy, they are critical in the impact that reducing barriers will have in stimulating trade within the SEM.

The Directorate-General, Economic and Financial Affairs (1988) classified these into four groups (as shown in Table 6.1) according to the level of price dispersion that identical products display across member states and the level of intra-Community trade. These two measures show how fragmented the EC market is for each sector and how severe harmonization is therefore likely to be. While we need not be concerned here with the more specific characteristics of these groupings (for a full account see Hendry 1993a), the implications the Directorate-General draws about the impacts of the SEM are important for HRM.

First, it does not, in general, expect there to be major dislocation in economic activity across the Community: 'The completion of the single market should . . . neither upset the mix of sectoral specializations across Member States nor lead to massive transfers of economic activities between geographic zones' (Directorate-General for Economic and Financial Affairs/ Employment, Industrial Relations and Social Affairs 1990: 4). Second, it assumes an increase in firm size and consequent internationalization. And third, it projects the development of European firms, noting, however, the tendency of member states to bolster national champions and the need to promote managerial mobility and cross-national representation on company boards to make such firms a reality. The rest of this chapter assesses progress towards these goals and what they mean for HRM in general and for the UK in particular.

EMPLOYMENT AND SKILLS IN THE SINGLE EUROPEAN MARKET

From the outset, it has been anticipated that there would be an initial loss across Europe of around a quarter of a million jobs for the first two years after

Table 6.1 The industrial sectors most affected by the SEM

NACE codes	Sector	Non-tariff barriers
	High-technology public-procurement sectors Group 1	
330	Office machines	high
344	Telecommunication equipment	high
372	Medico-surgical equipment	high
	Traditional public-procurement or regulated markets Group 2	
257	Pharmaceutical products	high
315	Boilermaking, reservoirs, sheet-metal containers	high
362	Railway equipment	high
425	Wine and wine-based products	high
427	Brewing and malting	high
428	Soft drinks and spa waters	high
	Group 3	
341	Electrical wires and cables	high
342	Electrical equipment	high
361	Shipbuilding	high
417	Spaghetti, macaroni, etc	high
421	Cocoa, chocolate and sugar confectionery	high
	Sectors with moderate non-tariff barriers Group 4	
	Consumer goods	
345	Electronic equipment	moderate
346	Domestic-type elec. appliances	moderate
351	Motor vehicles	moderate
438	Carpets, lino, floor covering	moderate
451	Footwear	moderate
453	Clothing	moderate
455	Household textiles	moderate
491	Jewellery, goldsmiths' and silversmiths' wares	moderate
493	Photographic and cinematic laboratories	moderate
495	Games, toys and sports goods	moderate
	Capital goods	
321	Agricultural machinery and tractors	moderate
322	Machine tools for metals	moderate
323	Textile and sewing machines	moderate
324	Machines for foodstuffs industry	moderate
325	Plant for mines, etc.	moderate
326	Transmission equipment	moderate
327	Other specific equipment	moderate
347	Lamps and lighting equipment	moderate
364	Aerospace equipment, manufacturing and repairing	moderate
	Intermediary goods	
247	Glassware	moderate
248	Ceramics	moderate
251	Basic industrial chemicals	moderate
256	Other chemical products for industry	moderate
431	Wool industry	moderate
432	Cotton industry	moderate
481	Rubber industry	moderate

Source: Panorama of EC Industry and estimates from Commission Services/Directorate-General for Economic and Financial Affairs/Employment, Industrial Relations and Social Affairs 1990: 24

the completion of the SEM as administrative barriers came down. Restructuring and the boost to trade were then expected to result in a net gain of between 1.8 and 5.7 million jobs after six years (Commission of the European Communities 1988). In these assessments, the UK was projected to suffer the most severe job losses (0.64 per cent of total employment compared with an average loss of 0.44 per cent), and to have the smallest net gains (1.39 per cent compared with an average 1.47 per cent across the EC). However, as Ramsay (1990: 13) comments, 'the loss of jobs is the most secure thing about 1992; and the subsequent gain in employment is the least reliable'. Rajan (1990) concurs with this view in his assessment of the SEM as a 'zero-sum game'.

Since then, the Institute for Employment Research at Warwick University has projected the effects of three possible scenarios (IER 1991). An 'efficiency' scenario, resulting from vigorous product-market competition and increased labour market flexibility, suggests an increase of 1.1 million jobs by the turn of the century – largely in service industries and part-time, low-paid jobs. A 'cost-cutting' scenario, where there is fierce price competition between European competitors, would effectively negate these benefits, affecting services and certain areas of manufacturing. A 'quality' scenario, in which Europe moves towards a high added value/high skill economy, would double the benefits and produce employment increases especially in chemicals, construction and banking.

The European Commission until recently continued to assume a modest impact on employment from the initial rationalization accompanying the SEM, noting in 1990 for instance that, 'the process of completing the Internal Market is taking place against a background of relatively strong output growth and even stronger job creation' (Directorate-General, Employment, Industrial Relations and Social Affairs 1990: 44). In the longer-term, however, it recognised that the real focus should be on impacts and responses at sectoral and regional level where any divergence would be most marked, while subsequent reports have begun to register the increase in unemployment (Directorate-General, Employment, Industrial Relations and Social Affairs 1991).

Very crudely, the Commission distinguished the northern from the southern states. In the northern states those among the forty sectors most likely to be affected tend to be capital-intensive high-tech (cars, pharmaceuticals, computers, telecommunications) and traditional heavy industries (electricity generating plant, railway rolling stock), both often being protected by public procurement policies. In the southern states, they tend to be labour-intensive industries such as clothing, footwear and textiles, which have also been highly protected. Figure 6.1 shows the relative concentration of the forty most affected sectors according to their relative strengths and their importance to employment in the twelve member countries.

The Commission's overall assessment of the affects on the UK is actually somewhat contradictory. One report first observes that the share of industrial employment concentrated in the poorly-placed sectors is greater (25 per cent,

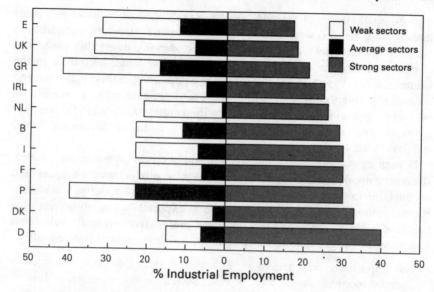

Figure 6.1 Share of industrial employment in sensitive sectors in the member states (1987)
Source: Directorate-General, Employment, Industrial Relations and Social Affairs, 1990: 48

as against 18 per cent), but then qualifies this by noting that the larger proportion of employment is concentrated in averagely performing sectors (Directorate-General for Economic and Financial Affairs/Employment, Industrial Relations and Social Affairs 1990: 34). On this basis, the UK has a reasonably balanced distribution of employment. However, Figure 6.1 and the report from which it is taken presents a more adverse picture, with only around a third of UK industrial sectors competitively strong. In this respect, the UK is in a similar position to Spain and Greece.

The inference is that the real gainers from the SEM, able to exploit the relatively strong position of their industries, will be Belgium, Denmark, France, Ireland, Italy and the Netherlands, which have proportionately more strong, as against weak, sectors – and Germany, where the share of well-placed sectors is highest and the share of poor or average-performance sectors is lowest. Thus, Germany has 73 per cent of its employment in strong sectors, and this in turn represents 40 per cent of total industrial employment. The positive and negative effects will cancel themselves out for Portugal and Greece. Taking the EC member states as a whole, therefore, the employment consequences for the UK are among the least favourable.

The real issue, however, is how member states respond and how the European Commission through the 1992 programme can help to bring about structural change. For the southern states, this means either specializing in the same kind of products as now but improving their competitiveness on world markets, but with the disadvantage that this will lock them into slowly growing markets. Or they could become less dependent on basic industries like clothing and footwear, and achieve an industrial structure more like the northern states. Spain already seems to be moving down this path. The challenge facing the northern states, on the other hand, according to the Commission, is to respond to international competition in their high-tech and industrially advanced sectors, while, at the same time, smoothing the shift out of declining heavy industries into growth sectors (Directorate-General for Economic and Financial Affairs/Employment, Industrial Relations and Social Affairs, 1990: 47–8).

In each case, there is an underlying presumption in favour of the 'quality scenario', involving capital investment in new production techniques and products, an expanding knowledge base, and a more highly skilled workforce. Running through the Commission's general expectations and objectives for the SEM is the enhancing of technological progressiveness and a belief that upgrading skills through increased training and development is essential:

> The importance attached to an education-training drive is not equally shared throughout the Community. Yet such a drive is essential as it must make it possible to renew existing qualifications, increase comparative advantages in terms of the ratio of real salary/level of qualification and therefore stimulate other types of investment (that is, not concentrated solely on industries with a high labour content).
> (Directorate-General for Economic and Financial Affairs/Employment,
> Industrial Relations and Social Affairs 1990: 99)

Other commentators have reached similar conclusions about the need to follow a high skill strategy (Rajan 1990; Lane 1991).

The response to the SEM through skills and training

The Commission sees primary responsibility for raising skills as lying with member states. Its own role is confined to (1) improving the level of basic education in certain states, such as Portugal and Greece, and (2) spreading scarce skills more efficiently across the Community.

Although OECD figures show the stock of people in the UK with degrees is among the highest, if not the highest, in Europe (OECD, *Employment Outlook*, July 1989), the participation rate in advanced secondary education and FE/HE has been among the lowest in the EC and OECD countries (Rajan 1990: 179, 223) – as Figure 6.2 shows. These figures are affected, however, by such factors as the length of degree courses, which tend to be shorter in the UK. Moreover, the British government has recently set targets to produce a substantial increase in the number of students in higher education in the UK, and in 1991–92 numbers expanded from 14 to 25 per cent of school leavers.

The importance of basic and advanced education lies in the throughput to firms. Clearly, any weaknesses here among member countries will become a major stumbling block in sustaining existing high-tech/knowledge based

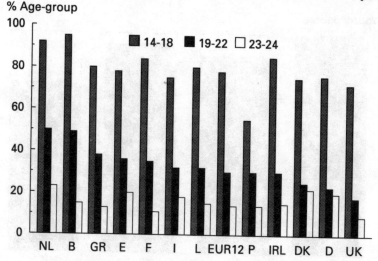

Figure 6.2 Share of young people in education in the member states (1988)
Source: Directorate-General, Employment, Industrial Relations and Social Affairs, 1990: 113

sectors and shifting more traditional sectors on to a similar footing. Equally important is the extent of post-school training young people receive alongside those who pursue higher education. Figure 6.3 shows that the UK lags considerably behind Germany, France and the Netherlands, with only 77 per cent of its young people in formal training or education beyond the school-leaving age, compared with virtually 100 per cent for Germany.

Figure 6.4 reinforces the picture of an underskilled workforce in the UK in its economic base, as it were, in terms of the numbers and proportions achieving craft-level qualifications. Equally, the numbers obtaining a technician qualification in 1985 in the UK at 80,000 contrasted with 140,000 in France and 185,000 in Germany.

Other failings of the British educational and training system include the narrow base of skills and knowledge developed in training, which limits employee flexibility, and the separation of roles in the system, as between employers and educational establishments (Esland 1990; Rajan 1990). The latter problem, however, is not confined to the UK, and considerable efforts have been made in the UK in recent years to overcome this (see Hendry 1993b).

Systematic data on how member states are responding to the call for an 'education-training drive' are beginning to emerge through the Price Waterhouse Cranfield Project reported in Chapter 7. One major problem, however, is that cross-country comparisons are bedevilled by different institutional systems. Company expenditure on training, for instance, reflects differences in who trains (companies or the state); whether or not there is legislative compulsion (as in France); and simply how efficient companies are at

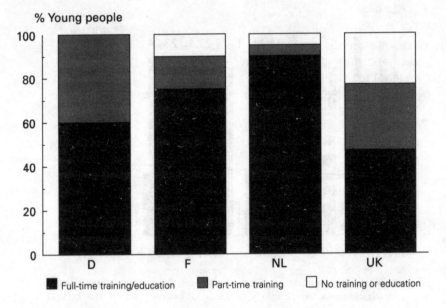

Figure 6.3 Proportion of young people receiving post-compulsory education or training by the age of 24 in some member states
Source: Directorate-General, Employment, Industrial Relations and Social Affairs, 1990: 115

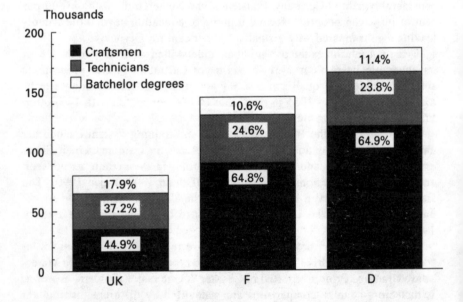

Figure 6.4 Number qualifying in engineering and technology in West Germany, France and the UK (1985)
Source: Directorate-General, Employment, Industrial Relations and Social Affairs, 1990: 116

accounting for training. As studies of vocational education and training (VET) in Britain have shown (Pettigrew, *et al.* 1989), there is enormous variability in what activities are counted as training and what elements of cost are taken into account. Holden (1991) confirms that this problem is not confined to Britain.

Moreover, only crude attempts have been made so far to project education-training responses at the sectoral level. The joint report (Directorate-General for Economic and Financial Affairs/Employment, Industrial Relations and Social Affairs 1990) sought to open up the debate by translating the prospects for groups of sectors – and therefore the kinds of business strategy that companies will need to follow – into implications for policies on skills and training. This level of aggregation, however, is too broad to be useful, partly because strategies for some sectors will differ between countries (and companies), according to how they are positioned in those.

Neither the first report from the Price Waterhouse Cranfield (1990) project nor Holden (1991) drawing on that, provide systematic data as yet on sectoral expenditure and trends (although Holden makes some broad comparisons over where European countries concentrate spending). We cannot therefore judge whether countries are investing in training in those sectors where they have a comparative advantage, or, indeed, whether companies are trying to upgrade skills in threatened sectors. The paramount question for policy makers is 'should one follow a national strategy of picking winners in allocating or encouraging the allocation of funds to training, in accordance with those sectors the European Commission has identified? Or would this simply produce a self-fulfilling cycle and deny dynamic firms in unfavoured sectors the opportunity to flourish?'.

There is scope for major comparative work on how sectors are responding to the prospects of the SEM, including the extent to which companies in different sectors are making use of training strategies to upgrade skills. One of the few studies so far to attempt this is Boyce's (1993) study of the food and drinks processing industry in the UK, France and Germany, which found the level of training had yet to respond to the SEM. Others, such as Wood and Peccei (1990) in their case studies of the furniture and insurance sectors, have confined their analysis to one country and/or to an assessment of broad HRM responses. The most substantial effort so far to relate business strategy and the HRM response on a European sectoral basis is the study by Calori and Lawrence (1991) and colleagues of four sectors (brewing, retail banking, book publishing, and the car industry). They endorse the view that 'training will more and more be seen as a strategic weapon' (ibid.: 77), as well as identifying the importance of specific management qualities such as inter-personal and intercultural skills. However, even this does not provide precise evidence of actual company responses or how the behaviour of exemplary individual companies compares with sector norms.

What we can say is that the UK falls short of the 'quality scenario' in two crucial respects – the level of wages and the level of productivity – which in turn reflect levels of skill, training, and the capitalization of its industry. Table 6.2 shows (a) that the UK ranks with Spain (plus Greece and Portugal) in having lower than average labour costs per employee (wage plus non-wage costs), but (b) has above average unit labour costs (that is, value-added per employee), implying a lower level of capitalization than its principal north European industrial competitors, France and Germany. In other words, the UK shows signs of being a low wage/low skill economy.

Comparative data on firms' performance and the way benefits are distributed reinforce this picture while also revealing a striking contrast between the corporate philosophies which animate the economies of Europe. The analysis by Lloyd *et al.* (1991) provides a devastating critique of UK national performance and the corporate values on which it rests. Taking the largest 500 European industrial firms as measured by sales (excluding those in the financial sector and utilities), they relate company profitability to the employee share of company wealth created. As Table 6.3 shows, the profit margins of large UK firms are much higher than their competitors on a company by company basis, higher across virtually all of eight principal sectors, and higher than the average taking all sectors together.

There are institutional factors which go some way to explain this disparity: for instance, the need to cover for higher inflation and interest rates, and the reliance on retained profit as a source of capital. As Table 6.4 shows, however, this does not stop large UK firms from distributing more of the added value to investors and less to employees than large firms do in any of the other EC countries.

Thus, British firms have the highest profit margins, pay the highest returns to investors, and give the lowest share of added value to employees. This raises the question, 'which type of corporate culture will Europe follow in the future?' – 'Will it be the low-margin German pattern or the high-margin UK

Table 6.2 Labour costs and unit labour costs in the member states

| Country | Percentage deviation with regard to the EC average in 1987 | |
	Labour costs	Unit labour costs
GR	−56.1	−24.4
P	−74.4	−13.9
I	1.4	−11.8
E	−25.8	−11.4
F	18.4	2.9
NL	27.2	2.9
D	22.2	3.3
IRL	−12.8	3.9
UK	−23.0	7.2
B	17.5	7.9
DK	14.0	8.5
L	15.7	19.8

Source: Directorate-General for Economic and Financial Affairs/Employment, Industrial Relations and Social Affairs 1990: 98.

Table 6.3 Sector margins in four EC countries

Sector	Italy %	France %	Germany %	UK %
Retailing	0.6	4.5	1.8	7.7
Food retailing	–	2.0	1.4	5.9
Motors/aerospace	11.5	5.7	5.7	6.4
Electricals/electronics	1.7	8.3	3.6	10.6
Engineering	5.0	5.0	4.2	9.3
Building materials	16.7	13.7	6.2	13.1
Chemical/pharmaceuticals	7.2	6.7	7.2	15.3
Food/drinks	0.8	11.0	3.3	10.3
Average	5.4	7.1	4.2	9.8

Source: *International Management*, April 1991, based on data supplied by Extel Financial's Micro EXSTAT European statistical service.

Table 6.4 Distribution of value added

Country	Companies listed	Investor share %	Employee share %
UK	201	8.1	60.2
Spain	10	8.1	65.6
Italy	25	7.3	64.1
Belgium	17	6.8	63.3
Netherlands	35	5.0	66.9
Denmark	15	4.3	69.8
France	111	3.7	69.2
Germany	81	2.7	75.7
Ireland	4	2.6	67.5

Source: *International Management*, April 1991, based on data supplied by Extel Financial's Micro EXSTAT European statistical service
Note: The rest of value added is accounted for by interest, tax and retained profit.

pattern? Or will the "European company" settle down to an intermediate margin closer to the French model?' (Lloyd *et al.* 1991: 60). Will it be one that rewards employees or investors? As they argue:

Financial sophistication leads to greedy investors, low wages, lack of international competitiveness and, ultimately, a less prosperous economy. The EC Heavyweights analysis points to a link between the strengths of various economies and the generosity of companies towards their employees.

It has always been assumed that high wages, such as those characteristic of Germany, are a result of prosperity, not a cause. The opposite may be the case. Countries with strong economies generally have companies that pay relatively large proportions of the value they create to employees, and relatively small proportions to investors. Companies in the Community's weaker economies are more likely to do the opposite.

(Lloyd *et al.* 1991: 54)

Ireland's experience of multinationals tends to confirm this in the exceptionally low unit labour costs (or high level of profit per unit of value-added), which the high-tech multinationals based there achieve (Directorate-General for Employment, Industrial Relations and Social Affairs 1990: 119). As critics of the European Community have long realized, increasingly internationalized economies require strong social controls – such as the Social Chapter is intended to provide – to prevent multinationals exploiting low wage economies. As a low wage economy and the most internationalized large economy in the EC (see below), the UK is especially vulnerable.

At the same time, the European Commission's initiatives to promote greater mobility and thereby greater efficiency in the labour market (through common vocational standards, transferability of qualifications, and student exchanges) may institutionalize such disparities while there are supply-demand imbalances between the weaker and stronger economies. Systematic data on imbalances at a sectoral level are not available, although Rajan (1990: 109) suggests recent economic recessions have led to people being employed at a level below their education and qualifications as well as tying up skills that could be put to better use elsewhere. Clearly, with the highest stock of graduates and higher levels of unemployment, the UK is vulnerable to a loss of its most educated workers to those countries like France which face particular shortages among, for example, electronics engineers and computer scientists (Directorate-General for Employment, Industrial Relations and Social Affairs, 1990: 50). This may well explain the keen interest in international graduate recruitment by the French which Keenan (1991) recently identified, although it hardly accounts for UK employers' relative indifference when the Institute of Manpower Studies (1989) was also, at that time, forecasting a dearth of new graduates in the UK.

FIRM SIZE AND INTERNATIONALIZATION

The SEM is expected to produce an increase in firm size as firms rationalize their operations internally and engage in cross-border mergers and acquisitions. This in turn is expected to increase their ability to operate in international markets in Europe and the world. From this point of view, the UK is seemingly well-placed, as it has one of the highest levels of industrial concentration and the most internationally-oriented economy in the EC.

Industrial concentration

As Table 6.5 shows, the UK has more employment concentrated in large firms and small to medium enterprises (SMEs), as against micro-firms (less than 10 employees), than the Community as a whole, while Germany also has a much larger SME sector (Bannock and Partners 1990). This disparity is especially marked in manufacturing where the UK also has a much smaller proportion employed in both SMEs (10–499 employees) and micro-firms.

Another way of looking at this is in the numbers of very large firms on a country-by-country basis. Thus, the UK has 40 per cent of the top 500 industrial companies in the EC in terms of sales, compared with Germany which has 16 per cent (Lloyd *et al.* 1991).

Table 6.5 Percentage of number of enterprises and of employment by size, class and sector (1986)

	Micro (1–9 employees)		SME (10–499 employees)		Large (over 500 employees)	
	UK	E-12	UK	E-12	UK	E-12
Enterprises						
All	90.09	91.34	9.74	8.56	0.18	0.10
Manufacturing	81.13	82.70	18.07	16.91	0.80	0.39
Construction	93.88	91.28	6.06	8.68	0.06	0.04
Services	90.47	93.03	9.42	6.92	0.11	0.06
Employment						
All	23.17	26.89	46.80	45.02	30.03	28.10
Manufacturing	6.92	11.14	38.83	45.95	54.26	42.91
Construction	43.05	39.53	43.49	50.57	13.47	9.90
Services	30.02	34.75	52.45	43.44	17.53	21.82

Source: Bannock and Partners 1990: para 6.8.

While the European Commission suggests greater concentration will be a good thing, this rather neglects the actual contribution of the SME sector to European economies and particularly its dynamic relationship with larger firms. Renewed interest in the idea of 'industrial districts' suggests a critical factor in dynamic, internationally competitive industries is the constellation of firms of varying sizes in customer–supplier relationships in close proximity, competing with one another (Porter 1990). (One of the things this sustains incidentally is a more vibrant market for skills.) While the UK is highly polarized in the size and importance of the large corporate versus SME and micro sectors of the economy as compared with France and Germany, there is also little interpenetration or integration between the two (Lane 1991). In other words, the conditions for a dynamic economy are wanting.

In terms of actual product, UK SMEs contribute only 32 per cent of private sector GDP compared with 46 per cent in Germany (Bannock and Albach 1991), while Table 6.6 using a different definitional base shows that the UK's large companies provide almost twice the proportion of GDP as equivalent size German firms. If one asks, then, which country benefits more, one observes first that the respective economies of the UK and Germany account for 15 per cent and 25 per cent of European GDP (Lloyd *et al.* 1991: 26), while Table 6.6 shows the UK, with its economy dominated by very large companies, is near the bottom of the league in terms of GDP per head of population. In other words, German economic strength rests on a wider company base, and the German economy is better served by this more even spread.

Table 6.6 Prosperity and corporate concentration

Country	GDP ECU bn	GDP/head ECU 000s	Companies listed	Total sales ECU bn	Sales % GDP
Denmark	97.8	19.1	15	18.9	19.3
Germany	1,111.1	18.2	81	507.5	45.7
Luxembourg	6.0	16.0	1	5.2	32.5
France	886.7	15.8	111	427.9	48.3
Belgium	145.9	14.7	17	48.8	33.4
Italy	831.6	14.5	25	98.8	11.9
Netherlands	208.6	14.1	35	166.2	79.7
UK	686.4	12.1	201	573.2	83.5
Spain	346.4	8.8	10	20.5	5.9
Ireland	31.3	8.7	4	4.9	15.7

Source: International Management, April 1991, based on data supplied by Extel Financial's Micro EXSTAT European statistical service

Since promoting the Single Market, the European Commission has taken on board the importance of the SME sector and has an active policy to encourage it to counteract, or complement, the development of larger firms. In this, as in any effort to promote SMEs, there are wide-ranging implications for HRM. These include difficulties for SMEs in gaining access to formal training provision, the character of skills in SMEs and appropriate forms of training, constraints on growth through limited management structures, and the means to develop managers (Hendry *et al*. 1991). The HRM community to date, however, has largely ignored the SME sector, preferring to focus on larger firms with recognizable HR activities and full-time professionals.

Internationalization

The UK already has the most internationally-oriented economy in the EC, as a result of acquisition activity by British firms abroad and by foreign firms in the UK, and until the recent recession depressed activity the UK continued to be at the forefront of this process. Figures for 1988–89 show British firms far and away the most active in mergers and acquisitions, accounting for 60 per cent of total transfrontier deals, compared with the French at 23.2 per cent, the Dutch at 5.5 per cent, Germany at 3.5 per cent, and Italian firms at 3.5 per cent (Directorate-General for Economic and Financial Affairs/Employment, Industrial Relations and Social Affairs 1990). Moreover, these figures relate to deals both within and outside the EC, with 85 per cent of all such activity by British firms being in the USA. Mergers and acquisitions (for industrial

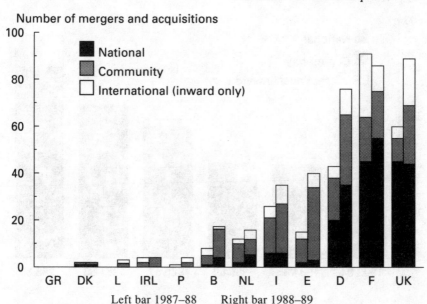

Figure 6.5 Mergers and acquisitions in the industrial sector in the member states (1987–88 and 1988–89)
Source: Directorate-General, Employment, Industrial Relations and Social Affairs, 1990: 52

companies) within the EC alone show the UK just behind France, but closing rapidly at the end of the 1980s (Figure 6.5).

More generally, as Figure 6.6 shows, the number of such deals within the EC as a whole has increased consistently through the 1980s, from around 150 in 1983–84 to nearly 500 in 1988–89. During this period, the growth in transnational mergers between industrial companies across European borders is particularly striking. Inward investment (by countries such as Japan and the USA) also accelerated as the prospect of an exclusive Single Market neared.

On the other hand, while mergers have grown at a similar rate overall in services, they are fewer (at around 175 in 1988–89) and they are far more confined within national borders. Recent service mergers have also been dominated by the banking and insurance sector. These trends show the European Commission's goal of larger companies being realized. In the process, there are powerful implications for HRM. On the positive side, there is the potential for considerable transfer of best work practices – a possibility which encouraged the UK government to attract foreign firms to the UK during the 1980s. On the negative side, the central issue is the difficulty of managing the merger process, including that of reconciling different company cultures. Adding national differences cannot make this any easier. Numerous studies suggest that mergers and acquisitions perform less well as a whole than companies pursuing a strategy of organic development (Fairburn and Kay 1989; Cutler *et al.* 1989). The performance of British firms in

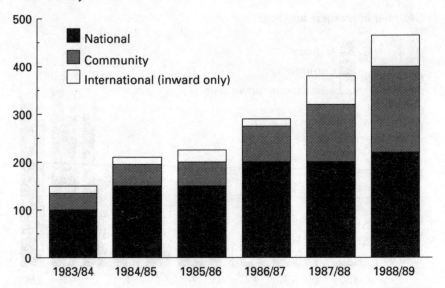

Figure 6.6 Mergers and acquisitions in the industrial sector in the community (1983–84 to 1988–89)
Source: Directorate-General, Employment, Industrial Relations and Social Affairs, 1990: 52

consequence has been generally depressed by past waves of merger activity (Kitching 1967; Cowling *et al.* 1980; Lubatkin 1983). Avoiding similar consequences on a pan-European scale is a significant challenge. Summarizing these effects, the EC observes:

> Quite considerable numbers of employees are being affected if only by changes in the pattern and structures of ownership of their employers. This may lead to changes in work practices as the products and services supplied change, as investment increases and as management styles alter.
> This may require considerable effort in the fields of human resource management and vocational training in order to ensure that the mergers are successful.
> (Directorate-General, Employment, Industrial Relations and Social Affairs
> 1990: 50)

THE DEVELOPMENT OF EUROPEAN FIRMS

The third aim which the European Commission has in view is the development of European firms. The increasing internationalization of large firms goes some way towards this, but much depends (a) on which way such firms face (that is, are they European firms or are they global multinationals), and (b) how far the 'European-ness' of such firms is cemented by management development practices.

European or global firms?

We have already seen that UK acquisition activity has been oriented to North America far more even than to Europe, and this has been a long-standing pattern through the 1980s. A second measure of firms' international orientation is who they trade with. As Table 6.7 shows, UK companies are, in fact, more oriented to markets outside the EC than are all other EC countries, except Denmark, although the proportion of UK trade within the EC has been increasing since Britain joined the Community in 1973.

Table 6.7 Percentage of exports to EC countries

Country	%	Country	%
Denmark	48.5	Greece	68.0
UK	49.4	Portugal	71.0
Germany	53.1	Ireland	74.0
Italy	56.6	Belgium/Luxembourg	74.5
France	60.4	Netherlands	75.1
Spain	63.8		

Source: OECD/Calori and Lawrence 1991: 12.

From one point of view, this might represent the way ahead, given that the object of larger European firms is to strengthen their competitiveness internationally and promote European trade with the rest of the world. We might also conclude that the UK is well-placed – better than most all others – to exploit markets outside the EC. A critical issue here, however, is the substitutability of exports by foreign direct investment. The quality of firms' exported goods and export strategies is central to this decision. Studies by Oulton (1990) and Williamson (1990) cast doubt respectively on the quality of British firms' exported goods and export strategies. This is likely to encourage globally-oriented British firms to transfer activities to overseas production and substitute this for exports from the UK. The shift in employment by UK firms during the 1980s to subsidaries abroad shows that this is precisely what has happened.

As a result, because of investment flows, UK firms are among the most internationalized in the location of employment. Ramsay (1990) cites ILO figures for the early 1980s which show UK multinational companies (MNCs) on average having a much higher proportion of employees abroad (40%), than German, American, and Italian multinationals (all at 25%), and French MNCs (20%) (UN 1988). Only those with small domestic economies, like Switzerland and the Netherlands, have more. The result is the relative absence of UK firms among Europe's biggest domestic employers. Only British Aerospace and GEC, plus the Anglo-Dutch Unilever, rank among the EC's top 25 manufacturers in the numbers they employ in Europe, compared with nine German and five French companies (Labour Research 1989).

The goal of developing 'European' firms is also a question of defending

European markets against world competition. Oulton's (1990) study, which is essentially a test of the quality of UK exports compared with imports, confirms the underlying weakness of UK industrial sectors in the considerable dispersion in 'relative unit values' between exports and imports in markets featuring British goods. In other words, the quality of British goods is very uneven and reinforces the picture of the UK having more weak and averagely performing sectors than most other EC countries.

One result is high import penetration and also greater exposure of the UK market to foreign investment (although there are clearly other factors in the eagerness of foreign firms to invest in the UK). Thus, the stock of foreign direct investment as a proportion of GDP is 23% in the UK, compared with 7% in Germany and France, and 4% in Italy (Directorate-General for Economic and Financial Affairs/Employment, Industrial Relations and Social Affairs 1990). Only the Netherlands has a higher proportion (at 36%). Throughout the post-war period, the UK has been the largest European recipient of American and Japanese investment. In other words, the pattern of inward investment confirms the 'global' rather than specifically European character of UK-based firms.

Both inward and outward investment and employment patterns show, then, why the UK is a strong supporter of an 'open door' policy on trade and investment within the EC. When taken with evidence on the internationalization of UK R&D (Cantwell 1990), British-owned firms are among the most internationalized in Europe. In turn, this highlights important differences in business culture between the UK and the other major EC countries. In Germany and France (not to mention others like Switzerland), there are strong institutional constraints to mergers and acquisitions generally and to acquisitions by non-indigenous firms in particular. Thus, there remain powerful barriers to the formation of European firms and a tendency still for member states to bolster national champions.

The 'European-ness' of European firms

Such barriers may continue to be reflected, even in pan-European mergers, in the dominance of national groups in the management of particular firms. For this reason, the European Commission has stressed the need to promote managerial mobility and cross-national representation on company boards to make such firms a reality.

Most studies suggest a growing importance for 'international' employees, and many commentators interpret this as meaning the development of a new breed of 'Euromanager' (Bruce 1989). Most fail, however, to discriminate between the different types of employee the SEM will affect. Atkinson (1989) argues that it is important to distinguish the characteristics of, demand for, and issues for recruitment and development in respect of four principal groups – senior managers, leading scientific and technical staff ('boffins'), younger managers on development programmes who could expect to experience international assignments at some time, and graduate recruits. Most studies identify the senior manager group as critical to the success of their businesses, but note suitably qualified managers are in short supply, partly because past management development practices geared to expatriate assignments are no longer appropriate. Much attention is now therefore concentrated on younger cohorts.

The development of the pan-European manager is addressed more fully in Section IV of this volume.

At the same time, most employees within European firms will not be mobile, even in major multinationals. Local conditions of employment will remain the norm for most people for the foreseeable future until the EC makes real progress in harmonizing employment standards through the Social Chapter. Confirming this, Wood and Peccei (1990), in their survey of medium-large organizations in the UK, found the development of common EC practices on employment was well down the list of firms' concerns. The three areas being given highest priority were equal retirement rights for men and women, provisions on health and safety, and equal terms and conditions for part-timers – areas where companies tended anyway to believe their own policies already met EC standards. In other respects, most firms were adopting a 'wait and see' attitude over the employment implications.

CONCLUSION

The three impacts of the SEM in terms of sectoral adjustment, increasing firm size and concentration, and the development of European firms will require HRM responses at both the company and institutional level. Paramount among these arguably is the development of high skill economies and firms to underpin a high added value industrial strategy. EC labour market policy has also been directed at realizing efficient use of scarce skills by encouraging labour mobility across the Community. The main objective, however, embraces the 'quality' scenario, largely by creating minimum common standards in employment across the Community through the Social Chapter.

The Social Chapter aims to discourage low skill/low wage economies from trying to improve their competitive position by lowering wage costs, cutting social benefits, increasing hours of work, reducing restraints on employers, or lowering direct wages (tactics which together have become known as 'social dumping'). However, although the Social Chapter was conceived with polarization between northern and southern Europe more particularly in mind, by consistently opposing it the Conservative government in Britain seems to have wanted to retain 'social dumping' as a policy option. The real losers, though, from an SEM pursuing the 'quality' scenario are likely to be those with low wage economies (or a preponderance of such sectors) and unregulated labour markets, so that existing disadvantages and sectoral specializations become institutionalized. From this point of view, the UK is well-placed to reap such disadvantages. Moreover, British-owned MNCs are heavily-biased towards non-manufacturing (Marginson 1992) and low technology industries (Stopford and Turner 1985), with a low level of skills and research activity. This suggests that Britain will continue to compete where its competitive advantage lies – in low wage, labour intensive, low skill, low productivity sectors.

REFERENCES

Atkinson, J. (1989) *Corporate Employment Policies for the Single European Market*, *IMS Report No. 179*, Institute of Manpower Studies, University of Sussex.

Bannock & Partners (1990) *Enterprises in the European Community*, Brussels/Luxembourg: Commission of the European Communities.

Bannock, G. and Albach, H. (1991) *Small Business Policy in Europe, Britain, Germany and the Commission*, London: Anglo-German Foundation.

Bower, J.L. (1988) *When Markets Quake: The Management Challenge of Restructuring Industry*, Boston: Harvard Business School Press.

Boyce, B. (1993) 'Human resources development training and the Single European Market: a case study of the food and drinks processing industries of the UK, France and Germany', in Shaw J.B. and Kirkbride, P.S. (eds) *Research in Personnel and Human Resource Management – Supplement 3 – International Human Resource Management*, Greenwich, Connecticut: JAI Press (in press).

Bruce, L. (1989) 'Wanted: more mongrels in the corporate kennel, *International Management* January: 35–7.

Calori, R. and Lawrence, P. (eds) (1991) *The Business of Europe: Managing Change*, London: Sage.

Cantwell, J. (1990) The internationalization of technological activities and its implications for competitiveness, working paper, Economics Department, Reading University.

Commission of the European Communities (1988) *Research on the 'Costs of Non-Europe'*, Luxembourg.

Cowling, K., Stoneman, P., Cubbin, J., Cable, T., Hall, G., Domberger, S. and Dutton, P. (1980) *Mergers and Economic Performance*, Cambridge: Cambridge University Press.

Cutler, T., Haslam, C., Williams, J. and Williams, K. (1989) *1992 – The Struggle for Europe: A Critical Evaluation of the European Community*, New York: Berg.

Directorate-General for Economic and Financial Affairs (1988) *European Economy: The Economics of 1992. An assessment of the potential effects of completing the internal market of the European Community*, Brussels: Commission of the European Communities.

Directorate-General for Economic and Financial Affairs/Employment, Industrial Relations and Social Affairs (1990) *European Economy: Social Europe. The impact of the internal market by industrial sector: the challenge for the Member States*, Brussels: Commission of the European Communities.

Directorate-General, Employment, Industrial Relations and Social Affairs (1990) *Employment in Europe*, Luxembourg: Office for Official Publications of the European Communities.

Directorate-General, Employment, Industrial Relations and Social Affairs (1991) *Employment in Europe*, Luxembourg: Office for Official Publications of the European Communities.

Esland, G. (ed.) (1990) *Education, Training and Employment, Volume 1: Educated Labour – The Changing Basis of Industrial Demand*, Wokingham: Addison-Wesley.

Fairburn, J.A. and Kay, J.A. (eds) (1989) *Mergers and Merger Policy*, Oxford: Oxford University Press.

Hendry, C. (1993a) *Human Resource Strategies for International Growth*, London and New York: Routledge.

—— (1993b) *Human Resource Management: A Strategic Approach to Employment*, London: Butterworth-Heinemann.

Hendry, C., Jones, A.M., Arthur, M.B. and Pettigrew, A. (1991) *Human Resource Development in the Small-to-Medium Sized Enterprise. Research Paper No. 88*, Sheffield: Department of Employment.

Holden, L. (1991) 'European trends in training and development', *International Journal of Human Resource Management*, 2 (2): 113–31.

IER (Institute for Employment Research) (1991) 'Employment in the Single European Market', Bulletin No. 10, University of Warwick.

Institute of Manpower Studies (1989) *How Many Graduates in the Twenty-First Century*, Brighton: IMS, University of Sussex.

Keenan, T. (1991) 'Graduate recruitment à la française', *Personnel Management*, December: 34–7.

Kitching, J. (1967) 'Why do mergers miscarry?, '*Harvard Business Review*, November-December: 84–101.

Labour Research Department (1989) *Europe 1992: What It All Means to Trade Unionists*, London: LRD.

Lane, C. (1991) 'Industrial reorganisation in Europe: patterns of convergence and divergence in Germany, France and Britain, *Work, Employment and Society* 5 (4): 515–39.

Lloyd, T., Carton-Kelly, A., and Mueller, M. (1991) 'EC heavyweights', *International Management*, April: 26–67.

Lubatkin, M. (1983) 'Mergers and the performance of the acquiring firm', *Academy of Management Review* 8 (2): 218–25.

Marginson, P. (1992) 'Multinational Britain: employment and work in an inter-nationalised economy', VET Forum Conference, Multinational Companies and Human Resources: A Movable Feast?, University of Warwick, 22–24 June 1992.

OECD (1989) *Employment Outlook*, (July) Paris: OECD (available on microfiche only).

Oulton, N. (1990) 'Quality and performance in UK trade, 1978–87', *NIESR Discussion Paper No. 197*, National Institute of Economic and Social Research, London.

Pettigrew, A., Hendry, C., and Sparrow, P. (1989) *Training in Britain: Employers' Perspectives on Human Resources*, London: HMSO.

Porter, M. (1990) *The Competitive Advantage of Nations*, London: Macmillan.

Price Waterhouse Cranfield (1990) *The Price Waterhouse Cranfield Project on International Strategic Human Resource Management: Report 1990*, London: Price Waterhouse.

Rajan, A. (1990) *1992: A Zero-Sum Game*, London: Industrial Society Press.

Ramsay, H. (1990) '1992 – The year of the multinational? Corporate behaviour, indus-trial restructuring and labour in the Single Market', *Warwick Papers in Industrial Relations No. 35*, Industrial Relations Reseach Unit, University of Warwick.

Stopford, J.M. and Turner, L. (1985) *Britain and the Multinationals*, Chichester: Wiley.

UN (United Nations Centre on Transnational Corporations) (1988) *Transnational Corporations in World Development: Trends and Prospects*, New York: UN.

Williamson, P.J. (1990) 'Winning the export war: British, Japanese and West German exporters: strategy compared', *British Journal of Management* 1 (4): 215–30.

Wood, S. and Peccei, R. (1990) 'Preparing for 1992? business-led versus strategic human resource management', *Human Resource Management Journal* 1, (1): 63–89.

7 Trends in European HRM
Signs of convergence?

Chris Brewster
Ariane Hegewisch
Lesley Mayne

'Europe' is increasingly seen as a single entity; particularly by the rest of the world. Common cultural and social traditions are emphasized and attempts are being made to fuse the countries together into a progressively closer European union. Chapter 5 (Brewster) has argued that, on an international perspective, human resource management can be seen to have a specifically European aspect. Closer up, however, looking within the borders of the continent, the question is raised as to whether the developing economic integration of Europe is being accompanied by a convergence of human resource management practices. Within the broader picture of similarity, how different are these countries on closer inspection?

Preliminary analyses of our data (Brewster and Bournois 1991; Hegewisch 1991; Holden and Livian 1992) show a number of trends common across Europe and a number of other areas where, despite much change, it is difficult to discern any consistent direction. This chapter draws on the research outlined in Chapter 5 (Brewster) to update this material and to identify the overall shape of developments in HRM in Europe. (Details of coverage, abbreviations used, etc. can be found on pp. 60–1.)

There is no area of human resource management where all organizations, whatever their sector, size or nationality, have moved in one direction: always there are at least some organizations moving against the general trend. With this caveat, however, there are four topics in HRM which currently have a high profile in the literature and which will assist us in examining the question of similarity and difference across Europe. These four topics are: developments in pay and benefits; flexible working patterns; equality of opportunity; and training. We also examine the question of responsibility for such human resource issues: is it located in the HR department itself or is it shared with line managers?

DEVELOPMENTS IN PAY

Pay is a central issue in human resource management. Trends in this area are clear; this section addresses the issues of the increasing decentralization of pay determination and the growth of flexible pay systems.

The decentralization of bargaining structures has taken place, both in countries with highly centralized systems of pay determination such as Denmark and Sweden (although not without some alternating moves towards recentralization) and in countries with greater decentralization such as the UK and France. In the latter two countries it is now only a minority of private sector organizations who are negotiating over basic pay at national or industry level, for any staff groups, including manual workers. These trends have been encouraged by employers' federations in both countries who in some industries have gone as far as withdrawing from industry negotiations, thus forcing company level bargaining (Hegewisch 1991). National or industrywide bargaining there is now mainly a public sector practice. In the UK for example only 22 per cent of private employers negotiate at industry-level for manual workers whereas 82 per cent of public sector employers implement national agreements.

Even in the UK, where there has been a concerted effort by Government and employers' associations and by many employers to drive pay determination down to the company level, there remain many organizations where basic pay for manual workers is established in national industry bargaining. This is consistent with other evidence from the UK. The Workplace Industrial Relations Surveys (Millward and Stevens 1986) and the more recent Marginson *et al.* (1988) research in the private sector both show a considerable degree of centralization in pay, and other related HR issues. More than that however the Marginson *et al.* work also shows that, in a typically informal way, many multi-site UK businesses maintain a considerable involvement from head office in HR decision-making. These conclusions are not uncontroversial; in a summary of these surveys, and his own research on the topic, Kinnie concludes that although there is some evidence of a move towards the decentralization of management and of bargaining structures in the UK 'these changes do not necessarily lead to an increase in decision-making discretion for establishment managers' (Kinnie 1989: 33). Morris and Wood (1991), however, have argued that this may underestimate the extent of change. (Recently, there has been some evidence of companies like Shell (*PM Plus* April 1992) and public sector organizations like Sheffield Council (*Personnel Today*, 5–8 May 1992) recentralizing personnel matters.)

The situation is of course fundamentally different in Denmark, the Netherlands or Sweden where over 60 per cent of employers still bargain at industry or national level (see Table 7.1). However, there has been a shift within multi-employer bargaining from national to industry level, with agreements which leave greater scope for company implementation (Ahlen 1989; Hegewisch 1991; Scheuer 1992; Visser 1992). Nevertheless the commitment to multi-employer bargaining with trade unions remains high. Least change can be discerned in Germany. Pay and conditions in Germany are regulated by collective agreements which are binding, through their membership of employers' associations, on 90 per cent of employers (Gaugler and Wiltz

1992). They allow, and even provide for, company level bargaining over implementation in several areas. However, the relationship between industry-wide and company level bargaining has been stable and there have been few signs of decentralization (for these reasons, and because much of collective bargaining procedures are written into co-determination legislation, the question on the determination of basic pay was not included in the German survey). It remains to be seen how far the German system will be able to cope with the drastically new situation caused by reunification.

Table 7.1 Levels of bargaining over basic pay for manual workers (percentage of organizations, 1991*)

	National/industrial collective bargaining	Regional collective bargaining	Company	Establishment/ site	Individual
Denmark	62	17	13	9	10
Spain	41	18	22	15	8
France	31	10	46	24	14
Italy	59	2	45	12	9
Norway	77	22	16	13	13
Netherlands	78	n/a	22	6	9
Sweden	68	8	32	11	13
UK	37	8	31	32	6

Source: PWCP
Note: * This topic was not included in German and Swiss surveys.

Levels of pay determination are one issue: the substantive pay arrangements made at the various levels are another. Reward management has been subject of much change and discussion over the last decade. The late 1970s and early 1980s were, in several European countries, a period of concern with high inflation leading to increased government attempts to control and keep down wage agreements; in Italy and France at least there were also linked policy objectives of greater pay equality, expressed through flat rate increases or agreements to higher increases for employees on lower grades. During the second half of the 1980s and the early 1990s the pendulum swung the other way. Human resource management theories stress the need to make pay more performance related, whether at individual or company level. Lower inflation has given companies greater scope for the introduction of performance rewards on top of cost of living increases; increasing competition and cash limits in the public sector have led more and more organizations to look for a direct link between rewards and contribution; and in some cases tight labour markets have increased the power of individual employees to negotiate particular deals. Within organizations variable pay, merit and performance related pay have increased across Europe.

A majority of organizations in all countries surveyed apart from the Netherlands and Norway increased variable pay in the three years preceding

1991; the number of organizations decreasing variable pay is very small everywhere, nowhere reaching even 10 per cent. There was a corresponding, though slightly lower, growth in the number of organizations offering increased non-money benefits (with the marked exception of France where there is a cultural and traditional preference for money payments and comparatively little development of fringe benefits).

In the research there is some correlation between those organizations who increased pay and benefits in response to recruitment difficulties and those who increased variable pay (Hegewisch 1991: 31), thus encouraging the assumption that at least some of the increases were a response to market pressures rather than a more fundamental shift in underlying payment philosophies. This impression is confirmed by organizational practices in terms of merit or performance related pay and other incentive payments. The practice of merit or performance related pay is least common in the Scandinavian countries; even for managerial staff less than a fifth of organizations in Norway and less than a sixth in Denmark and Sweden use this approach (see Table 7.2). In France, Italy and the UK over two-thirds of organizations use merit pay for managerial staff and, at least in France and Italy, a third and more do so for manual workers. In Italy it has been estimated that the share of merit pay in white collar wage packages between 1983 and 1988 grew from 13 per cent to 20 per cent (*IDS Focus* 1989: 10); similarly the uptake in France has been extensive, encouraged partly by taxation policies. Marsden (1989) suggests that much of this increase in performance related pay was a reaction to pay policies at the beginning of the 1980s which in both Italy and France led to a flattening of differentials. Overall, however, while this is an area of considerable cultural difference across Europe, undoubtedly the practice has become popular during the second half of the 1980s, with obvious consequences for both collective bargaining and the role of management.

There has been much less uptake of other forms of incentive pay, particularly those forms that link pay awards to company performance.

Table 7.2 Use of merit/performance related pay for managerial staff (percentage of organizations) (1991)

Switzerland	65
Germany	24
Denmark	14
Spain	48
France	70*
Italy	85
Norway	18
Netherlands	27
Sweden	13
UK	68

Source: PWCP
Note: * French figures are for 1990; 'managerial' includes some professional staff.

Practices such as profit sharing or employee share options in most countries are offered by only a minority of employers, even at managerial level. Employee share options have become popular in the UK, being offered to management in 40 per cent of companies and by 25 per cent of organizations to manual staff; the number of organizations offering share options in any other of the countries surveyed falls well below 20 per cent. Profit sharing is a little more common and more widely spread; in France over two-thirds of organizations offer profit sharing, to all levels of staff – a result largely of favourable tax incentives. In Germany over 60 per cent of organizations have profit sharing schemes for managers, and in Switzerland over 40 per cent (with much lower proportions for other staff groups); in the Netherlands and the UK slightly under one third. In the remaining countries, particularly Denmark, Norway and Italy, this is a rare practice.

The issue of incentive payments thus illustrates that, in spite of some common trends towards more variable pay and pay decentralization, national and cultural differences remain strong in remuneration policies across Europe. The trend towards pay flexibility should not hide the continuing importance of institutional pay bargaining systems and even legislation in the field of pay determination – a common feature of pay bargaining in most European countries. Most countries in Europe have some form of national minimum wage (or a system of generalizing collective agreements across an industry). In most countries in Europe legislation sets a framework for collective bargaining, by regulating the levels of bargaining, the status of agreements, the role and rights of bargaining partners as well as mechanisms of arbitration (Brewster *et al.* 1992; IDS/ IPM 1992). While the 1980s might have seen a shift in the power of the negotiating partners, our data provide little evidence of a major threat to systems of bargaining overall. It remains to be seen how far greater flexibility in payment structures and decentralization can survive the recession that has now hit most of Europe; this will show whether there will be a lasting shift towards a more performance related pay culture or whether flexible pay was a reaction to good times and tight labour markets, and only worked when it led to increases in pay.

FLEXIBLE WORKING PRACTICES

'Atypical' work patterns or contracts, such as temporary, casual, fixed-term, home based and annual hours contracts, are continuing or are on the increase in every country in our survey despite differing legal, cultural and labour traditions (Brewster *et al.* 1993). Many of the highest increases (i.e. where more than half of all the organizations in the country have increased their use of a particular form of flexible working) occur in countries where there has traditionally been less use of such forms; indicating a levelling out and more widespread use of flexibility across Europe.

Flexible working packages tend to be used as a response to the changing demographics within the labour market. The lack of a skilled labour force in some countries has forced a greater use of time flexibility. Schemes offering all or certain groups greater access to part-time work, job sharing, term-time employment and career breaks have been seen as a means of retaining or enticing back into the labour market categories of staff unable to work full-time, such as working mothers, carers or older workers.

A perhaps more widespread rationale for flexibility arises from increased international competition. The effect of this trend is to put additional pressure on managements to increase productivity with reduced wage costs. In the public sector a reduction in public spending would also see organizations using flexible working practices as one contribution to maintaining services. The same practices have been used in both private and public sectors as a response to cost-saving measures which result in cuts in permanent posts or 'headcount'. The innovative use of working arrangements also assisted organizations in making better use of their capital equipment and resources by extending working hours to cope with increased demand. The increase in variable work patterns increases the cost-effective use of labour by reducing employee costs and matching work provision more closely to work re-quirements. However, the provision of labour on this basis does not always benefit the employees. Indeed, in many cases it operates directly against their interest; leaving many flexible workers with substantially reduced pay and with reduced protection in terms and conditions of work.

This potential exploitation of some workers on these forms of contract is causing increasing concern within the Commission of the European Community. The Social Chapter includes a provision to extend workers' rights to individuals on atypical contracts; and the European Court of Justice has been making judgments under the equal opportunities legislation which are restricting the cost advantages of employing workers on these contracts.

The debate about these practices has been influenced by the 'flexible' firm model developed by Atkinson and associates at the Institute of Manpower Studies (Atkinson 1985). This argued that firms could be seen as developing a core of full-time permanent workers (who provide the competitive or central proponent of the organization's work, and are therefore treated as a key asset, with appropriate terms and conditions of employment, training and careers) and a periphery of 'atypical' workers (who are, in effect, dispensable). The flexible firm model has attracted the criticism of commentators such as Pollert (1988); a key issue being whether the increase in the use of such practices as part-time and temporary labour is a strategic decision within the organization to create a flexible workforce or whether the growth is a result of short term responses to outside influences beyond the control of managers, such as high unemployment, reduced trade union influence or competitive pressures.

The data from our research confirm the more anecdotal or partial views of many commentators who have failed to find any evidence of explicit strategies aimed directly at the creation of a core/peripheral workforce. We found little or no correlation between corporate or HR strategies and the increased or decreased use of flexible working practices. In broad terms therefore our data fail to show that flexibility is in any overall sense linked to a strategic approach to HRM. Of course, this does not mean that certain individual organizations may not be operating in such a strategic fashion.

Whatever the rationale, one simple fact is clear. Despite the fact that trends in the use and increase in flexible working tend to vary by country, by sector and by size of organizations, there is, in almost all subcategories, a picture of continuing growth (see Table 7.3).

Table 7.3 Organizations having increased or decreased the use of certain working arrangements over the last three years (%) (1991)

	Part-time work	*Temporary/casual*	*Fixed term contracts*
Switzerland	80	58	43
	(1)	(5)	(5)
Germany	47	31	54
	(5)	(11)	(7)
Denmark	18	20	16
	(14)	(24)	(2)
Spain	22	51	49
	(8)	(9)	(7)
France	29	40	46
	(7)	(14)	(12)
Italy	49	19	43
	(6)	(6)	(5)
Norway	30	35	43
	(11)	(26)	(17)
Netherlands	58	66	20
	(3)	(5)	(20)
Sweden	17	25	24
	(24)	(15)	(1)
UK	48	36	28
	(6)	(12)	(4)

Source: PWCP
Note: Figures in brackets represent decreases.

Seven out of the ten countries surveyed showed their largest growth figures to be in the use of part-time, temporary or fixed term contracts, rather than, for example, in shift working, over-time working or weekend working. Atypical contracts frequently apply to workers who enter the labour market for the first time, like young people, or re-enter after they have had a break, for example to have children. Shiftworking, overtime or weekend work (at least outside the retail sector) are much more often used for traditional workforces. However, other forms of 'atypical' contracts such as homeworking or annual hours which were widely predicted to increase rapidly, continue to be used by only a small minority of organizations, across all countries surveyed. The lowest percentage of increase was in the use of homeworkers, where no country had as much as 10 per cent of organizations increasing their use.

Only in Sweden had there been a significant decrease in part-time working.

In that country part-time work is being converted into full-time work. At least six in ten employers in France, Denmark, Norway, the Netherlands, Spain, Switzerland and the UK increased either temporary or fixed term employment during the previous three years. (There is, of course, some trade-off between temporary and fixed-term contracts, depending partly on local legal requirements. For an individual on a short fixed-term contract the distinction may be of little importance.) A reduction in use of these forms occurred in only a minority of organizations. However, in the large majority of organizations the use of temporary or fixed term employment remains, even with the high rates of increase, rather marginal (see Table 7.4). High temporary users are still signficantly less than 20% of organizations in nearly all countries.

Table 7.4 Percentage of organizations having more than 10 per cent of employees on forms of atypical contracts (1991)

	Part-time	Temporary/casual	Fixed term
Switzerland	37	4	10
Germany	20	1	12
Denmark	37	4	8
Spain	3	23	26
France	13	9	15
Italy	6	3	10
Norway	41	8	11
Netherlands	35	18	3
Sweden	44	14	1
UK	24	7	5

Source: PWCP

Further analysis of the data indicates variations in the spread of certain forms of flexible work within countries. Public and private sector employers use flexible working in different proportions and in different ways, the contrast being particularly marked in the UK (Bruegel and Hegewisch 1993). While part-time work, for example, has grown particularly in the public sector, there are still stark country differences in the utilization of part-time workers, reflecting varying employment norms operating within public administration systems.

As mentioned above, while flexible employment contracts might benefit the individual employer, the same does not necessarily hold for the employee. Nor are such working practices costless for the economy as a whole, given that the state is likely to have to fund the bill for unemployment due to interrupted working patterns or training for workers whose lack of attachment to any one employer makes investment in their training unlikely. The European Commission has expressed its concern at the social consequences of flexible contracts and has put forward a number of proposals for greater protection of flexible workers (Lockhart and Brewster 1992; Brewster *et al.* 1993).

When organizations were asked if they thought that full implementation of the EC Social Chapter would require a change in personnel policies towards flexible working practices, the results varied across countries (see Table 7.5). A greater percentage of organizations in non-EC countries felt that EC initiatives regarding working hours and shifts would have an impact. The greatest impact on working hours and shift work was anticipated in Sweden. Legislation regarding the use of part-time, temporary and fixed term contracts was anticipated to have the biggest effect on personnel policies in France, Spain and, particularly, Italy.

Table 7.5 Percentage of organizations expecting effects of EC Social Chapter in relation to working hours and flexible employment (1991)

	Working hours/shifts	Use of part-time, temporary, fixed term contracts
Switzerland	63	40
Germany	59	53
Denmark	58	47
Spain	45	62
France	53	63
Italy	31	70
Norway	60	55
Sweden	74	47
UK	58	47

Source: PWCP

All of the results emerging from our survey suggest that organizations across Europe are moving towards greater flexibility, even if they are starting from different positions. The assumption is that the benefits of flexible working outweigh the disadvantages. At an organizational level flexible patterns require a more definite focus on the actual work rather than the job, with more relevance and less costs providing a greater competitiveness and opening up opportunities for new sources of labour.

Disadvantages for managements of flexible working within the organization have been paid less attention in the past, but in certain areas are very real. Administratively, flexibility is more complicated, requiring greater complexity in such areas as recruitment, training and work organization. Recent research has shown that 'flexible workers' can be more expensive overall than 'standard workers' (Nollen 1992). Furthermore the commitment of flexible workers may be less certain. By definition these workers have a lesser time commitment to an organization and often a lesser psychological commitment too. This in turn raises issues of motivation, confidentiality and communication between managerial and non-managerial employees. Effective management (and the skills to perform as an effective manager within a flexible workforce) remains a predominant issue.

In the policies of a clear majority of organizations across Europe, however, the disadvantages are outweighed by the advantages outlined at the beginning of this section. It seems likely that the total dominance of 'standard' working contracts has gone forever and that we can anticipate a continuing spread of atypical working.

EQUALITY OF OPPORTUNITY

The equality of men and women in employment is one of the key tenets of European social policy, set out in the pay equality section of the Treaty of Rome in 1957 and expanded by several equal treatment directives in the 1970s. As a result all EC member states have sex discrimination and equal pay legislation. Nevertheless the area of equal opportunities, of practices and of support for working women, is one of the most divergent within Europe. In countries such as Denmark and France, and in the non-EC Scandinavian countries, childcare and caring facilities are widespread; most women with children combine paid work with domestic responsibilities. In the Scandinavian countries women's participation in paid work is now very nearly as high as that of men. At the other end of the spectrum are the more southern European countries such as Greece or Spain where women are only a third of the labour force and where public childcare and caring provisions are limited.

Whatever the proportion of women in the workforce, vertical and occupational segregation of women is a feature of all European countries, including the Scandinavian countries. Women work in female dominated jobs, and they rarely reach positions of senior management. Another characteristic common to most European countries is women's predominance among part-time workers; although levels of part-time work vary substantially between countries (Bruegel and Hegewisch 1993).

During the last decade increasing attention has been focused on the continuing underutilization of women in the labour market. This was not least because of demographic changes, mainly the falling birthrate, which results in a drop in the number of school leavers and thus is forcing many employers to reconsider how to fulfil their future labour needs. Added to this, at least in countries such as Germany, since the late 1970s there have been increasing political and social pressures on companies to change employment practices and give a more prominent role to women. This has encouraged, for example, some of the larger banks in both Germany and Britain from the early 1980s to re-examine their graduate entry programmes and try to increase the number of women in senior positions. Even more active were local authorities who, from that time, started to develop equal opportunities policies, positive action plans and set targets for changes in the composition of their workforce. However it has only been in the second half of the 1980s that such initiatives have been taken up by a broader number of organizations. Over half of the organizations in the UK and the Netherlands and over a third in Germany, Norway, Sweden and Switzerland monitor the share of women in recruitment and, even though the numbers are smaller in all countries, around a third of organizations also monitor the gender distribution of training and promotions (see Table 7.6). Such activities in the field of equal opportunities are markedly lower in France, Italy and Spain – significantly so for France, where in fact employers are legally bound to establish these statistics but where there is little enforcement to ensure that the legislation is implemented.

Table 7.6 Percentage of organizations monitoring the share of women in the workforce in recruitment, training and promotion (1991)

	Recruitment	*Training*	*Promotion*
Switzerland	39	28	32
Germany	37	18	14
Denmark	11	8	11
Spain	24	14	16
France	25	22	24
Italy	29	14	17
Norway	41	33	31
Netherlands	50	31	34
Sweden	41	37	39
UK	53	27	33

Source: PWCP

Equal opportunities policies of course do not refer solely to gender inequality. In the English language the term is generally understood as including discrimination on the basis of race and ethnic background, as well as disability. Most European countries have some quota system for the employment of people with disabilities (although there is no general anti-discrimination legislation on the grounds of disability). Discrimination on the grounds of race or ethnic origin in employment is much less of a concern in most European countries although there is strong evidence that because of discrimination, black and ethnic minority people are not utilized to their full potential. In Britain and the Netherlands the issue of race discrimination in employment has been more prominent with employers during the last few years although, as can be seen from Table 7.7, much less so than equal opportunties for women. The level of migrants, immigrants and black and ethnic minority people in the workforce in European countries varies from about 5 per cent in the UK and the Netherlands to 8 per cent in France and Germany and 25 per cent in Switzerland. But awareness and concern among employers about race discrimination in many countries remains low.

TRAINING

The field of training provisions in Europe is one of considerable government intervention, but also one where levels of provision (in terms of numbers of university graduates, institutes of vocational qualification) vary considerably between countries. However in most countries the issue of training is seen as

Table 7.7 Percentage of organizations monitoring the share of black and ethnic minority people in the workforce for recruitment, training and promotion

	Recruitment	*Training*	*Promotion*
Switzerland	33	15	7
Germany	25	7	3
Denmark	3	0	0
Spain	4	2	1
France*	n/a	n/a	n/a
Italy	9	2	1
Norway	3	5	2
Netherlands	39	19	14
Sweden	9	5	1
UK	52	20	23

Source: PWCP
Note: *Topic not included in France.

critical in the long-term strategy of organizations in terms of manpower planning, human resource allocation, fulfilling skills needs in the light of change, the development of management succession and career path planning, and as a means of aiding or substituting for recruitment (Holden 1991). Our data show a Europe-wide increase in investment in training at all levels, particularly for managerial and professional staff.

Whether training is treated as a cost or, as many organizations now claim it should be, as an investment, details of both expenditure and benefits are important. However, across Europe (with the exception of France, where the law requires organizations to spend at least 1.2 per cent of their pay bill on training: Bournois 1992) many organizations are unable to identify the actual percentage of wages and salaries spent on training (see Table 7.8).

Being unable to calculate these figures could be in part a consequence of the move to more decentralized training provision and the devolution of HR responsibilities as a whole. The increased responsibility of line management

Table 7.8 Average proportion of wages and salaries spent on training in each country and percentage of organizations which did not know training expenditure

	Average training expenditure	*Don't know*
Sweden	2.2	25
Germany	2.5	24
Spain	2.2	18
France	3.8	2
Italy	2.0	24
Norway	2.7	30
Netherlands	2.6	23
Sweden	3.8	44
UK	2.8	38

Source: PWCP

for training may result in a lack of information about the subject gathered centrally. This lack of information is not only found in European organizations. Grosseilliers (1986: 46) revealed that in the USA '31 per cent of education directors at the largest corporations said they didn't know how much their companies spent on Training and Development'. This raises questions about how organizations actually evaluate the effectiveness of their training programmes when this basic information is not available.

However, many organizations in Europe are spending considerable amounts of money on training (Table 7.8). They are devoting substantial amounts of time to this purpose as well. Table 7.9 uses manual workers, the group that receives least training, as an example. Even here, in eight out of the ten countries more than 10 per cent of the organizations devote five or more days – out of a presumed working year of around 200 days – to training.

Table 7.9 Average days training per year given to manual workers (percentage of organizations not including 'don't knows') (1991)

	<1	1–3	3–5	5–10	10+
Switzerland	36	40	17	5	2
Germany	38	35	15	9	4
Denmark	25	31	27	12	5
Spain	14	20	25	22	19
France	13	37	25	20	6
Italy	22	41	19	14	5
Norway	20	28	28	17	8
Netherlands	14	32	29	17	8
Sweden	73	20	5	2	0
UK	21	37	24	13	6

Source: PWCP

To some extent differential training provisions externally are reflected in organizations' training efforts internally. The high number of days employees spend on training in Spain, for example, is due to a level of State education insufficient for organizations' requirements; they have to supplement training internally. Similarly the high quality of provision in Germany explains the comparatively low level there.

Information on expenditure or on days spent on training is not enough: organizations also need to be able to assess the benefits – the need for training and the extent to which such needs are met. More than half of all organizations across Europe stated that they systematically analysed employee training needs. However, the methods most frequently used for this assessment tended to be the less formal ones such as line management and employee requests.

Generally our data show that across Europe organizations are trying to organize training which meets both of two, possibly conflicting, goals: those of the organization and those of individual employees. In France, Germany,

Switzerland and the Netherlands the balance tends to be towards employee demands. These countries are much less likely to analyse their employee training needs via a projected business or service plan than other countries.

Comparing the analysis of training needs to the evaluation of the training once given, we find a slightly smaller overall percentage of organizations assessing the latter. Once again however, where organizations do evaluate training it tends to be done in an informal manner. Evaluation of training is more likely to be conducted by informal feedback via line management or the trainees themselves than by tests or formal evaluation. These informal methods of analysis and evaluation could be linked to growing line management responsibility in this area. A more cynical interpretation is that much training is still done as an 'act of faith' with no real expectation that the organization will be able to measure the resultant benefits.

Where is this training commitment most intensive, and on what topics? Our data show that managers in general receive more training than any other occupational group. Around one tenth of organizations provide management training of ten days or more. Further, the amount of money spent on management training over the last three years has increased by more than half in every country, though in Germany, Italy, the Netherlands, Spain and Switzerland provision for technical and professional staff has increased even more.

There are some interesting differences in what the HR or personnel departments see as constituting their main training requirements in the next three years. In all countries apart from Denmark, Italy and Spain the highest priority was people management and supervision. Both Spain and Denmark saw their main requirements in training for computers and new technology with Italy concentrating on the management of change.

The high percentage of organizations looking at the provision of training in people management and supervision may reflect the decentralization of HR issues to line management and the growing responsibility they are needing to take on board. What it also shows is that, within Europe as a whole, HR departments themselves are becoming more aware of the need to train managers for the increased role they are now being asked to perform in human resources. It is to this issue of the relationship between personnel specialists and line managers in taking responsibility for HR issues that we turn next.

Overall, the subject of training is seen as a high priority by personnel specialists across Europe. Despite the differences in external provision through the Government-supported education and training systems in each country, there is a common trend towards the expansion of training provision.

THE HR DEPARTMENT

The position of the HR department within the organizational structures has been covered in Chapter 5 (Brewster). Beyond the extent of integration of the specialists within the general senior management structures of the organization there is the issue of the responsibilities of the HR department itself. There has been considerable speculation, particularly within the UK, that many 'personnel management' tasks are being devolved to line managers; the managers whom most employees work to on a day-to-day basis and who, within decentralized cost or profit centre arrangements, are increasingly responsible for the overall value of the human resource. There is now, perhaps, a developing orthodoxy that HRM as a concept should include a reduced role for personnel or HR specialists and an expanded role for line managers.

Defining and identifying devolvement of HR management is perhaps relatively straightforward (Hoogendoorn and Brewster 1992). Two clear indicators are available from our data: the first is the extent to which line managers are involved in certain HR practices and the second the related issue of how many personnel specialists there are for a given number of employees.

The respondents to our survey were asked to identify the position of their own organization on six issues: pay and benefits; recruitment and selection, training and development; industrial relations; health and safety; and work-force expansion or reduction. In each case they were asked whether responsibility for major policy decisions rested with line management; line management with personnel or HR department support; with the personnel or HR function with line management support; or with the personnel or HR department alone. An overall comparison provides a simple means of analysis and enables us to develop a comparative rating (Hoogendoorn and Brewster 1992; Brewster and Holt Larsen 1992). The results show some very interesting variations and are shown in Figure 7.1.

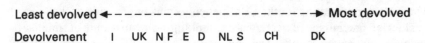

Figure 7.1 Relative devolvement rankings of ten European countries

The results show that in Denmark and Switzerland devolvement is the norm for most organizations. Denmark is rated first or second in terms of the extent of line management responsibility on all of the aforementioned issues, with Switzerland always being among the top ranked four countries with most widespread devolution. Sweden and the Netherlands are also above the 'devolution average'.

Five out of the ten countries fall in a cluster at or below the 'devolution average'.

Variations within the group of five do exist despite the close overall ranking. Somewhat of a surprise to many commentators is the position of the UK. It is one of the least devolved countries in our sample. Italy, as one can see from the table, stands on its own and has by a clear majority the fewest organizations devolving issues to the line.

We also assessed changes in line management responsibility for HR issues; and found in all countries a trend towards more devolution. The countries that have shown the least obvious trend in this direction over the last three years are Italy, which is at the extreme of this scale, and Germany. This would fit in with the common stereotype (Randlesome 1990; Lawrence 1991) of German employers being conservative and stable.

The second indicator within our data is the proportion of personnel specialists to the total numbers of employees. A higher number of personnel specialists is likely to be correlated with less devolvement to line management. There are naturally many other related issues such as the degree to which line managers are trained to undertake these duties, but in general we find a close correlation between the devolvement ranking and the number of specialists per thousand employees (Fig 7.2).

Low ←									→ High
Devolvement	I	UK	N	F	E	D	NL	S	CH	DK
Personnel functionaries per 100 employees	18.2	13.9	12.8	13.8	14.9	14.5	18.5	15.6	12.5	10.7

Figure 7.2 Devolvement and proportion of personnel specialists
Source: PWCP

The table shows that Denmark and Switzerland have the lowest percentage of personnel specialists and are the two most devolved countries. The least decentralized country, Italy, shows up as having one of the highest number of specialists. There are some conflicting results in this table, such as those of the Netherlands. The table shows them as lying towards the more devolved end of the rankings but also having a high number of personnel specialists. The results illustrate that a high level of devolvement can occur in different situations. Two organizations with very different perceptions of HRM, might both be characterized by a high level of devolvement. The first organization might find HRM too important not to be integrated fully with all line management issues, whereas the second may simply feel that it is a waste of resources to invest in a separate and well staffed human resources department.

Devolvement of HRM issues to the line also shows an interesting contrast with the influence of national or regional level bargaining on pay. The northern European countries are the most likely to have pay bargaining centralized above organizational level and in broad terms they tend to be the countries with higher devolvement rankings. There is some correlation between centralization of pay bargaining outside the organization and the extent of devolvement within it. There are two possible explanations. One is that the perceptions reported by the data are not reflected in reality: what seems to the respondent to be devolution is only so in comparison to a tightly restricted external environment. The second is that a high degree of centralization above the level of the organization and devolvement within it are actually compatible; it is within clear, established and predictable frameworks of labour cost that line management are able to take on and accept a more substantial role in human resource issues.

SIMILARITY OR DIFFERENCE?

In summary, then, we have drawn on data from across Europe to identify the four key areas of pay, flexibility, equal opportunities and training. In all four areas the evidence indicates major differences between countries – but also indications of common directions of change. When we move from HR issues to the HR departments which handle them, however, it is much harder to identify commonalities other than a slight tendency – from very different bases – towards more devolution.

The findings we have reported vary, as we have shown, by country. Space has not permitted us to develop one interesting, and unexpected, finding from our research. This is that the differences between countries are in the majority of cases greater than the differences between industrial sectors or different size bands of organizations: at least for organizations above 200 employees on which our survey is based. Within particular countries sector and size may be important differentiators, but an international perspective shows that national differences are great. The influence of national cultures, economic circumstances, history, employment legislation and fiscal policies cannot be ignored.

This drives us back to our question about convergence. To what extent can we see similarities and differences in the way that European countries handle human resource management? Overall it seems clear that the increasing cohesion of the European market will lead to the development of a specifically European labour market – but only amongst top level managers, certain technical skills (computing specialists, biochemists, nurses, etc.) and low-skilled jobs (hotels and catering for example). There will be a developing influence of the European Community – probably through the European Court at least as much as via the policy makers. The increasing influence of multi-country organizations will also develop gradually. There is, therefore, a general drive towards convergence.

However, our general view of the strength of the different European cultures, and our research evidence which shows how differently the various countries in Europe handle human resource management, leads us to suggest that extensive convergence will not occur. Over the next decade or so we anticipate increasing steps towards a common European understanding of the key issues in human resource management – but a continuing divergence in how organizations handle these key issues.

REFERENCES

Ahlén, K. (1989) 'Swedish collective bargaining under pressure: inter-union rivalry and incomes policies', *British Journal of Industrial Relations* 27 (3): 330–46.

Atkinson, J. (1985) *Flexibility, Uncertainty and Manpower Management* IMS Report No 89, Brighton: Institute of Manpower Studies, University of Sussex.

Bournois, F. (1992) 'France' in Brewster, C., Hegewisch, A., Holden, L. and Lockhart, T. (eds) *The European Human Resource Management Guide*, London: Academic Press.

Brewster, C. and Bournois, F. (1991) 'A European perspective on human resource management', *Personnel Review* 20 (Issue 6): 4–13.

Brewster, C. and Holt Larsen, H. (1992) 'Human resource management in Europe – evidence from ten countries', *International Journal of Human Resource Management* 3 (3): 409–34.

Brewster, C., Hegewisch, A., Holden, L. and Lockhart, T. (eds) (1992) *The European Human Resource Management Guide*, London: Academic Press.

Brewster, C., Hegewisch, A., Lockhart, T. and Mayne, L. (1993) *Flexible Working Practices in Europe*, London: Institute of Personnel Management.

Bruegel, I. and Hegewisch, A. (1993) 'Flexibilisation and part-time work in Europe', in Brown, R. and Crompton, R. (eds), *The New Europe: Economic Restructuring and Social Exclusion*, London: UCL Press.

Gaugler, E. and Wiltz, S. (1992) 'Germany' in Brewster, C., Hegewisch, A., Holden, L. and Lockhart, T. (eds) *The European Human Resource Management Guide*, London: Academic Press.

Grosseilliers, L. (1986) 'What companies do to evaluate the effectiveness of training programs', in Bernhard, H.B. and Inglois, C.A. 'Six Lessons for the Corporate Classroom', *Harvard Business Review* 66 (5): 40–8.

Hegewisch, A. (1991) 'The decentralization of pay bargaining: European Comparisons', *Personnel Review* 20 (6): 28–35.

Holden, L. (1991) 'European trends in training', *International Journal of Human Resource Management* 2 (2): 113–31.

Holden, L. and Livian, Y. 'Does strategic training policy exist? Some evidence from ten European countries', *Personnel Review* 21 (1): 12–22.

Hoogendoorn, J. and Brewster, C. (1992) 'Human resource aspects of decentralization and devolution', *Personnel Review* 21 (1): 4–12.

IDS Focus (1989) 'The European view', No. 53, December.

IDS/IPM (1992) *Pay and Benefits: European Management Guides*, London: Institute of Personnel Management.

Kinnie, N. (1989) 'The decentralization of industrial relations?: recent research considered', *Personnel Review* 19 (3): 28–34.

Lawrence, P. (1991) 'The personnel function; an Anglo-German comparison', in Brewster, C. and Tyson, S. (eds) *International Comparisons in Human Resource Management*, London: Pitman.

Lockhart, T. and Brewster, C. (1992) 'Human resource management in the European Community' in Brewster, C., Hegewisch, A., Holden, L. and Lockhart, T. (eds) *The European Human Resource Management Guide*, London: Academic Press.

Marginson, P., Sisson, K., Martin, R. and Edwards, P. (1988) *Beyond the Workplace: the Management of Industrial Relations in Large Enterprises*, Oxford: Blackwell.

Marsden, D. (1989) 'Developments of pay level patterns and flexibility in Western Europe', paper presented to the Eighth World Congress of the International Industrial Relations Conference, Brussels.

Millward, N. and Stevens, M. (1986) *British Workplace Industrial Relations 1980–1984*, Aldershot: Gower.

Morris, T. and Wood, S. (1991) 'Testing the survey method: continuity and change in British industrial relations', *Work, Employment and Society* 5 (2): 259–82.

Nollen, S.D. (1992) 'The cost effectiveness of contingent labor', in *Proceedings of 9th World Congress – Volume 6 (Communication Abstracts)*, International Industrial Relations Association: Geneva.

Pollert, A. (1988) 'The flexible firm – fixation or fact?', *Work, Employment and Society* 2 (3): 281–316.

Randlesome, C. (1990) *Business Cultures in Europe*, Oxford: Heinemann.

Scheuer, S. (1992): 'Denmark: return to decentralisation', in Ferner, A. and Hyman, R. (eds) *Industrial Relations in the New Europe*, Oxford: Blackwell.

Visser, J. (1992): 'The Netherlands: the end of an era and the end of a system', in Ferner, A. and Hyman, R. (eds) *Industrial Relations in the New Europe*, Oxford: Blackwell.

Wareing, A. (1992) 'Working arrangements and patterns of working hours in Britain', *Employment Gazette*, March: 88–100.

8 HRM and human resource information systems in Europe 1992
Hopes and reality

Michael J. Kavanagh
Christian Scholz

INTRODUCTION

HRM over the past decade has been rapidly changing and will likely continue to change in the future. It was not surprising that, in his latest book, Porter (1990) observed that the effective application of labour (and its ideas) to other factors of production leads to the generation of profit and wealth for companies. The advances in computer technology for HRM during the past decade have assisted companies in more effectively managing their labour, their human resources. Perhaps one of the most significant changes facing the HRM community is the creation of Europe 1992 (EU92), the planned economic cooperation among the twelve countries of the EC. Numerous directives and laws will affect the way in which HRM functions in any company doing business in the EC. This holds true both for EC-based companies as well as for non-EC-based companies.

Many managers and HRM professionals in US firms are convinced that the recent political changes in Europe and Russia mean there will be a 'United States' of Europe with the advent of EU92. The implication is that many of the HRM practices and programs will be transferable, with some minor modifications, within the EC. Since a common currency as well as unified compensation and benefit directives are being planned for EU92, a further hope, especially for non EC-based HR managers, is that this will simplify the current problems that MNCs have in dealing with differences in exchange rate and 'social security' regulations across European countries. In fact, most textbooks (Dowling and Schuler 1990; Mendenhall and Oddou 1991) tend to treat EU92 as a single entity, and the arrival of EU92 as a solution to some of the difficulties that MNCs have in the personnel and HRM (PHRM) arena. Thus, in sum, the hopes are that EU92 may simplify the application of established HRM practices and programmes across the EC since it will create a 'United States of Europe'.

However, the reality is that this will probably not happen. There are strong cultural differences across European countries that need to be considered in examining the implications of EU92 for HRM. These strong cultural differences may make the application of HRM practices and programs much more complex. The implications of this reality, of a different, multicultural vision of EU92 on the PHRM function are enormous. These are independent countries, with lengthy histories that have established separate cultural values. To expect that employees of MNCs across European countries will react in the same way to common personnel programmes may be false hopes in the face of reality.

In this chapter, we will describe how the changes in EU92 can be represented in a model of organizational functioning that includes the HRM function with an human resource information system (HRIS), a strategic management system (SMS), and, most important, cultural factors. We will then describe the reality of EU92, and the implications for HRM. In the light of both the hopes and reality of EU92, we will then examine the use of HRISs in terms of some of the HRM problems that will be created in EU92. Finally, we will describe two possible, but different, future scenarios for HRM in EU92.

A MODEL OF ORGANIZATIONAL FUNCTIONING

In Figure 8.1, modified from Kavanagh, Gueutal, and Tannenbaum (1990), a systems model of organizational functioning is presented that is applicable for understanding HRM in EU92. There are important characteristics of this model for this chapter. First, the organization functions within an environmental envelope, and thus, must be sensitive to changes in the important aspects of that environment. For EU92, both the national culture in the external environment and the corporate culture within the internal environment of companies take on increased importance, particularly for MNCs. Second, the organization's SMS, as well as its HR management system (HRMS), is driven by the goals on the right-hand side of Figure 8.1. In reality, the organization over time is driven by variances from expected goals through the feedback loops depicted in the model. In EU92 these variances from expectations could be the differences between hopes and reality of US managers and HRM professionals. Further, and most important for EU92, these goals are embedded within a corporate culture, and are thus, directly affected by it.

The double arrow linkages underline the importance of having an HRM strategy and system that is consistent with, and supports the business strategy of the firm. The necessary interrelationship between business strategy and HRM strategy and practices for successful organizational functioning has been well established in the literature (Schuler 1987). The linkages in Figure 8.1 that lead to goal accomplishment reflect this thinking. However, an important addition is the corporate culture factor internal to the firm. This factor influences the way in which the HRM strategy and practices are developed relative to the business strategy. Further, the entire organization is influenced by the external environment, and a critical factor is the national culture. A central thesis of this chapter is that the national culture has such a pervasive effect on the external environment for firms that successful functioning is highly dependent on maintaining important features of the national culture.

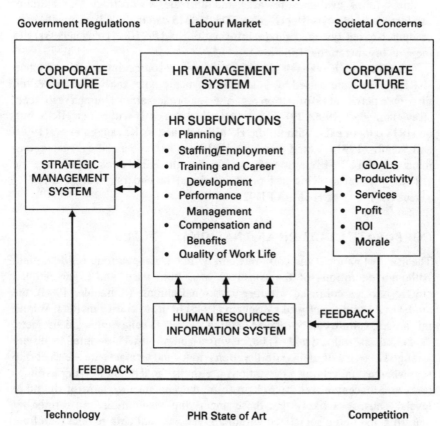

Figure 8.1 A model of organizational functioning

The SMS and the HRMS are interlinked. Thus, there must be congruence between them, if the company existing within EU92 is to function effectively. Further, the HRIS and the HR subfunctions are interlinked. The changes being brought about by EU92 are so complex that it is *a central point of this chapter that the existence of some type of HRIS, closely linked to changes in the HR subfunctions, will be critical for firms, and their HRM departments, in order to manage their employees in the EC.* As Downey (1990) notes, Europe 1992 will create additional HRM problems and require complex changes in order to manage workers for both European and US companies. The use of an HRIS should help to resolve some of these problems.

The following definitions help to understand the model in Figure 8.1 better. The SMS is the organizational function that generates both the long- and short-term goals for the organization, frequently referred to as strategic and operational goals. The HRMS, is the organizational function that plans for, acquires, trains, evaluates, rewards, and motivates a workforce for maximum productivity and cost-effectiveness. The HRMS can include both manual and computer-based systems of data, information, and decision rules necessary to meet its organizational function.

According to Kavanagh *et al.*, 'A human resource information system (HRIS) is the system used to acquire, store, manipulate, analyze, retrieve, and distribute pertinent information regarding an organization's human resources' (Kavanagh *et al.* 1990: 29). Thus, the HRMS can exist without an HRIS, but, an HRIS cannot exist without the HRMS. Further, as Kavanagh *et al.* (1990) and Scholz (1991a) noted, using an HRIS has become a critical resource in managing the HRM function effectively, but, the HRIS does not manage the HRMS, people do. This last point is critical in understanding the reality versus the hopes of HRM in EU92.

CORPORATE CULTURE AND NATIONAL CULTURE

The usage of national and corporate culture in this chapter requires definition. Although definitions of the construct of culture vary, and organizational culture is often confused with organizational climate (Schneider 1990), the model of culture developed by Schein (1985) helps to clarify matters. Within this model, culture can be defined at three levels: (1) behaviours and artefacts; (2) beliefs and values; and (3) underlying assumptions. These three levels are arranged in terms of their visibility. Behaviours and artefacts are the easiest to see, whereas underlying assumptions are invisible. The underlying assumptions are conceptualized by Schein to be the guidance system for the other levels. Thus, it is likely that these underlying assumptions are formed by maturing and being socialized within a given national culture, and therefore, a national culture can encompass and impact on all three levels. Finally, these three levels interact. In new situations, for example, in a new company with its own special culture of shared behaviours and beliefs, normative behaviours, artefacts and values can impact on the underlying assumptions, and vice versa.

Examining the work of a variety of writers and researchers from both anthropology and organizational studies, Rousseau (1990) observed that it is not that different researchers use widely different definitions of culture, but rather, the types of data they collect on culture differs. She identifies five levels of the elements of culture, varying from the easy to observe to the difficult to measure. The first level, artefacts, are seen in such observables as company logos and slogans. Patterns of behaviour comprise the second level, behavioural norms the third, and values the fourth level. Typically, researchers focused on these levels use self-report questionnaires. The final level, fundamental assumptions about human nature are probably inferred from other measures, rather than being directly assessed (Rousseau 1990). Treating culture in terms of the types of data one collects to measure it helps clarify the construct, and provide additional insight as to how national cultures differ entially influence organizational functioning. But of central importance is the fact that the corporate culture of the firm is determined by the employees within that firm, and these individuals were socialized within a given national culture.

Going one step further, corporate culture must be understood as the implicit consciousness of an organization, which develops out of its members' behaviour, and which influences their behaviour (Scholz 1987). This dualistic model of organizational culture, therefore, calls for two directional influences. On one side, organizational culture results from organizational behaviour; while on the other side, organizational culture directs individuals' behaviour. In this sense, the HRMs and the HRIS are a function of the corporate culture, and, on the other side, influences growth and change of culture.

Corporate culture is shaped by, and embedded within national culture. People from different cultures bring their shared values, beliefs, and underlying assumptions to the workplace. Also, each company has its own corporate culture as well as sub-unit cultures within a company. It is interaction of these sub-unit cultures, corporate and national cultures that gives the countries of EU92 their uniqueness. This uniqueness cannot be overlooked in implementing the directives of Europe 1992.

Support for this argument can be found in the work of Hofstede (1980) and Laurent (1983). Hofstede (1980) demonstrated the existence of specific national cultures along the following dimensions: (1) power distance; (2) uncertainty avoidance; (3) individualism/collectivism; and (4) masculinity/femininity. For example, in Eastern cultures, great emphasis is placed on the group or collective, on social versus task concerns, and on the hierarchy. Western cultures focus more on the individual, task concerns, and the hierarchy is considered less critical. Furthermore, research by Hofstede (1980) and Laurent (1983) demonstrates that there are differences on these dimensions within the EC. Austria has low power distance and high masculinity, while Sweden is high on femininity. Finally, the British are high on individualism, whereas the Portuguese are high on collectivism. Even though a number of EU92 directives are known (Downey 1990), how to implement them successfully across countries is uncertain. It is in the implementation of these directives that the corporate and national culture differences will come into play.

EU92 DIRECTIVES, CULTURE, AND REALITY

The basis of EU92 is the creation of a Single Market, the term used to describe an economically unified EC. This unified economy will be governed by a variety of laws and directives, some of which will have serious impacts on the functioning of HRM. Downey at the time he wrote his article, indicated that:

(1) More than 200 of a total 300 directives setting up the Single Market have already been adopted in the EC; (2) more than 100 customs documents have been consolidated into a single set of EC-wide customs regulations; and (3) more than 100 standard setting bodies have been established to develop regulations that harmonize hundreds of thousands of technical standards for thousands of products.

(Source: Downey 1990: 38)

In addition, Downey provides details on fifteen directives specifically aimed at HRM in order to help bring the labour force regulations in congruence with the thinking behind the SEM. As Downey (1990) notes, the net effect of these many directives will essentially eliminate country-to-country differences in the legal requirements for HRM, that is, along with standards for production, human resource regulations will also be harmonized. This is, of course, a complete turn-around from the way in which the laws and regulations for HRM currently exist for the European Community, i.e. different ones for each country.

Our impression of the reality of EU92 can be summarized in the following two points (Scholz 1991b):

1 The new Europe, EU92, will not be 'united' as the USA is. Nor can EU92 be handled in the same manner as recommended for the traditional evolution and growth of MNCs.
2 EU92 legal directives will lead to harmonization and a labour market with less barriers. However, the national cultures will impact on the cultures inside the organizations. Thus, an incentive plan that might be quite successful in Germany could be a miserable failure in Italy.

Although the hopes of US managers and HRM professionals is that the 'United States of Europe' will emerge from EU92, the reality is that this will probably not happen. There are extremely strong cultural differences across European countries that Americans fail to appreciate. The roots of European society have a long history, and the marked cultural differences will not be erased by the implementation of shared laws and regulations. Thus, it is not surprising that Americans, with a much more common history, do not completely understand the changes that are occurring with EU92, particularly in the area of HRM. As noted earlier, the notion of a different, multicultural vision of EU92 is somewhat inconsistent from the view espoused in textbooks (Dowling and Schuler 1990; Mendenhall and Oddou 1991).

Comparing business operations between the EC and the USA must take into account the greater homogeneity within the USA. This is not only true for the shared culture within the USA, but can be seen in other areas such as language, legal systems, school systems, organizational practices and structures, and management systems. Although there are differences across geographic areas within the USA in these spheres, there are still a great many similarities. These similarities have made it possible to transfer successful HRM and HRIS practices from state to state and region to region. This homogeneity simply does not exist for the countries within the EC. Differences in legal and school systems alone will create difficulties for easily transferring HRM and HRIS practices from one country to another. But in many ways, it will be the cultural differences – behavioural norms, values, and fundamental assumptions about human nature – that will make it difficult to homogenize HRM and HRIS practices for firms doing business within the EC.

Konrad (1991) reported strong differences across countries in terms of employees' descriptions of the culture of their organization. These differences were particularly marked when contrasting employee perceptions from northern and southern European countries, and Konrad argues that a conceptual model relating national culture to corporate culture is needed to understand his results.

EUROPEAN BUSINESS ANALYSIS

Preliminary data from another continuing large-scale project, the European Business Analysis (EBA) study show strong differences in terms of length of service and age structure for managers, staff, and workers from Germany, Italy, and Spain. In addition, managers from these three countries differ significantly in terms of the number of companies in which they have worked, and, also, in terms of their work experience abroad. For example, from Table 8.1, it can be seen that 91 per cent of managers in the Spanish sample had no work experience abroad, whereas almost all of the managers in the German sample had some work experience abroad. Thus, the early findings from the Konrad and EBA studies would reinforce our argument that 'united' Europe in terms of shared employee experiences and values is not going to appear magically with the passage of the laws and directives that are part of EU92.

Table 8.1 Work experience of managers abroad

Experience Abroad	Germany (%)	Country Italy (%)	Spain (%)
None		77	90
<10 per cent of work experience abroad	48		
		14	4
10–30 per cent of work experience abroad	36	4	1
> 30 per cent of work experience abroad	16	5	5

Perhaps the most important finding from the EBA study is not found in the statistics. In sampling from just three countries, Germany, Italy, and Spain, creating a common database was enormously difficult, and, *this was data being collected for research only.* This holds true even more for the whole group of researchers who are participating in the International Industrial Observatory (IOO). This includes researchers from France, Great Britain, Netherlands, Spain, Sweden, Italy, and Germany. For example, trying to communicate, and collect data on, the notion of decentralization or autonomy in a company, was severely hampered by language and cultural differences in what actually was meant by the term. Think about the implications of this difficulty when we try to combine databases across the EC, an issue to which we now turn.

THE ROLE OF HRIS

Before considering more specific HRM directives, we will address the general implications of these wide-spread changes in EU92 on HRM. One clear implication will be an increase in personnel record keeping requirements. New legislation in the USA, for example, has always been accompanied by increased record keeping and reporting. This will be more complicated in the EC, particularly where reports will most likely need to be combined for companies that have manufacturing or service locations across countries. The obvious language differences will complicate matters severely, and, as Triandis and Vassiliou (1972) have demonstrated in terms of employee selection, language represents culture. Thus, the language differences, particularly colloquialisms across countries and cultures will create major problems.

Perhaps the most significant contribution of an HRIS, from a time-saving perspective, is its ability to complete repetitive reports based on personnel records quickly (Kavanagh *et al.* 1990). This does not mean that all difficulties will disappear, particularly when one considers the hardware and software differences that exist across countries. However, these technical difficulties can be overcome, although it will be costly. However, the problems of language differences, and thus, differing terms for the same HR programme, will still need to be addressed, like the problems we encountered in the EBA study. For example, it is unlikely that 'bonus pay', 'incentive system', or 'total quality management' will have the same meaning across countries. In fact, something simple like 'home address' could cause problems, particularly with transient employees working in one country while their families live in another.

The power of an HRIS will help here. Although the definition and consistent use of terms will take a major translation effort, the computer system always records and remembers the term once it has been entered. Thus, dealing with language and culture differences must be aided within the HRIS by 'help' functions and data dictionaries that would translate the same term into the appropriate language. Is this possible in EU92? Our future scenarios at the end of this chapter will be based on this question.

In addition, the changed laws and new directives for EU92 will impact in general on other HRM areas for MNCs, such as payroll and benefits administration, time and attendance reporting, recruiting and selecting, and internal promotion and career development. More specifically, many of the directives aimed at HRM will create a EC-wide labour market with fewer barriers between countries. This legal *harmonization*, a term frequently used in reference to standards for the advent of EU92, will make both recruiting of new employees and transferring current employees between countries easier. Naturally, the difficulties that will arise because of different corporate cultures and business practices across countries will complicate matters. The different procedures for reporting new hires, transfers, or terminations across countries are reflective of the cultural differences. The meticulous Germans, for example, document every incident on the employees' records, whereas the Spanish and Italians are much more leisurely about these records.

In dealing with these cultural differences, but taking advantage of the common labour market, an HRIS could also be quite useful and a variety of stand-alone and HRIS application software is currently available (Frantzreb 1990). For example, powerful HR planning applications are available that can record and forecast position openings and surpluses within a company, whether they are within a single country or an MNC. This software can also record employee skills, training experiences, and career development paths for employees. However, these applications do require a common use of HR terms and a common database, and this problem may be solvable as discussed above. The HRIS should give MNCs a greater ability to take advantage of a common labour market and its trends.

CONCLUSIONS AND TWO POSSIBLE HRM/HRIS SCENARIOS FOR EU92

It has been the argument of this chapter that EU92 presents both challenges and opportunities for HRM. The directives and laws currently being enacted will create the SEM in economic terms for EU92. Will this occur for HRM? The ideas for a 'United States of Europe' clash with the reality of national and corporate culture differences across companies in the EC. Any firm operating in the SEM must be aware of these cultural differences, particularly in light of legal harmonization and the common labour market that is being created by EU92 directives. What will be the changed role of HRM, and more specifically, how will the powerful tools available in an HRIS be used to assist companies in dealing the complex HR problems in EU92? We are not certain, but offer the following two possible, but different future scenarios for HRM and HRIS in EU92.

Scenario 1 – minimum HRM/HRIS

In this scenario, we envisage the problems caused by cultural differences across countries in the EC, both national and corporate, are so great that it would cause a breakdown in any sophisticated HRM/HRIS functioning, e.g., recruiting and applicant tracking. Thus, the HRM/HRIS will be engaged in only simple level functions like headcount and total FTE budgets. Naturally, because of the EU92 directives and law, mandated records on payroll, unemployment benefits, and other 'social security' information will need to be maintained. However, in this minimum scenario, this latter information would be kept country-by-country, and not combined across the EC. Thus, reports to the European Commission would be done by country, necessitating the task of interpretation of these reports in terms of common, harmonized, laws and directives to the Commission itself. In addition to this, European institutions will call for some new, standardized, data, such as 'percentage of other EC-nationalities' among the employees, or 'ECUs spent on training in languages'. These new data requirements increase the pressure in management to reduce its HRIS to an absolute legal minimum, which will be quite low, since Europeans are usually very reluctant in agreeing to any joint standard.

Scenario 2 – Sophisticated HRM/HRIS

In this scenario, the reality of EU92 would blend with the hopes of US managers, some HR practitioners, and most HR academicians. This would require a very sophisticated HRIS to support the HRM function. Language translation software for HRM terms would need to be created, at a minimum, and this by itself is an enormous task. Coordinating hardware/software configurations across the EC would probably mean new designs for both architectures and platforms. Under this scenario, for example, it would be possible to develop and use a HR planning model software package that would enable an MNC to utilize fully the entire labour market defined by EU92, with possible additions from Eastern Europe (e.g., Slovenia and Serbia). The full utilization of this level of HRM/HRIS will be extremely costly.

But why should European companies move in the direction of this long and stony road? Many European companies currently perform rather well and are good players in the global market. Part of the competitive advantage these 'good players' enjoy is definitely caused by their existing HRM/HRIS. Therefore, why should these companies give up their competitive advantage? European companies will recognize that by increasing the magnitude of their current HRM/HRIS, they will be able to outperform non EC-based companies.

Concluding comment

Which of these scenarios is most likely? Or, is there another one that could occur? We feel at this time that the first, minimum level, scenario will be the most prevalent for MNCs doing business within the EC. It is simply too simplistic to assert that as of 1 January 1993, common HRM practices are being adopted that would allowed more sophisticated HRIS to emerge. Our earlier comments regarding the influence of different national cultures based on language, educational, and legal differences on corporate culture will prevent sophisticated HRIS developing immediately. However, if companies doing business within the EC expect to compete in the global, as well as the domestic, marketplace, they must efficiently utilize their human resources. The cost-effectiveness of sophisticated HRIS have been demonstrated in both the private and public sector in the USA. We fully anticipate that, within ten years, the HRIS in use by firms in the EC will be extremely sophisticated.

REFERENCES

Dowling, P. J., and Schuler, R. S. (1990) *International Dimensions of Human Resource Management*, Boston: PWS-Kent.

Downey, T. (1990) 'What to do now for Europe: 1992', *Computers in HR Management* 1 (3): 34–42.

Frantzreb, R. B. (1990) *The Personnel Software Census*, Roseville, California: Advanced Personnel Systems.

Hofstede, G. (1980) *Culture's Consequences: International Differences in Work-Related Values*, Beverly Hills, California: Sage.

Kavanagh, M. J., Gueutal, H. G. and Tannenbaum, S. I. (1990) *Human Resources Information Systems; Development and Application*, Boston: PWS-Kent.

Konrad, E. (1991) 'Cultural differences in Europe 1992: preliminary results from FOCUS92'. Invited paper presented at the State University of New York at Albany, March.

Laurent, A. (1983) 'The cultural diversity of Western conceptions of management', *International Studies of Management and Organization* 13 (1–2): 75–96.

Mendenhall, M. and Oddou, G. (1991) *Readings and Cases in International Human Resource Management*, Boston: PWS Kent.

Porter, M. E. (1990) *The Competitive Advantage of Nations*, New York: Free Press.

Rousseau, D. M. (1990) 'Assessing organizational culture: the case for multiple methods', in Schneider, B. (ed.) *Organisational Climate and Culture*, San Francisco: Jossey-Bass, pp. 153–92.

Schein, E. H. (1985) *Organizational Culture and Leadership: A Dynamic View*, San Francisco: Jossey-Bass.

Schneider, B. (ed.) (1990) *Organizational Climate and Culture*, San Francisco: Jossey-Bass.

Scholz, C. (1987) *Strategisches Management: Ein integrativer Ansatz*, Berlin: Walter de Gruyter.

—— (1991a) *Personalmanagement, Informationsorientierte und verhaltenstheoretische Grundlagen*, Munich: Verlag Franz Vahlen.

—— (1991b) 'Corporate culture and Europe 1992', *Hallinnon Tutkimus, The Finnish Journal of Administrative Studies*, 3: 222–6.

Schuler, R. S. (1987) 'Personnel and human resource management choices and organizational strategy', in Schuler, R.S. Youngblood, S.A. and Huber V., (eds) *Readings in Personnel and Human Resource Management*, 3rd edn, St Paul, Minnesota: West Publishing.

Triandis, H. C. and Vassiliou, V. (1972) 'Interpersonal influence and employee selection in two cultures', *Journal of Applied Psychology* 56: 140–5.

Part III

Developments in Eastern Europe

9 The transition to a market economy and its implications for HRM in Eastern Europe

Joseph Prokopenko

It has been almost seven years since East European countries joined Western countries in a structural adjustment process. For many, structural adjustments are not only macro-changes, they also include a state of mind, a productivity and quality-oriented culture, a system of values and attitudes to work and, certainly, democratization of economic and political life (Prokopenko 1989). In Eastern Europe, restructuring entails revolutionary changes, basically intended to completely overhaul and modernize entire economies that are inefficient and poorly maintained with outdated technology and organizational structures (Sadore 1989).

Traditionally, managers in this region were not sufficiently concerned with the main business issues, since central governments had always tightly controlled the goals of enterprises and the way they functioned through the central planning mechanism. The reforms are intended to drastically change all of this. These changes have already influenced management approaches and HRM practices in companies and will continue to do so to an ever greater extent.

TRADITIONAL MANAGEMENT PRACTICES

The grand 'socialist' experiment, which started in Russia in 1917 and after 1945 was spread to East European countries, has failed. There is a deepening crisis in these countries as recession and unemployment grow and the failure of the ex-USSR, traditionally a huge market for most of the East European economies, is aggravating the situation (Panov 1991). Poor economic and social conditions, political instability, nationalist separatism and scarce consumer goods and resources create a lot of difficulties and confusion for HRM practices and strategies.

Traditionally the job of a 'socialist' manager was to fulfil the Plan established by the ministry and to request funds for inputs. Many decades of meeting the Plan produced managers who were motivated only by increasing production. Quality, cost and timeliness have not been important criteria (McCarthy 1991). Competition is virtually a new concept to 'socialist' managers. Marketing, financial management and cost control were not in the lexicon of these managers. Key decisions were heavily influenced by the state and party representatives. Since all centralized economies were 'scarcity economies', and all input components were difficult to obtain, a manager's major operational objective was to secure reliable supplies of money, materials, equipment and labour from the State. As most enterprises were monopolies and the only supplier of their product, managers of receiving enterprises had to develop strong bargaining skills (Pearce 1991). Thus, there was an extensive focus on bargaining, and the best negotiating position was to have 'good connections' with key Party officials and state bureaucrats.

Socialist-style hierarchical, centrally controlled organizations are still the norm and they retain characteristics of traditional authoritarianism: obedience to authority, lack of trust in outsiders, attention to rank and status and belief in a powerful, punitive legal system. Centralized control is pervasive in large and small organizations with unfortunate consequences for HRM practices. There remain conflicting attitudes with regard to success. It is still not quite acceptable to make money and especially not a lot of it. A no-risk attitude is still common among East European managers. Although by mid-1991 support for privatization in Poland had risen to 45 per cent, Poles were even less supportive if thought it would affect them personally (World Bank 1991). Although Hungary had a full command economy for only about 20 years, the Government still owns nearly 85 per cent of the country's capital stock. Privatization, as in all Eastern Europe, is proceeding slowly (Pearce 1991).

Despite this, *perestroika* has brought substantial changes to the jobs of these managers. They are now expected to manage in a far more market-oriented, competitive environment. They have to recognize the complexity of social, political and cultural dimensions of the market relationships, competitiveness, democratization and human rights aspects. They are also changing their beliefs about personnel practices.

HRM: WEST AND EAST EUROPEAN CONTEXTS AND TRENDS

The essence of HRM is that people are regarded as a competitive asset to be led, motivated, deployed and developed, together with the firm's other resources, in ways that contribute directly to the attainment of the firm's strategic objectives. HRM, in effect, reflects and becomes part of the organization's corporate culture (Handy *et al.* 1989). It involves all management decisions that affect the nature of the relationship between the organization and employees; it regards people as the most important single asset of the organization; it is proactive in its relationship with people and it seeks to enhance company performance and employee wellbeing (Poole 1990).

Against this definition we would like to review some global trends in HRM and compare them with the East European ones along the lines of the most important tasks (or functions) of HRM such as selection and staffing; motivation and rewards; performance appraisal; training and development;

communication and labour relations (Hendry and Pettigrew 1990; Rand 1986; Wilhelm 1990).

To compare the maturity of HRM in the West with that in the East is difficult because of the diversity between Eastern and Western countries and companies. However, using the adapted Meshoulam and Baird (1987) HRM matrix, which demonstrates relationships between stages of human resource management (reflecting company maturity) and main HRM components, it is possible to outline the general area of main differences between West and East European companies (see Figure 9.1).

Methodologically it would be even better to consider the transition of HRM culture and practices from state-owned companies to private ones, with market-oriented culture. From this point of view the global trends in HRM practices are very similar in the West and in the East as seen in Table 9.1.

As a consequence of privatization, top management attitudes will also change dramatically. Instead of considering employees as production and cost factors, managers will view them as a vital creative resource to meet customer expectations, as a source of revenue.

In addition there are a number of other trends and shifts which we need to consider:

- Personnel managers increasingly become internal consultants in the process of transition from personnel policy to HRM. East European companies use more external consultants to perform some of the HRM functions such as head hunting, designing motivation systems, management development and even introducing cultural changes.
- Nationalism and separatism is another important factor. Whereas in Western countries this problem becomes less and less evident, in East European countries, it often becomes one of the main agenda items of personnel policy, often involving human rights problems (Ukraine, Russia, Estonia, Latvia, Lithuania, etc.).
- The shift towards integral management is becoming an essential trend. Market orientation directs management practice towards the primary process of the organization. This leads to a re-evaluation of staff services. For example, despecialization (Tissen and Bolweg 1987); growing investment in hardware and software and new technology; also increase the strategic importance of the integration of well-trained and motivated employees around main business objectives.

The majority of Western companies today are still traditionally oriented towards personnel management and not towards HRM (Krulis-Randa 1990). For example, of 1,266 Swiss business firms contacted in 1989 by the University of Zurich continuing survey, 41 per cent of respondents indicated that they had a formal personnel policy, and none claimed to operate a strategic HRM policy. The situation is much worse in Eastern Europe. However, the marketization of Eastern European companies is likely to cause substantial changes after 1992 and will force them to move closer to strategic

Stages/components	I Initiation	II Functional growth	III Controlled growth	IV Functional integration	V Strategic integration
Management awareness	Awareness of functions administrative role	Aware of function's broad role but not committed	Aware, often frustrated at fragmentation	Cooperative and involved	Integrated
Management of personnel function	Loose, informal, often none	Personnel manager, programme orientation, manage conflicts among subfunctions	Personnel executive. Business orientation, measurement, goals	Function orientation. Long-range planning, line/staff relations collaborative	Company orientation consistent/integrated with business strategy
Portfolio of programmes	Basic salary and benefits administration, basic record keeping	Many new programmes added responding to business needs, revisiting basic programmes	Management control, budgets. Portfolio reevaluated in measurable terms, advanced compensation	Inter-disciplinary programme. Focus on goals. Productivity, change management, flexible planning	Cultural, environmental scanning long-range planning emphasis on effectiveness
Information technology	Manual employee profile, record keeping	Automated salary and basic profile. Advance record keeping	Automated personnel work, mainly profiles, tracking, basic statistics	Utilize computer for projection, planning, analysis and evaluation	Long-range planning. 'What if' questions linked to personnel and organizational data
Personnel skills	Administration, routine and housekeeping	Functional specialists	Increased professionalism in function and managerial skills	Integrating activities, skills in systems, planning and analysis	High-level involvement in organization, macro skills
Awareness of internal and external environment	Not aware	Aware of environment and corporate culture but do not incorporate them into functions	Aware of risks and opportunities in environment, address some in programmes.	Aware, react, incorporate into planning environmental changes	Systematic search for environmental impacts, take active role in decision-making

EAST

WEST

Figure 9.1 The dividing line between HRM maturity levels of Eastern and Western European companies

Table 9.1 Differences in HR purpose and practices in state-owned and private organizations

State-owned companies	Private companies
The purpose is to ensure that jobs are allocated to the right people at the right time.	The purpose is to match available human resources (skills and potentials) with the corporate mission and goals.
Personnel polices aim at trade-offs between economic and social objectives.	The HR policies aim at developing a coherent 'strong' culture and balancing current and future needs.

Adapted from Krulis-Randa 1990

HRM. This means moving away from vertical management and the centralized personnel function of a personnel department to horizontal management and a decentralized personnel function involving line management.

CHARACTERISTICS OF PERSONNEL PRACTICE IN EASTERN EUROPE

These global trends create an environment or a scene for HRM changes in companies of both the West and the East. However, some specific characteristics of personnel practice in East European countries deserve special consideration.

Selection and entry

Traditionally, in most East European countries the process of selection was rather passive. Workers and technical staff were recruited through advertising vacancies, managerial staff through promotion from within the company and through recommendations by party committees. Labour market mechanisms did not exist. During the last few years the situation has changed. A number of private and state organizations has emerged that deal with labour force searches. Recruitment of workers and engineering personnel is not difficult. There is a relatively large skilled, well-educated labour pool. However, experienced professional, market-oriented managers are in short supply for two major reasons. The first is that, in the most cases, centralized educational institutions provided good administrators, not market-oriented managers. Second, the best self-made entrepreneurs and managers prefer to run their own business and are not interested in working for a large, usually state-owned company. Traditional lack of mobility (mainly because of scarce housing) is another difficulty in recruiting managers.

The principles of selection are now also changing dramatically. The most important criteria for private and even for some state companies (with a high degree of independence) are competence, experience and trainability and not so much good connections. Personnel management techniques such as the probationary period, temporary jobs, labour contracts, part-time employment and other approaches with reduced job security, are becoming normal practice (Van Ham *et al.* 1986).

Motivation and rewards

The lack, in state-owned enterprises, of incentives and pressures for high level achievement (productivity and quality) is widely known. The problems at present with incentives can best be understood in the light of the major expectations of the Eastern European workforce during this transition period. Here, three major groups emerge.

The first, expects order and discipline, more direct, authoritative, traditional management styles, and a high level of social protection and paternalism from the Government. This group is not well-educated and not ambitious. It is content with existing or slightly improved personnel management systems, which provide job security and minimum social protection.

The second group believes that the market economy is the only way to economic and social development. It expects more entrepreneurship, participation in decision-making, payment by results and greater democracy.

The third group is represented by people who believe in a balance between the first and second types of expectation: social-oriented market economy with strong state intervention. A major shift in expectations is taking place from the first to the second and third groups. Let us consider these shifts in three major areas: job security, compensation, performance appraisal and promotion.

Full employment

Full employment has traditionally been a primary objective and a characteristic feature of the centrally-planned economy. It was achieved by a combination of a low-wage policy, a high rate of fixed capital, a centrally-dictated output growth and an incentive structure that encouraged a high demand for labour.

Current economic reforms are expected to reverse this. The removal of price and enterprise subsidies, freeing prices and unifying exchange rates make many existing enterprises, particularly large ones, hopelessly uneconomic. The closing down of a large number of plants and/or their down-sizing would seem unavoidable in the near future. This is being increasingly accepted by part of the Eastern Europe labour force as a natural feature of the market economy, however undesirable. At the same time a huge proportion of the workforce still expects the Government to provide guaranteed employment. This is one of the reasons why general public opinion is still very suspicious about privatization (Braverman and Yutkin 1992).

Remuneration and incentives systems

The prevailing egalitarian appreciation of work reflected in the remuneration and incentives systems, results in compensation levelling between highly skilled and unskilled workers regardless of individual performance and in the subsequent loss of motivation for top level performance. The unwritten social norm of 'equal pay for everybody' in the same work group still exists in most Eastern European companies and has led, to a large extent, to management losing its basic means of motivation.

Managers get a bonus even if they do not make any profits. The Soviet idea of an incentive scheme is that everybody earns more (Wynd and Reitsch 1991). In his recent empirical study of cultural values in Czechoslovakian science-intensive companies, Landa (1990: 220) mentioned the prevailing lack of economic recognition for outstanding job performance. Social peace in an organization was felt to be more important than income differentials which may lead to improved efficiency, but could cause a turbulent social environment.

Given the excessive demand for labour and the high survival rate of firms (even when making large losses) in a centrally-planned economy, workers can virtually rule out the possibility that they will be made redundant. They actually have a relatively strong bargaining position with employers to hinder such moves. Hence, the issue of management is how to stimulate workers and employees to improve performance in the transition period while keeping the wage level from inflationary growth. Although this traditional wage system grew out of former distorted economic conditions, many newly established private enterprises have been quick to adopt it.

This creates continuous bargaining and distrust between managers and subordinates. It is very well illustrated by conventional Hungarian wisdom (which could be applied to any East European country) that 'workers get their salaries for just showing up, if the supervisor wants them to do any work he must "pay for it"' (Pearce 1991: 81).

Some managers have learned that they must always 'hold some of the bonus money back' for unexpected demands. Employees know about it so they strive to gain more through bargaining. Only very recently have some state-owned and private enterprises begun tying bonuses, particularly for executives, to enterprise earnings, with clear performance measures.

There is a special feature of the compensation policies of joint-venture companies in East European countries. Over and above the salary, fringe benefits are critical and traditional compensation in Eastern European countries where shortages of consumer goods and services prevail. For example, in CIS countries, a bigger 'soft' rouble salary is a weak motivator: there are too many roubles around and almost no consumer goods. A wide variety of bonuses and premiums are awarded ranging from holidays and year-end type bonuses to commission-type and hardship travel premiums.

There are other fringe benefits which are very important for the East

European situation. For example, a tax-free clothing allowance, amounting usually to 20 to 30 per cent of basic salary, is traditionally paid into clothing or food hard currency stores. Some companies allow accumulation of the monthly clothing allowance to cover payments to mail order Western department stores. In Russia employees ask for their fringe benefits to be increased rather than their salaries. Most JVs have found it necessary to match the social benefits such as housing, holiday accommodation and even schooling for children. Recently some JVs have begun distributing rare items like shampoo, coffee and cigarettes to their workers.

Among non-monetary incentives some JVs are suggesting such items as a company car, a PC or a laser printer for use in the office, or other high-technology products through internal JV distribution channels. A trip abroad for training or another business purpose constitutes one of the best incentives today.

There is another famous personnel policy instrument which is specifically East European, the so-called 'management by special favours' (Pearce 1991). This is the practice by which managers allow employees to 'break the rules' by turning a blind eye to employees' use of organizational resources for their own purposes and to their absenteeism.

Performance appraisal and promotion

Performance appraisal systems in Eastern European companies are nearly always seen to be accompanied by a great deal of bureaucratic, administrative and often unnecessary paperwork. Those who are appraised seldom seem to find the procedure stimulating and all too often there is no clear relationship between appraisal and subsequent improvement of performance, payments or promotion. Personnel directors find it very difficult to interest their colleagues in completing the evaluation forms unless the managing director issues a directive to do so. But this is now beginning to change. Differentiation of rewards and more transparency result in better justification of any changes in rewards and promotions.

Promotion in East European countries was often determined for political considerations, and for loyalty rather than merit, professionalism, competence or potential. Of course, it would be wrong to state that the latter never had any meaning, but the former always dominated. Another important factor was personal connections as opposed to a focus on results or performance.

Until recently, many state-owned companies were forced to fill top-level managerial positions with senior party committee members from different central and local organizations. Sometimes this was to accommodate a failed senior party politician, but the official explanation was to 'strengthen enterprise management'. Recently, these criteria have changed in private and relatively independent public companies, but the approach, though not so straightforward, still exists and influences personnel practice.

CHANGES IN VALUES AND ATTITUDES

HRM practices can be better assessed if values and attitudes are analysed as well. Managerial values are normally the result of combined, complex inter-action between traditional and organizational cultures. Traditional culture is a long-term phenomenon which essentially changes very slowly, yet organizational culture is the factor which influences management the most dynamically even within an unchanging traditional culture. From this perspective it is easy to understand that management practices can be changed faster in small, entrepreneurial private firms than in large, state bureaucratic and hierarchical organizations. There are many dimensions to consider when differentiating between Eastern and Western value systems. Let us limit ourselves to a few important ones within the framework of 'bureaucratic (East)' versus 'entrepreneurial (West)' cultures. The main difference between the value systems of the two categories can be judged in the light of the priorities of a bureaucrat and of an entrepreneur (Table 9.2).

As can be seen, the entrepreneurial obsession with the customer dictates a radically different set of priorities. In the large bureaucratic East European organizations, the customer orientation has been systematically squeezed out of existence. The major differences in value systems which have been developed for many years under the influence of traditional cultures, political systems and organizational structures can be summarized as in Table 9.3.

Table 9.2 Bureaucratic and entrepreneurial priorities

Priority	Bureaucrat (East)	Entrepreneur (West)
1	Managers themselves	Customers
2	Employees	Shareholders
3	Shareholders	Employees
4	Customers	Managers themselves

Table 9.3 Value systems in West and East

East	West
Equity is more important than wealth	Wealth is more important than equity
Group unity is emphasized for motivation	Individualism is emphasized for motivation
Education is an investment in prestige	Education is an investment in personal development/success
Protocol, rank, and status are important	Informality and competence are important
Personal conflicts are to be avoided	Conflict is creative energy to be managed

However, cultural changes in private companies are now becoming more noticeable as Eastern Europe increasingly moves towards a market system. Thus, the main characteristics mentioned above are slowly transferring from the left (East) to the right (West). These conclusions are also supported by Vlachoutsicos and Lawrence (1990) in their comparison of cultural values between American and Soviet managers.

There are other essential differences in mentality. Most East European managers think in terms of production and quantity. In the West, managers talk about quality, marketing, profits and sales. Another important East European feature is the concept of collectivism. The core of the traditional collective could be any group charged with specific tasks. Members of the group normally show cohesion, solidarity and loyalty to one another and to their leader. It is difficult to penetrate this group from the outside. Giving any information to outsiders needs the leaders' approval, which results in excessive compartmentalization and the tendency to give priority to group interests over organizational ones. Normal networking, which has just recently started to take place among the cooperative and private enterprises in Eastern Europe, is unusual and often considered as a 'Mafia' by the public.

HRM practices in Eastern Europe are often faced with widespread avoidance of responsibility and ambiguity. For example, 'no' could simply mean 'try something else', 'find a way around it' (Wolniansky 1990). This is understandable because if a bureaucrat says 'yes' and makes a mistake he falls from grace and there is usually no going back. This is why managers, particularly in public agencies, try as much as possible to avoid responsibility and risk. One of the reasons was mentioned previously: if managers gained their positions through party connections, not competence, they are afraid to display their ignorance. Besides, in highly centralized systems it is difficult to discover who has made which decision. Thus, East European managers and workers are more inclined to respond to specific and precise orders from superiors and not to take any initiative in innovations or changes.

Scarce and imprecise communications are also an enormous constraint not only to the enterprise structural reform, but to the introduction of HRM practice as well. In large state enterprises managers have had little opportunity to understand other colleagues' problems because communication is mainly vertical. Lateral problems can only be solved by special appeals to higher-level management which take a lot of time and frustrate subordinates. Practically all information flows downward, resulting in endless bureaucratic delays.

NEW EAST EUROPEAN TRADE UNIONISM

Personnel practices cannot be understood without discussing the role of new trade unionism. Prior to the recent wave of reforms, trade unions in Eastern Europe were deeply embedded in governmental institutions. They were not independent and were closely interwoven with the ruling party at every level of the hierarchy. In this situation, trade unions had two basic but conflicting roles; to promote the achievement of production targets and to represent the interest of employees. Inevitably, this dual task was a source of tension. As a result of economic and political reforms unions have almost completely divorced themselves from the Party and state. They have been democratized to a certain extent. Their role has now been reduced to representing only workers' interests (Sziracki 1990).

Increased opportunities for negotiation and the prospect of real collective bargaining has induced unions to begin to develop effective communication channels and closer contacts with the rank-and-file membership. The shift away from large industrial monopolies towards small firms and the growth of the private sector have required a new union structure. Furthermore, the introduction of new forms of self-management and worker participation has undermined the unions' exclusive authority in 'interest representation', prompting unions to re-examine their strategies. Workers have been drifting out of trade unions in large numbers. In strikes, which are now frequent events in all East European countries, workers often prefer to bargain directly with the management in full assembly or through their working councils.

Participation is becoming an important trend in management and trade union practice, which has certain important implications for the whole HRM strategy and for managerial styles. There have already been some attempts made in private and JV companies of Eastern Europe to move from traditional collective bargaining towards a more effective joint consultation system, which could be considered as a new though still very weak trend.

HRM'S MOST URGENT TASK: MANAGEMENT DEVELOPMENT

The ambitious programmes to restructure economies in the East European countries are being hampered by a lack of market-oriented management competence. This resulted from several factors including disregard for managerial competence in the command economy, political priorities over rational thinking in decision-making and the weakness of existing management education and training systems (Ford Foundation 1991). An increasing number of market oriented companies in Eastern Europe are beginning to give due recognition to the fact that the talent and commitment of their employers and managers are their greatest assets.

Management training needs

To a large degree, the new changes conflict with present dominant East European management practices and styles, which could be described as authoritative with excessive emphasis on discipline and hierarchical subordination and centralized control.

At the same time, structural changes have already had a dramatic effect on the management style of a number of managers from private, cooperative and even some state companies. They now feel less inhibited by state control and party bureaucrats are almost forgotten. They find market orientation refreshing and stimulating.

Such economic and political reforms and their main structural elements will greatly impact future managerial approaches and styles. For example, globalization and internationalization make the economy more interdependent. East European managers will have to overcome organizational impediments to global strategy and be able to integrate the activities of partners to cope with global problems and thrive in widely diverse cultural environments.

Innovation and technological changes require more integrative skills to identify priorities with regard to personnel policy, motivation, management development, worker participation as well as the management of subcontractors and competitors. Conceptual management skills and creativity will become increasingly important.

Sectoral labour market structural changes will require managers to better understand the divesting process to motivate labour market mobility and apply new personnel and human resource development policies involving the active support and cooperation of both workers and employers. It is increasingly important that managers possess very good negotiating and advisory skills. Personnel practices, such as limited terms of employment, unfilled vacancies, relocation, transfer, overtime and part-time secondment, temporary leave, voluntary (early) retirement, subcontracting, management buy-outs, cooperatives, etc., call particularly for flexible management styles and attitudes. Growing labour market flexibility will call for economic, social and psychological skills to attract some employees and demotivate others.

The move from large to small enterprises, the channelling of production towards small units, deregulation, privatization and profit centres calls for improved delegation, training and development, employee initiative and creativeness.

Among the most powerful trends changing managerial approaches is the move from bureaucracy to entrepreneurship. Such forms of entrepreneurship as introducing new products and setting up new businesses, enterprises or joint ventures, are dramatically influencing managerial patterns and styles. First of all, in order to minimize bureaucracy and segmentation, entrepreneurs' objectives, policies, procedures and orientations are becoming more flexible, customer-oriented and less formalized. The powerful trend towards entrepreneurial activity is resulting in the managerial profile changes shown in Table 9.4.

A general move from bureaucratic to entrepreneurial in the managerial style of Eastern European executives has already started and will continue. The profile changes in Table 9.4 could be considered as long-term management development needs and the main challenge of HR professionals in East European companies. However, there are also more immediate and extensive training needs such as:

Table 9.4 Bureaucratic and entrepreneurial managerial profiles

Bureaucratic	Entrepreneurial
Repetitive behaviour	Creative, innovative behaviour
Short-term focus	Long-term focus
Subsistence-seeking	Wealth-seeking
Adverse to opportunity and risk	Opportunity and risk acceptance
Analytic	Intuitive
Low concern for quality	High concern for quality
High concern for process	High concern for results
Focus on efficiency	Focus on effectiveness

- General management (in market conditions).
- Strategic management (including planning, portfolio analysis and feasibility studies).
- Industrial restructuring (down-sizing, privatization, business valuation, small enterprise development).
- Marketing and sales management (including pricing, advertising, distribution, international markets).
- Financial management (sources of funds, equity, capital markets, cash flows).
- Accounting and auditing.
- Organizational development and change management.
- Problem analysis and decision-making.
- Innovation, technology transfer and product design management.
- HRD and motivation.
- Information technology (MIS and computerization).
- Environmental management.
- Productivity, value added concepts, profits, quality management.
- Negotiating skills.
- Business law.

Quantitatively, management development has an enormous market. It is safe to state that all managers in all sectors, including public administration, have to be retrained or receive updated, basic management education. This means that the present management development system does not even come close to meeting existing qualitative and quantitative management training needs.

Training approaches and methodologies: problems and prospects

Management development in Eastern Europe is still more of a teaching process through memorizing and testing than the integration of new management skills, attitudes and behaviour, or an organizational culture through practical-oriented, action learning approaches. Management consulting, which plays an important role in actual organizational changes and management development through action learning, is still in its initial stages of development. No East European country has yet taken a strategic approach to the development of managerial resources and improving managerial practice in companies.

It may be suggested that management development is still too centralized. There is little emphasis on the responsibility of enterprises to improve management potential and managers' own responsibility for self-development. There is also a lack of good professional trainers, modern training equipment and facilities, as well as programmes, training materials and literature on management. Many trainers come from the university system and tend to emphasize lecturing and standardized programmes. Training needs analysis and tailor-made programme designs are still uncommon.

Voluntary associations for management education and training are still non-existent, or play no apparent role in promoting management development expertise and information. There are no specialized periodicals devoted to management education issues.

There is also an important strategic problem to be solved which is a balance between long-term management education (MBA type) and practical, result-oriented short term programmes for present managers. Certainly, the long-term programmes are better, but restructuring is taking place now and acting managers do not have time and often the money for long-term courses.

Problems of foreign assistance in management development

The present strategy of Western assistance to Eastern Europe is mainly to remove managers from the recipient country environment for two to four weeks of training in the West. The result of this is not particularly good. During this time trainees, at best, obtain a very general impression of the business school or institution and not much more. Among other frequently mentioned shortcomings in Western assistance (see also Chapter 10), are the following:

- Focus on an academic and less on a pragmatic approach.
- Transfer of Western materials into the local culture without proper adaptation.
- Lack of a permanent foreign faculty in East European training centres.
- Too much lecturing, not allowing sufficient participation.
- Lack of jointly designed programmes, management literature and information in local languages; including programmes for mixed (East and West) groups.
- Lack of attention to developing local management training capabilities (trainers, and training systems).
- Finally, neglect in providing adequate language training is a major problem which often makes even an excellent programme useless.

Suggestions for strategies and policies

The directions and quality of HRM in East European countries depend to a large extent on general management development strategies, including international assistance. Our analysis suggests that the following strategies and policies promote both effective HRM and enterprise management:

- Developing local management training and education institutional mechanisms and capacity. This includes setting up new, improved training centres and institutes, training trainers abroad, assisting in acquiring modern educational technology and equipment.
- Concentrating on management development in recipient countries, rather than taking managers abroad, with the active participation of foreign and local faculty (preferably trained abroad). Better impact on the transition to a market economy would be made by emphasizing the training of top-level public service administrators as well as managers of large enterprises in the areas of deregulation, privatization, market creation and HRM.
- Developing training methodologies, materials and programmes through the joint efforts of local and Western specialists.
- Providing diversified management training programmes with the participation of Eastern and Western managers. This could create a better setting for learning, interaction and cultural integration between participants. Action and experiential learning methodologies could be better applied.
- Recognizing that while basic management education (MBA-type) is an important long-term strategic objective of Eastern European HRM policy, the present focus should emphasize more urgent short-term programmes to retrain practising managers in order to prepare them now to move their enterprises into the market economy as soon as possible.
- Emphasizing language training as one of the most important starting points for meaningful transfer and adaptation of Western management experience to local management development practice.
- Sufficient effort should be oriented to develop owner-managers or entrepreneurs representing companies with high potential for growth.
- Too much effort in management development is concentrated in East European capitals. These efforts, including help from the West, should be more decentralized and directed to other industrial cities, often distant from the capital, and where there could be more enthusiasm and readiness to accept and absorb it.

PROSPECTS FOR THE FUTURE

So far, unemployment has been relatively low, but will increase as uneconomic, state-owned enterprises are forced to close. Older workers are particularly at risk of becoming the long-term unemployed. Unemployment will particularly strike women. Skills shortages are a general problem throughout Eastern Europe, particularly professional and managerial skills. The situation is even worse in the ex-USSR where people have no collective memory of free enterprise, where 'the communist tradition goes back to 1917 and no Soviet grandfather was a merchant' (Rajan and Graham 1991).

Despite generally high educational levels, there will be a lasting problem of retraining and refocusing resources on the private, consumer-oriented sectors from state-owned, militarized industries. Thus, massive redeployment of human resources will need an intensive retraining programme. Increased efforts have already been under way in many East European nations to augment and reward employee skills despite the fact that performance appraisal is often hampered by the absence of a proper definition of responsibility and by an inadequate control system. Many enterprises have already started to develop new personnel and HRM policies and to accumulate positive practical experience. These developments, and their continued progress, will be essential in the macro-level structured adjustment processes in Eastern Europe.

REFERENCES

Barnevik, P. (1991) 'Change comes to Poland – the case of ABB Zameck', *Harvard Business Review*, March–April: 102–3.

Braverman, A., and Yutkin, A. (1992) 'Russia on the starting line', *Business in the ex-USSR*, January: 25.

Ford Foundation (1991) *Management Education and Training in Central and Eastern Europe and the Soviet Union*, New York: Ford Foundation, pp. 22–3.

Handy, L., Barham, K., Panter, S. and Winhard, A. (1989), 'Beyond the personnel function: the strategic management of human resources', *Journal of European Industrial Training* 13 (1): 13–18.

Hendry, C. and Pettigrew, A. (1990) 'Human resource management: an agenda for the 1990s', *International Journal of Human Resource Management* 1 (1): 17–43.

Krulis-Randa, J. (1990) 'Strategic human resource management in Europe after 1992', *Human Resource Management*, September 1 (2): 136.

Landa, O. (1990) 'Managerial culture in Czechoslovakia', in Management Centre Europe (eds) *The International Management Development Review*, MCE, Brussels, pp. 216–22.

McCarthy, D.J. (1991) 'Developing a programme for Soviet managers', *Journal of Management Development* 10 (5): 26–31.

Meshoulam, I. and Baird, L. (1987) 'Proactive human resource management', *Human Resource Management* 26 (4): 483–502.

Panov, V. (1991) 'The Russian economy in 1992', *Business in the ex-USSR* 23: 48.

Pearce, J. (1991) 'From socialism to capitalism: the effect of Hungarian human resource practices', *Academy of Management Executive* 5 (4): 76–82.

Poole, M. (1990) 'Human resource management in an international perspective', *International Journal of Human Resource Management* 1 (1): 1–15.

Prokopenko, J. (1989) *Management Implications of Structural Adjustment*, (MANDEV/54) Geneva: ILO.

Rajan, M. and Graham, J. (1991) 'Nobody's grandfather was a merchant: understanding the Soviet commercial negotiation process and style', *California Management Review*, 33 (3): 40–57.

Rand, J. (1986) 'HR management: an integrative perspective', *Personnel*, June: 51.

Sadore, R. (1989) 'A note on industrial restructuring in socialist countries: changing management's psychological outlook', *Public Enterprises* 9 (2): 148–58.

Sziracki, G. (1990) '*World Employment Programme Research*', Working Paper No. 46, Geneva: ILO.

Tissen, J. and Bolweg, J. (1987) 'Personnel management in the Netherlands: recent development and trends', *Personnel Review* 16 (3), 3–8.

Van Ham, J., Williams, P. and Williams, R. (1986) 'Personnel management in a changed environment', *Personnel Review* 15 (3): 3–7.

Vlachoutsicos, C. and Lawrence, P. (1990) 'What we don't know about Soviet management', *Harvard Business Review*, November–December: 50–63.

Wilhelm, W. (1990) 'Revitalising the human resource management function in a mature large corporation', *Human Resource Management* 29 (2): 130–1.

Wolniansky, N. (1990) 'Mastering the Soviet chessboard', *Management Review* 79 (3): 25–8.

World Bank (1991) 'Poles support market economy – with caution', *Transition* 2 (9): 5.

Wynd W., and Reitsch, H. (1991) 'Soviet and American business students: similarities and differences', *Journal of Education for Business*, July/August: 339–40.

10 The transfer of managerial knowledge to Eastern Europe

Jean Woodall

INTRODUCTION

The 1989 'Revolutions' in what is now known as Eastern and Central Europe were followed by a wave of new measures of technical assistance from the West: the British Government Know-How Fund directed initially to Poland and Hungary (and Bulgaria after 1990), US Aid, the World Bank, United Nation's Economic Development Office (UNEDO) and the EC's TEMPUS and PHARE programmes. A primary focus of these initiatives has been to assist these countries with developing the organizational infrastructure and individual human capability to manage the 'new businesses' of Eastern and Central Europe.

However, where is this all leading to? What is the purpose of all this activity devoted to the education, training and development of Eastern and Central Europe's 'new' managers? What sort of managers are wanted? Are the skills that are being transferred those that will enable them to deal with the problems of their own organizational and cultural context, or are they designed more to enable managers to 'participate' (if not exactly compete) in international business? Is the West passing on the best 'know-how' in respect of latest thinking on management education, training and development, or have 'models' been eschewed for 'muddle' and the opportunity to develop new methods cast aside in favour of old solutions?

This chapter will try to answer some of these questions, by reference to the experiences of Eastern and Central Europe in general, and to the approach adopted by the British Know-How Fund (KHF) in particular. The main argument will be that:

- In the 'West' we have developed a great deal of knowledge about achieving effective management learning in recent years, but in general, this appears to be disregarded in the process of transferring know-how to Eastern and Central Europe.
- Like other Western assistance programmes, the KHF has adopted a very pragmatic approach, but one which nonetheless does start with preconceptions about what is needed in METD in Eastern and Central Europe.
- Most KHF initiatives have adopted a very conventional approach to

meeting METD needs. Yet these needs should be seen as being met more broadly than the provision of courses – as indeed is the current trend in the UK.

- Effective meeting of these METD needs should avoid the temptation to start 'with a clean slate'. Account should be taken of the economic, organizational and cultural context of management prior to 1989.
- Effort is needed to ensure that 'opinion formers' in the field of METD in Eastern Europe are brought fully into contact with the broader community of METD professionals in the West and are encouraged to develop their own solutions, rather than rely on Western professionals as 'gatekeepers'.

EFFECTIVE MANAGEMENT LEARNING AND THE TRANSFER OF KNOW-HOW

Over the last twenty years, management development specialists have devoted a great deal of time to analysing the process of managerial learning. In particular, there has been a move from management development programmes that teach managers how they ought to think and behave, to programmes which aim to help managers learn from experience. The work of David Kolb (1984) provided the theoretical underpinning for this shift of focus, and the practical work of Peter Honey and Alan Mumford (1982, 1983) provided the main means of dissemination of the ideas to management development programmes. The process of learning from experience, and recognising and compensating for different learning style preferences has become a commonplace at the outset of most management development programmes.

We also have been made aware that the methods of management development that we select involve ready-made assumptions about the learning process, but that at the same time, these methods are not set in tablets of stone: methods that are currently popular (e.g. experiential or work-based methods, case studies, etc.) have evolved by trial and error to meet the needs of particular situations. The main justification for choice of learning methods, should be a pragmatic response to the following questions: what underlying theories of learning appear to apply to the situation; how do we intend to apply the use of these methods?

On the other hand, most of what we know about the transfer of learning has come out of the studies conducted by occupational psychologists focusing upon craft and operative skills, rather than managerial work (Annett and Sparrow 1985). Here the focus has been upon the use of a previously learned skill in a new setting, or the attempt to reduce training time and effort due to the trainees' need to 'unlearn' previous training or experience. In practical terms, we know that learning transfer can be enhanced by:

- Avoiding rote learning.
- Promoting learning that is meaningful to the learner.

- Making use of existing learner abilities.
- Including relevant content.
- Integrating theory and practice.
- Using varied examples and experiences.
- Promoting 'discovery' learning.
- Providing reinforcement and motivation.
- Providing follow-up in the workplace.
- Neutralizing negative peer pressure in the workplace.

However, it is widely recognized that in the case of management development when the time interval before practical application of learning is unpredictable, the transfer of learning cannot (nor should) be so precisely prescribed as in the case of more task-specific work. There is a long standing terminological debate in the West centred around management education training and development. Rather than rehearse that here, it is possible to use one recent definition from a summary of the recent UK debate:

> Management Training is defined as the process by which managers acquire the knowledge and skills related to their work requirements by formal structured or guided means. Management Education is the structured formal learning process which often takes place in an institutional framework. Management Development is the broader concept concerned with developing the individual rather than emphasising the learning of narrowly defined skills: it is a process involving the contribution of formal and informal work experience.
>
> (Training Agency and Deloitte Haskins and Sells 1989: 3)

Collectively these three activities can be described as 'management education, training and development' (METD) to indicate the broad scope of current thinking on how the managerial learning process should be supported in the West. However, this debate does not yet appear to have informed current assistance to Eastern and Central Europe.

THE PRAGMATIC APPROACH ADOPTED BY THE BRITISH KNOW-HOW FUND

Because assistance of this kind to Eastern Europe was unheard of since the days of the United Nations' Relief Funds (UNRRA) and US Marshall Plan of the late 1940s, there were no pre-existing methods to administer it. A Joint Assistance Unit was set up between the Foreign Office and the Overseas Development Administration (ODA), with the collaboration of the British Council, to act as a managing agency and assist in bringing prospective partners together and in preparing joint bids. Not surprisingly, the strategy adopted was one that had been followed by the ODA in its work on projects with developing countries: namely bringing together UK and host country partners.

In the cases of Poland and Hungary, the initial idea was to invite proposals for either the direct training of managers or 'management trainer training' which were to be scrutinized as to their worth. The latter judgement proved to be difficult to make and there was a natural tendency for most project proposals to be centred on the capital cities and traditional higher education institutions, or else dependent upon independent Western consultancies. A survey commissioned to review this policy reported in favour of building up Polish and Hungarian METD around an institutional focus. This was to be achieved in the case of Poland by means of creating four regional management centres (RMCs) at Lodz, Poznan, Gdansk and Lublin. The concern was to create an institutional framework that would define a range of METD activities suitable to meet regional needs.

Typically, these RMCs have involved a consortium between a key sponsoring academic institution, an independent foundation and associated consultancy activities. They were 'matched' up with partner institutions in the UK which were selected by a process of inviting applications from consortia of UK higher education institutions and other organizations, such as publishing companies and software houses, and then drawing up a short list. The aim was that they should eventually be run as self-financing small businesses with a very market-driven portfolio of activities: delivery of MBA programmes, executive development and other in-service management training; business information consultancy and English language training. All four centres have drawn up detailed work programmes for a three-year period from 1991 onwards.

A number of smaller scale projects were also set up outside of the RMC framework such as:

• UK government support to assist with the creation of an employment service.
• Joint Industrial and Commercial Attachment Programme sponsored by the CBI offering short work placements in the UK for East European managers from six countries.
• Productivity Improvement Initiatives – involving direct work between UK consultants and companies in Poland with the aim of generating a demonstration project to diffuse technological innovation and marketing knowhow throughout an industry.
• Regional Accountancy Training Project working in two centres; Krakow and Lodz.

The KHF approach to Hungary was different. Because awareness of Western management techniques was seen to be at a higher level there, direct links could be established between Hungarian and British higher education institutions. There are British-Hungarian academic links centred on four separate higher education institutions in Budapest, and others in regional centres in Miskolc and Pecs. In addition there are a number of private sector initiatives – especially in distance learning, in-company development, and a joint venture in 1989 to set up an international management centre in Budapest sponsored by a consortium of Western higher education institutions.

The boundaries between KHF activity in METD and other areas of collaboration, such as public administration and local government, are as blurred as they are between the KHF and other international initiatives to provide support to Eastern and Central Europe, such as those directed through the World Bank and US Aid (mainly focusing on sponsoring joint ventures and privatization). The general impression is of an eclectic and pragmatic approach which is cautious to avoid an over-concentration of efforts in certain cities and institutions and to avoid directly creating long term dependency on Western support.

The KHF is avowedly agnostic when it comes to prescribing approaches to METD. The explicit purpose is to create an infrastructure for the Poles, Hungarians and others, to find their own solution to their management training needs. Even its management advisers are cautious to avoid commitment to models or methods of METD. Nonetheless, a preliminary review of METD needs in Poland, in April 1991, indicated three areas:

- 'Technical' skills in finance, personnel, production, etc.
- Management organization – how to put these together for market decision-making
- The basic business attitudes and values required for success.

The key 'technical skills' of management were, in order of priority: accounting and financial management; marketing; production management; personnel management; management information systems; and investment appraisal and planning. In particular, the second and third areas of need were seen as very important, but as very difficult to meet.

It is interesting to reflect on this analysis. It is a pragmatic response to what exists 'on the ground' in a country like Poland. However, nowhere in all of this has there been an attempt to draw upon what we know in the West about management learning, nor to review the baseline from which these Polish managers start. There seems to be little concern to investigate what skills these managers might already possess and the manner of their previous education and career development. If this were done, the KHF priorities for skill transfer and methods of achieving it might well be different.

METHODS OF METD USED IN POLAND AND HUNGARY

Most of the initiatives funded by the KHF place a great deal of emphasis upon conventional course delivery via existing higher education institutions, with the involvement of Western faculty, leading to an accredited qualification (usually the title 'MBA', but occasionally lower level qualifications such as diplomas and certificates of management). This trend is encouraged very much by prevailing values in the client country where the possessor of an MBA, who knows even the rudiments of investment appraisal or company law, can be assured lucrative business as a 'consultant' to other firms. Outside this, senior managers from local large firms come on executive development programmes and those with a business opportunity embark on small business start-up courses. Curiously, it seems that the Western partners involved have left behind all the nostrums of 'good practice' that we have developed in the West in respect of METD and equally have chosen to ignore what their clients have already learned prior to 1989.

Needs have been analysed by Western providers

In terms of 'what we think they ought to know' and managers are treated as an undifferentiated group. This practice would be deemed unacceptable among METD professionals operating in the UK. In general, Western providers lack knowledge about the economic, organizational and cultural context of management in Eastern and Central Europe (see below). Also, little account is taken of differences between managers in terms of the structure and ownership of their enterprises (from the 'old' state-owned companies, to newer small and medium sized enterprises, joint-venture partners, and owner-managers) and in terms of age and experience (Csath 1988).

The key focus is upon imparting knowledge and understanding

It is separated from developing the competence to carry out and transfer skills back to the workplace. Currently, this is a major concern in the UK, and should be all the more so in the case of Eastern and Central Europe. Again, age and experience of managers needs to be taken into account (Csath 1988). For example, the older generation from state-owned enterprises might be conservative and risk-averse, and so methods suited to attitude change such as action-learning and self-development could be appropriate. On the other hand, the 'reform generation' might be more in favour of work-based learning assisted by in-company training centres. Finally the owner-managers with little opportunity to take time out for study, and who are mainly from the younger generation may need continuous development facilitated via personal development plans and distance learning. Very often this group consists of highly educated people, who none the less have a distrust of academic institutions, but more respect for independent consultants.

The learning process is given scant consideration

The culture of 'passive learning' is well ingrained in the former state socialist societies of Eastern and Central Europe and is reinforced by the preference for formal lectures and presentations adopted in such management education centres that came into operation in the late 1960s. Moving to a more 'student-centred' approach will not be easy given the learning culture and resource constraints, but management development experts have long acknowledged that the appraisal and selection of appropriate management development methods needs to be related to the application of explicit theories of the learning process in a specific context (Burgoyne and Stuart 1991). There is little evidence that management development programmes have universally adopted this approach.

Some pioneering projects are using participative methods

These include methods such as case study analysis, business games and role plays. Unfortunately, most of these are based on Western organizations and are steeped in a Western management cultural perspective. Interesting isolated cases of successful practice linking knowledge transfer with the development of trainer facilitation and consultancy skills are occasionally published (Wallace *et al.* 1988).

Workbased methods are seldom used

This is understandable as, to be effective, they require the support of workplace management. Action learning, secondment, mentoring, self-development cannot operate effectively without this. However, given that most Eastern and Central European managers will not be able to leave their workplace to attend courses, such techniques have the potential to be an essential part of a mid-term strategy to disseminate management know-how and change company practices.

Bringing Eastern European managers over to the UK or other Western countries

Doing this on short attachments to business can be a very good shock tactic of raising awareness, but follow-up benefits are unclear.

However, exposing these managers to Western style executive development programmes does not always produce the desired results. This was the experience of an eminent business school who took their Russian managers on an outdoor training course designed primarily to develop communication, leadership and team work. Unfortunately, the group's operation was characterized more by 'command and control' style behaviour rather than 'action-centred' leadership. This was because many of the managers' previous experience of outdoor training was on active military service in Afghanistan! Such anecdotes only serve to illustrate the width of the cultural gulf between the trainers and the trained. There could be some progress towards overcoming this, if only Western partners in joint projects made adequate use of the knowledge and expertise of those who have made a detailed study of the systems of economic planning and management, education and social structures, and cultures of the countries for which they are providing METD.

THE ECONOMIC, ORGANIZATIONAL AND CULTURAL CONTEXT OF MANAGEMENT

The process of transferring Western management know-how to Eastern and Central Europe necessarily requires the involvement of management specialists. While this appears to state the obvious, nearly all of those experts will have had scant knowledge, understanding and experience of the operation of state socialist centrally planned economies. Exceptional cases arise where the accidents of birth, family connection, higher education and previous business connections have brought such specialists into close recent contact with Eastern and Central European economy and society. Thus, for most management experts the transfer of know-how has to be a two-way process. Again, there are considerable grounds for doubt as to the depth of learning about the preceding development of the economy and business structures achieved by Western specialists. The following section now indicates how important it is for Western management experts to move up this learning curve.

THE OPERATION OF A CENTRALLY PLANNED ECONOMY

A significant difference that must be fully addressed is the operation of a centrally planned economy (CPE). This is seldom appreciated in full as the tendency of Western economic observers has been to confuse the 'model' with the 'muddle' that existed (Nove 1983). The path followed by the Eastern and Central European economies has largely been conditioned by the experiences of the USSR. This is popularly portrayed as the 'Stalinist model' which entailed the following.

- A legally binding and centrally determined plan that dominated all economic activity, created a sellers' market and provided the sole yardstick of business success. Exact fulfilment of the plan was rewarded more highly than 'over-fulfilment'.
- The establishment of an extensive bureaucratic hierarchy through which communication tended to follow vertical channels and control over production units was assured, by the principle of 'one-man-management' backed up by tight communist party control over senior management appointments (the *nomenklatura* system). At each level of the hierarchy a single person was accountable for performance to his superiors. Usually this necessitated a three-tier hierarchy: industrial enterprise, central administration/industrial association and industrial ministry, but also entailed the creation of large monopolistic conglomerates (Woodall 1982).
- Planning took place in physical terms or 'volume' of output rather than through a measure of 'value' such as the price mechanism. The major instrument for achieving co-ordination of national plans was the set of 'material balances' (a set of tables linking physical inputs and outputs throughout the production process). Where used in the process of transactions between production units and the economic administration, prices served mainly as a unit of account or a means of evaluation of performance.

- Economic planning and management was carried out on behalf of workforce interests, rather than by them. Their interests were 'represented' by trade unions whose main role was to mobilize labour and to attend to social welfare needs. Workforce motivation was to be achieved by ideological commitment and, to a lesser extent, by material rewards tied to the achievement of the overall enterprise plan targets, rather than their own performance and involvement.
- Giving priority to heavy industry (especially defence-related) with emphasis upon collectivization of agriculture for the purpose of transferring resources to industry (Lovenduski and Woodall 1987: 77–8).

Yet the 'Stalinist model' of economic planning and management was not the original point of departure and subsequent destination for the economic development of most of Eastern and Central Europe after 1945 and only between 1948 and 1956 could it be said to prevail. The operation of a more mixed economy during the period 1945–48 and political and economic reform movements in Poland and Hungary in 1956, in the German Democratic Republic in 1962, in the USSR in 1965, in Czechoslovakia and Hungary in 1968, focused on integrating 'plan and market' in very different ways. These reforms had a limited success and were followed by revisions or recentralization in the 1970s and 1980s. Even so, the main point is, that the 'Stalinist model' never achieved the full centralization aimed for and in fact encouraged patterns of managerial behaviour resisting such central control that outlived its demise and reform.

ECONOMIC MANAGEMENT IN A CENTRALLY PLANNED ECONOMY

As outlined earlier, efforts at tight control in fact induced evasive behaviour patterns and a mode of operation at the organizational level that had its own unintended logic. For example, industrial enterprise management preferred targets that could be achieved comfortably with the aid of guaranteed supplies, but central planners preferred an incremental increase over the previous year's output. Thus, enterprise managers tended to understate their productive capacity while the central planners endeavoured to raise targets as high as possible. The resulting 'taut planning' made it increasingly difficult for firms to secure scarce supplies for which demand had become overheated.

Indeed, fulfilment of plan targets took precedence over everything else, as individual employee wages at all levels had a large 'at risk' bonus. Supposedly an exercise in precise economic forecasting integrating developments over a five-year period, planning in practice looked more like budgeting. The annual plan was far more important than the five-year plan and sometimes the major operational objective would be achievement of quarterly or even monthly output targets (Lovenduski and Woodall 1987: 82).

Thus, what might seem by Western business standards to be irrational managerial behaviour became entirely rational in the context in which it occurred.

- Managers aimed for the least demanding plan targets, and the minimization of risk.
- Cost-effectiveness was disregarded as long as targets were met. This could mean both hoarding materials and labour, keeping high inventories of finished goods, and tolerating wide fluctuations in output, with 'storming' towards the end of the plan period.
- Search for and acceptance of any available supplies on the grounds that they were tradable.
- Disregard of quality, marketing and financial considerations, as the 'customer is captive, and the producer is king'.
- Excessive bargaining between superiors and subordinates.
- Pervasive distrust.
- A tendency for managers to evade responsibility (Lovenduski and Woodall 1987; Pearce 1991; Woodall 1982) and hide behind bureaucratic rules and regulations.

THE NATURE OF MANAGERIAL JOBS

Managerial jobs in centrally planned economies were as variable as they are in the West – size, divisionalization of enterprises, proximity to the effects of privatization and joint ventures with the West – are some of the most important influences. However, in general, managerial jobs were characterized by the following.

Structured internal labour markets within larger organizations

This meant that there were fewer ports of entry at lower levels but more at senior levels, and a very hierarchical grade structure with ambiguous accountability.

The influence of particular educational experiences on recruitment

The pattern of a strong correlation between a higher education in engineering and senior management career opportunities was set in the USSR in the late 1920s and extended to Eastern Europe in the late 1940s. An additional strong correlation was established between type of higher education experience, social background and subsequent management career path. By this, the most technically qualified would be more likely to seek posts in R&D and other support functions (where work was less pressured) and avoid posts in production and operations. Similarly, it is from this latter group that most of the younger owner-managers are drawn.

An inverse relationship between responsibility and rewards

Because of the immediacy of plan targets, line management jobs in production and operations would be highly stressful, yet at the very junior levels of first line managers, pay was often lower than that of skilled manual workers. At senior levels frequent turnover was not uncommon (albeit of a voluntary nature, rather than due to dismissal). In all cases, a large part of take-home pay was bonus-related, the proportion increasing with seniority, but payment was unrelated to individual performance.

The influence of the nomenklatura *system upon managerial career development*

This involved local communist party control over succession planning, by constructing lists of incumbents and potential 'reserves' for key management jobs. Promotion was based upon 'connections' and not assessment of performance or procedural justice (Pearce 1991; Woodall 1982). Also, this system left managers little control over the selection of their immediate colleagues, making the concept of team development rather hollow.

The machinery of central planning and administration put considerable pressure on managers. Far from being mere ciphers passing on central instructions they adopted a variety of roles as:

'Jugglers' of competing interests

These originated from both within and outside the firm. With low employee motivation, the crude performance-related pay needed to be delivered to achieve plan targets. Local government and communist party interests needed to be placated. Most of enterprise managers' time was spent dealing with problems that arose from outside of the workplace.

Managers of information

They monitored information received from outside, interpreting, processing and transmitting this on; they 'fudged' the information sent to the centre about the firm's capacity in order to secure manageable plan targets.

Resource managers:

They hoarded scarce supplies and traded them on the 'grey markets'; making decisions about the internal allocation of resources.

Indeed, it is possible to apply a Western framework for analysing enterprise directors' roles such as Mintzberg's (1973). What is striking is, that so many of the roles of senior managers in a centrally planned economy were analogous to his categories. The difference lies in the purposive focus of the behaviour viz: managers know a lot about how markets operate because they are constantly trading (see above), but at the same time being 'entrepreneurial' meant risk minimization rather than risk taking. In any case a detailed audit of management roles under the 'old system' must be a prerequisite for designing METD for the 'new system'.

PRE-EXISTING EXPERIENCE OF MANAGEMENT DEVELOPMENT AND AWARENESS OF WESTERN MANAGEMENT SCIENCE

Contrary to popular belief, the centrally planned economies were never totally insulated from knowledge of Western management science (Beisinger 1988). Indeed, Taylorism gained considerable popularity in the USSR during the 1920s – to the point that it was applied far more assiduously than it ever was in the West. To some extent this enthusiasm was tempered by the Stalinist suspicion of scientific experts and preference for the 'heroic' ideological motivation of manual workers, as exemplified in the 'Stakhanovite' movement in the USSR and the purges of management schools in the 1930s. Furthermore, in the Eastern and Central European countries 'liberated' by the USSR after 1945, there had been a pre-war tradition of social and management science that never quite died and was subsumed into official Marxism-Leninism – for example, operations management, industrial sociology and economics in Poland, and administrative science and industrial sociology in the German Democratic Republic and Hungary.

While social and management science, such as economics and applied psychology, bore the scars of the Stalinist years in the USSR and Eastern and Central Europe, academic interest in Western ideas revived again after the late 1950s. The constraints of official communist party policy meant that such 'bourgeois science' was seldom allowed to leak out beyond these circles, but nonetheless links with Western business schools and the publication of the works of a number of management 'gurus' (for example, J. Humble, P. Drucker and J.K. Galbraith), accompanied the major attempts to reform centrally planned economies after the early 1960s. Unfortunately, few practising managers were exposed to these ideas and academics had little valid experience of management.

Management schools were founded throughout Eastern and Central Europe in the 1960s, beginning with the German Democratic Republic in 1962, followed by the rest by 1968. Uusally set up outside of the system of academic higher education the emphasis was upon 'leading managers', and hence stressing the importance of following 'politically correct' Marxist-Leninist policy. In some countries, there were different management training centres for individual industries. In all cases, only senior and middle managers (usually those trained as engineers) participated, expected (and usually received) formal training by means of didactic methods, and were exposed to a range of subjects including forecasting, operations management, cost-accounting, social sciences (including economics and social psychology), but not marketing or finance. While ILO assistance in Romania (1967) and Poland (1972) supported the foundation of university-based management schools, these brave attempts never reached the scale needed to encompass all but a few senior and middle level managers. It is as if policy makers and academics were:

> Drawn to imported theories of management science and to grandiose technocratic schemes as surrogates for market reform.
>
> (Beisinger 1988: 16)

It was only after the 'Revolutions' of 1989, that the biggest expansion of management education occurred, mainly outside of the higher education system (except for Hungary) and largely funded through Western assistance programmes and joint ventures. Nonetheless, Western management advisers are advised to build on what has gone before, and not to assume they are starting with a clean slate.

CONCLUSION: THE WAY FORWARD?

If the transfer of management development know-how to the countries of Eastern and Central Europe is to become embedded in management practice, then the following matters need to be addressed.

Equal partnership in the transfer of know-how

Western advisers must acquire a detailed knowledge and understanding of the experience of management in a centrally planned economy. There is no better place to start than with an audit of the existing systems of METD.

A professional analysis of training needs and management roles

A detailed audit of management roles at various levels under the old system and in the new organizations that are making the transition to a market economy, is the prerequisite for development of new attitudes, skills and behaviours. Development driven solely by Western management curricula and qualifications should be avoided.

Design of development programmes based on an analysis of management learning

The existence of passive learning needs to be recognized and the move to active learning supported. Long academic programmes may have low face validity with participants compared with short courses or work based on action learning. Materials need to be customized to the economic, organizational, and cultural context.

Development of closer international links at a professional level

Professional management organizations in the West can assist more actively in the exchange of know-how, and assist in the dissemination of good practice.

NOTE

1 The author would like to thank officials at the ODA, the British Council and Noel Hibbert of Coventry Polytechnic for their advice and assistance.

REFERENCES

Annett, J. and Sparrow, J. (1985) *Transfer of Learning and Training*, Research and Development Series No. 23, Manpower Services Commission.

Beisinger M. (1988) *Scientific Management, Socialist Discipline and Soviet Power*, Boston: Harvard University Press.

Burgoyne, J. and Stuart, R. (1991) 'Teaching and learning methods in management development', *Personnel Review* 7,1: (reprinted in *Personnel Review* 20 (3): 27–32).

Csath, M. (1988) 'Management education for developing entrepreneurship in Hungary', in Davies, J., Easterby-Smith, M., Mann, S. and Tanton, M. (eds) *The Challenge to Western Management Development*, London: Routledge, pp. 137–51.

Honey, P. and Mumford, A. (1982) *Manual of Learning Styles*, Maidenhead: Honey.

—— (1983) *Using Your Learning Styles*, Maidenhead: Honey.

Kolb, D. (1984) *Experiential Learning: Experience as the Source of Learning and Development*, Englewood Cliffs, New Jersey: Prentice Hall.

Lovenduski, J. and Woodall, J. (1987) *Politics and Society in Eastern Europe*, London: Macmillan.

Mintzberg, H. (1973) *The Nature of Managerial Work*, New York: Harper & Row.

Nove, A. (1983) *The Economics of Feasible Socialism*, London: George Allen & Unwin.

Pearce, J.L. (1991) 'From socialism to capitalism: the effects of Hungarian human resources practices', *Academy of Management Executive* 5 (4): 75–88.

Training Agency and Deloitte Haskins and Sells (1989) *Management Challenge for the 1990s*, Sheffield: Training Agency and Deloitte Haskins and Sells.

Wallace, J, Razvigorova, E., Kalev, J. and Boulden, G. (1988) 'Management and organizational development in Bulgaria', in Davies, J., Easterby-Smith, M., Mann, S. and Tanton, M. (eds) *The Challenge to Western Management Development*, London: Routledge, pp. 238–48.

Woodall, J. (1982) *The Socialist Corporation and Technocratic Power*, Cambridge: Cambridge University Press.

11 Realities, paradoxes and perspectives of HRM in Eastern Europe

The case of Czechoslovakia

Marián Kubeš
Peter Benkovič

INTRODUCTION

East European countries are undergoing major changes that are most obvious in their political and economic systems. These changes also have an inevitably significant impact, which is not so readily visible and understandable to an outside observer, on everyday lives. HRM is one of the most dramatically affected areas. The old HRM practices are no longer compatible with the requirements of a rapidly changing environment; the absence of relevant theory is a major shortcoming in all our attempts to make the best use of human potential.

We believe that the best way to represent the situation and current trends in HRM in the former Eastern bloc, and specifically in Czechoslovakia, is to set out certain realities and paradoxes of the former regime and to compare them with the realities, paradoxes and perspectives of the present.

THE PAST

In 1970, the Central Committee of the Communist Party resolved that the main criterion for promotion into any managerial position would be loyalty to the ideology of the Communist Party; the standard way to demonstrate that loyalty was membership of the party. Therefore HRM, rather than serving the functional needs of the organization, came to serve the requirements of the political ideology. An interesting and vital consequence of this process was the shift of focus in HRM, from objective productivity indicators, to the more subjective (and more rigid) objectives of the ideology. The realization of the Central State Plan, an operational ideological document, took priority over the realities of market forces.

Dictate of the plan

The Central Plan encompassed everything, including the sorts of goods to be produced, their quantity, their prices, numbers of employees and apprentices, and salaries. Even the number of university students was prescribed. The plan for each successive year was set up as follows. The production output of a specific year was taken as next year's base and that base was raised by 3–5 per cent as the target for the next year. If an enterprise exceeded the plan by 20 per cent the base for next year was 120 per cent. Various enterprises came to realize that the smaller the percentage by which they exceeded the plan, the better. The system had a built-in stagnation factor.

The direct consequence for HRM was the selection and promotion of persons who were most likely to meet the requirements of the Central Plan, whether or not that plan made sense in local conditions. Indirectly, the consequence was to discourage the development of new products and their source – the free thinking, creative type of manager willing to take the occasional risk.

The Central Planning function, i.e. the governmental bureaucracy responsible for the plan, eventually recognized the need for innovative changes. The bureaucrats tackled the need in typical fashion. A central committee passed a resolution about the need to be more innovative. The resolution resulted only in the capacity to generate slogans and to pay lip service to its aims. It did not generate the output needed. The stifling, by a monolithic central control system, of individual differences and of incentives for taking risks led to the devaluation of the very human resources upon which industrial productivity ultimately depends.

At the level of the firm, the personnel office found its proper functions perverted. Instead of identifying and sharpening individual differences in ability that could be put to the service of the firm, the human resources department functioned to select individuals who were most likely to conform. The training function was perverted to serve ideological indoctrination rather than to develop individual skills. In both cases, the traditional HRM activities were prostituted to the service of the Communist Party. The director of the personnel office was, without exception, required to be a member of the Communist Party. No special education or training in human resources was required. The only requirement was to follow the instructions of the Central Committee. The effect of this contrived reality, with its associated paradoxes, was a lack of confidence in a future under communist rule, where the Central Plan, right or wrong, took precedence over the realities of the local situation.

But the control from the centre was not absolute. There were those in the system, not necessarily the brightest or the best in their fields, who found it impossible not to assert their individual views and feelings about their work and their futures. These individuals gravitated together into small groups in various firms and organizations, to form what later came to be called 'islands of positive deviation'. Often working in small groups within groups, these 'deviant individuals' supported one another in constructing an alternative view of the realities of their lives and of their work, an alternative often reflecting more accurately the local situation in their firm, school or academic discipline. These were the men and women who developed new thought and attitudes during and after the now famous 'Velvet Revolution'.

Change towards a complex environment

The most general and permanent change introduced by the November revolution was the changed external environment in which organizations have to operate. It has been a change towards the complexity so typical of free market economies. In Western countries, the complexity of the business environment has been growing gradually over past decades. Even radical changes in the external environment, described by Toffler (1980) as changes from a 'second' to 'third' wave organizational context, were substantially in line with the previous principles of organizational functioning. That of the free market economy was perhaps the most important. In contrast, the November revolution introduced a more radical change of the external environment from a centrally planned to a market driven economy. This change happened very quickly. It has resulted in the inability of the organization simultaneously to change internally and to cope with the external changes effectively. Figure 11.1 illustrates the giant jump into a more complex environment and, at the same time, the discontinuity gap indicating the scale of change needed *within* organizations. They now operate in a complex environment closely similar to the environment in which Western organizations operate. In contrast to their Western counterparts, however, they have little or no experience in coping with this environment and lack the skills necessary to manage key resources, including human resources, successfully.

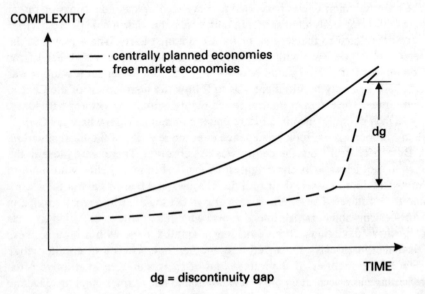

Figure 11.1 Changes in external environment

Research background in HRM

We have investigated the research background of HRM in Czechoslovakia by bibliometric analysis of the journal *Psychologie v ekonomicke praxi (Applied Industrial Psychology)*, the main Czechoslovakian medium where researchers and practitioners can publish the results of their studies. The journal has been published quarterly since 1966. The backgrounds of the contributors embrace universities, research institutions and enterprises where psychologists have been employed. We carried out bibliometric analysis of the contents to identify the scope of HRM and related topics in Czechoslovakia.

During the period 1966–91 (26 volumes, 104 issues) 379 articles were published, including proceedings from two conferences. Ten articles written by foreign contributors were excluded from the analysis. We were able to allocate most of the articles to two major categories, i.e. industrial/ organizational psychology and organizational behaviour on the one hand, and personnel and human resource management on the other. The remainder could be categorized into organizational development and effectiveness, management (general issues), marketing and consumer behaviour, and miscellaneous topics. In the latter category appeared articles on ergonomics, transport psychology, sociology, research methods and statistics, young worker issues, and issues affecting women, as well as several ideological articles written on the occasion of anniversaries and political events.

As we can see from Table 11.1, only 11.3 per cent of articles were concerned with personnel and human resource management. In this category more than one third of the articles were concerned with training and development issues. Although labour turnover is right at the bottom of Table 11.2 (measured by the number of articles) the practitioners in different industries were in fact

Table 11.1 Number of articles published in *Psychologie v ekonomicke praxi (Applied Industrial Psychology)* during the period 1966–91

Category	No.	%
Industrial/organizational psychology, organizational Behaviour	166	43.8
Personnel and human resource management	43	11.3
General issues of management	16	4.2
Organizational development and effectiveness	12	3.2
Marketing, consumer behaviour	5	1.3
Miscellaneous	137	36.1
Total	379	100.0

preoccupied with this issue. The reason for this, as seen from the communist ideology point of view, was that the higher the turnover, the less control could be exercised over the work force. Of course, the authorities soon recognized that high turnover also had negative impacts on effectiveness and productivity. In many companies the turnover was much higher than was tolerable. There were two main reasons. The first was that moving from one company to another, was the best and, in many jobs, the only way to get a

Table 11.2 Number of articles in the category 'personnel and human resource management' referred to in Table 11.1

Article	No.	%
Training and development	17	39.5
Performance assessment	6	14.0
Handicapped workers	6	14.0
General issues of P and HRM	5	11.6
Selection, recruitment	5	11.6
Labour turnover	4	9.3
Total	43	100.0

Table 11.3 Number of articles in the category 'industrial/organizational psychology, organizational behaviour' referred to in Table 11.1

Article	No.	%
General issues of industrial/organizational psychology	21	12.7
Stress	19	11.5
Motivation	15	9.0
Group performance, group processes	13	7.8
OB diagnostic	12	7.2
Creativity, innovation	12	7.2
Job description, job analysis	12	7.2
Individual differences	11	6.6
Leadership	10	6.0
Decision-making, problem solving	6	3.6
Perception	6	3.6
Information processing	6	3.6
Human relations	5	3.0
Job satisfaction	4	2.4
Work conditions	4	2.4
Communication	4	2.4
T-groups, sensitivity groups	3	1.9
Organizational climate/culture	3	1.9
Total	166	100.0

salary rise. The second reason was even more important. It was the absence of a strong organizational culture. This is also obvious from the analysis in Table 11.3 where only a few articles (3) are concerned with this topic. The overall orientation of the organizational development category was towards the maintenance and improvement of existing structures, not towards changing them.

PRESENT

The Velvet Revolution brought a change in the political regime. It also brought a change in organizational culture. There was, as might be expected, a great deal of re-shuffling in top management. Almost without exception, throughout the industrial and commercial complex, the first to go was the personnel director, a recognition of the critical role which such individuals had in maintaining the old system. The key to the maintenance of the old system was the human resource function; paradoxically the key to the future was seen to be that same human resource activity. Now there are serious problems in establishing a new HRM environment and mentality after forty years of its service as the handmaiden of the Central Planning ideology. Several examples of such problems illustrate the current reality in Czechoslovakia.

Organizations are not equally aware of the necessity to change. Usually, only a small core group realizes the seriousness of the situation and is also willing to accept the greater risks accompanying the change process. Most organizations, when trying to introduce change, exaggerate the importance of technical equipment, foreign investment, and changes in technology. They underestimate the importance of HRM and of creative leadership.

The newly appointed personnel directors have no training. Despite the best of intentions and long hours, the typical personnel director suffers from a lack of formal education in personnel management. Furthermore, he or she has had no opportunity to get the necessary training after university. It is, of course, superfluous to note that on-the-job training under the old regime is counter-productive in an open system.

The gap in expertise in the new environment is currently being filled from two sources. On the one hand, there have sprung up a number of consultancies originating out of the former 'islands of positive deviation'. These benign and well-intended individuals make themselves available for consultation in human resources. Some are quite effective; some have not had the training and experience necessary to come into an organization and design constructive interventions. Unfortunately, existing personnel directors are not always able to evaluate the effectiveness of their consultants and their proposals. They simply accept them in blind faith.

On the other hand, there has been an influx of human resource 'messiahs' from the Western bloc. Changes towards complexity in their own countries have stimulated development of new theories and new strategies for management development and human resource management which are not, however, readily applicable in the cultures of former communist countries. These outside consultants often have excellent credentials and admirable experience in their home cultures. What they may lack is experience in the particular culture of the former Eastern bloc nations. This is a serious disadvantage, a disadvantage of which the consultants might be aware, but of which their customer, the local personnel manager, might not. So we have a situation where proposals, ostensibly sound by the usual standards of the external consultant, may not be workable in the culture of the local firm.

In addition, we believe that we can detect a certain bias in the source and orientation of foreign consultants. Most of them tend to come from Austria and Germany. This is not necessarily a bad thing, except that we can detect an orientation among those consultants towards the mentalistic, as opposed to the behaviouristic, approach to HRM. We find little interest, for example, in behaviour assessment techniques and in assessment or developmental centres. We find most of these consultants to be uninterested in longer term training projects. They seem, rather, to be interested in selection functions based upon a mentalistic test philosophy. This particular emphasis is somewhat dated, at least in the United States, where equal rights legislation has forced users towards more objective, behaviour measures as compared with the mentalistic assessment devices of earlier days (pre-1960s). It is our view that the day of the mentalistic test has passed. The behaviour assessment approach not only has more validity and fewer legal hazards in the selection and promotion context, but it lends itself more easily to the design of training programmes where those individual differences, identified in selection and job classification, are sharpened and developed.

Finally, it is important for us to report that the Velvet Revolution was not a spiritual exorcism. That brilliantly executed change at the political level did not automatically translate itself into impressive changes at the level of the working psychology of the manager, the personnel director, or the worker. Forty years of being alert (or careful) to serve the needs of a distant bureaucratic planner left many of us in human resources with the tendency to look for someone to 'tell us what to do'. We are perhaps too ready to adopt the changes recommended by our consultants, whether or not they are suited to our local circumstances.

And that may be the final and potentially fatal paradox – a readiness to seek and accept change without the necessary ('human' may we say?) resources to evaluate the suitability and the efficacy of the changes proposed. It is conceivable that sometimes it is better to do nothing than to do something which is inappropriate. If only we knew which was which!

The one guiding principle we should have is perhaps that both the old and the new, the Eastern bloc and the West, have something to contribute to HRM. Surely job security, a feature handled so well by the Eastern bloc Central Planning model, is an important ingredient for any human resource package. And certainly the tendency of the Western bloc to acknowledge, to respect and to take advantage of individual differences, maximizes the value · of precious and scarce human resources. What we should set our hearts and minds to, in both the Eastern and Western blocs, is to select and develop the best from both models. If communism was, after all, just a massive social experiment then capitalism must be also. Let us examine the results of these experiments as carefully as we can, to help us design a system of HRM that takes advantage of both the successes and the failures of both experiments.

FUTURE

The view of the future can best be seen from two perspectives. The first perspective, that of the researcher in human resources, management and creativity, gives some notion of the knowledge base upon which the future of HRM will develop. The second perspective is that of the practitioner, the person responsible for using the scientific research base in the solution of human resources problems. The present authors would like to share their good fortune of having experienced both aspects of human resources work.

A theory needed

There are many sources of theoretical thinking in HRM in Western countries that influence the processes of establishing its theory and practice in post-totalitarian countries. From the range available both researchers and practitioners take out, more or less randomly, what they feel would be 'the best' for each particular case. There is, therefore, an urgent need for the development of a comprehensive theory reflecting reality in the recently re-established democracies. Such a theory must take into account developments during several past decades with their heritage including people's experience, attitudes, beliefs, values, and work ethics.

The present authors, in their efforts to build a theoretical background for their training and consultancy activities, tried several approaches amongst which the most influential were:

- High performance managerial competencies – theory and developmental programme (Schroder 1989)
- Adaptation–innovation theory of cognitive style (Kirton 1989)
- Productive workplaces (Weisbord 1987)
- Learning organization concepts (Pedler *et al.* 1991; Senge 1990)
- Basic approaches to creative problem solving (Isaksen 1991)

A managerial competency approach

Schroder's approach (Schroder 1989) is based on his work identifying the characteristics of team members which were consistently associated with superior team performance. He also identified managerial behaviours (competencies) which are essential for creating and managing the new organizational structures required to achieve superior performance in the new, more global and rapidly changing technological environments. Later, a system of measurement was designed to identify an individual's profile in the eleven competencies and a management development programme, based on the high performance competencies, emerged.

The competencies cover four areas of a manager's behaviour: the cognitive competencies (information search; concept formation; conceptual flexibility); the motivating competencies (interpersonal search; managing interaction; developmental orientation); the directional competencies (self-confidence; presentation; impact); and the achieving competencies (proactive orientation; achievement orientation).

Although it can be argued that every job contains managerial elements, this development programme aims at the top management function in the first instance. And this was another reason, besides its sound theoretical background, why we have, in Czechoslovakia, introduced this approach. As we described earlier, after November 1989 new, young and inexperienced top managers found themselves in turbulent and dynamic environments.

Adaptation–innovation theory

The adaptation–innovation theory of cognitive style (Kirton 1989) concerns a basic dimension of human personality – the preferred mode of tackling problems, making decisions and creativity. Its implications for the life cycles of organizations and social systems have also been studied and it contributes to our understanding of the problems connected with change processes. Although adaptors and innovators, the two extreme representatives of the adaptation–innovation continuum, differ in their preferred way of solving problems, they are both essential for the successful functioning of any social system. A habitual adaptor tends to accept generally recognized policies and tends to 'do things better'. The characteristic style of an innovator is to 'do things differently' and to reconstruct the problem.

A consultancy theory

M.R. Weisbord is a partner of Block-Petrella-Weisbord, Inc. a management consulting firm. In his book *Productive Workplaces* he describes a new approach to organization and management consultancy based on the integration of his many years of experience as manager and consultant, together with the histories, theories, and methods of leading management innovators, all resulting in new guidelines for productive workplaces. His guidelines involve three aspects. The first is that improving the economics and technologies of our work should be done through cooperation. The second is that a world which is changing too fast, generates problems which are hard to solve without creating many others. The way out is to shift from improving systems by experts towards improving systems by 'everybody'. The third aspect is that tension in working together derives from our inner dialogues between authority and dependency, individuality and the need to belong. His approach is excellently integrated into a simulation 'The Flying Starship Factory' (Copyright BPW, Inc., W.O. Lytle and M.R. Weisbord). The FSF simulation is a powerful tool in managing change consultancy. The present authors are certified users of the FSF in Czechoslovakia.

Learning organization approaches

Another concept we have found very useful for our work is that of the learning organization. The books by Peter M. Senge (1990) and Pedler *et al.* (1991) have offered both an excellent theoretical framework and examples and illustrations of how organizations are adopting this approach. We believe that our organizations in Czechoslovakia necessarily need a totally new philosophy in transforming themselves. The communist ideology suppressed almost everything which is typical of a learning organization. In state owned firms 'nobody learned and nobody was allowed to learn'. The learning approach to organizations could help us to reduce the gap which has been created by very fast changes from stability to a complexity in environments (see Figure 11.1).

Creative problem solving

The reader may well ask how we can implement learning organization theory and principles into post-communist practice, when, even in Western companies, it sounds strange to many workers and managers. A good tool for introducing the learning organization concept into Czechoslovak organizations is the creative problem solving process. We have been strongly influenced by the work of S.G. Isaksen (1990) and have developed our own programme synthesizing the creative problem-solving process and the learning organization concept.

Some observations

Our research in creativity has taught us several important things about HRM. First, it has demonstrated that the creative potential of our people is no different from that of those in the West. Measures of level and style of creativity have been shown to be normally distributed without significant differences in the mean and the standard deviation as compared to comparable Western populations (Kubes 1992).

Second, under the pressures of the communist regime, selection of managers was skewed towards the adaptive, i.e. non-innovative (Kirton 1976), end of the spectrum of styles of creativity. We are sure that this artificial, politically motivated selection bias will be corrected in the future.

Third, the swing away from the conforming adaptive type of the past, towards the innovative type in the future, will reach a limit where the weaknesses of the innovator, for example, his distaste for the detailed planning necessary for an established system, must be overcome by appropriate development, training and team building techniques.

Fourth, on the basis of the research on high performance managerial competencies (Schroder 1989), we have found our managers to be particularly deficient in the competencies of 'presentation', 'self-confidence' and 'impact'. These competencies are crucial to effective negotiation with foreign counterparts and in internal communication with employees. We expect that a full range of experiential learning techniques will be deployed to help redress these critical defects.

Fifth, it is clear to us now that training techniques that have proved to work well in the West, will not automatically work effectively in our situation. The techniques developed in the West must be adjusted appropriately for use in our particular social and cultural setting. The first attempt in this direction, using the competency-based management development programme (Schroder 1989), seems to be positive.

Sixth, participative management was recognized some time ago as a useful tool for managers in the period of transition from second- to third-wave types of organizations. After long experience of not being allowed to contribute to the processes of decision making, employees in East Europe find it extremely rewarding if they are involved in problem-solving and decision-making about the functioning of their organizations. This, however, does not happen automatically as the tradition of directive management and highly hierarchical structures are still typical features of many institutions.

Perhaps the most critical lesson we have learned is that there is no quick imported solution to the problem of changing our organizational culture. To send two top managers to a course on employee motivation in Pittsburgh does not begin to address the problem. Upon their return home the trainees face total indifference in their customer, the worker, who has never heard of Pittsburgh. What is required is an intensive, sustained, and massive effort to change the microculture at all levels of the local organization. We find that there is simply no 'quick fix'. There is no 'silver bullet'. There is only full participation of all staff in the business of changing and sustaining positive work attitudes and commitment to quality output. That task cannot be contracted out to consultants or left to glamorous courses.

In Figure 11.1 we have demonstrated the shift of the whole society towards a more dynamic environment. The implications of this shift for organizations were discussed. Adaptation–innovation theory was successfully applied in the work context and through the lenses of this theory we can also describe the problems that East European countries face in human resource management.

Every system has a strong tendency to become more and more adaptive. To some extent it has to be adaptive if it wants to be effective and achieve continuity. In the case of Czechoslovak organizations there was one additional factor that drew organizations towards adaptiveness. It was the political and economical environment (see Figure 11.1) which was kept stable, and even rigid, artificially. Besides their natural tendency towards adaptiveness, institutions were stimulated not to introduce changes that would aim at 'doing things differently'. After November 1989 a strong pressure from the environment towards changes occurred – not surprisingly towards innovativeness. Now we experience what Kirton calls in his lectures 'the pendulum effect': after being artificially held in one extreme position the pendulum has a strong tendency to swing too far in the opposite direction. This is at least as dangerous for the system as the previous one. It is also one of the critical tasks of management to manage human resources so that the productive range of the pendulum swing is maintained (in terms of adaptation–innovation impact on the system; see Fig. 11.2).

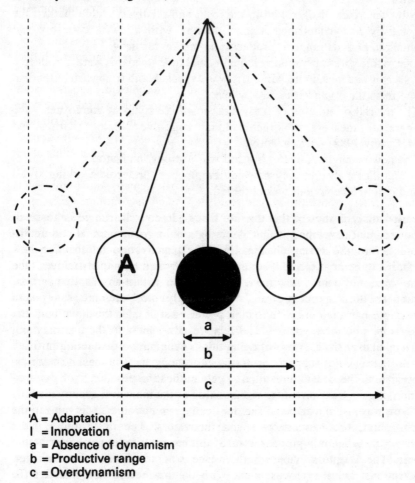

A = Adaptation
I = Innovation
a = Absence of dynamism
b = Productive range
c = Overdynamism

Figure 11.2 The pendulum of change

Case study

One example from our consultancy practice illustrates how changes in the external environment have an impact on the internal life of the organization and also in influencing HRM practices. The present authors were asked to discover the reasons for growing turnover in a small (about 100 employees) applied research software and electronic equipment company. The problems, as seen by the top management, were high turnover and increasing job dissatisfaction (especially with salaries). The company had been in the business for ten years when the request for external help came. The introductory analysis revealed that:

- A new managing director had been appointed approximately one year before.
- After ten years of operation in the local and relatively stable market, the company had established a joint venture with a Swiss company and enlarged both its range of products and market territory.
- Due to foreign cooperation new quality and time standards were introduced.
- As a consequence, more flexibility was expected both from each individual and from the organization as a whole.
- The overall orientation of individual cognitive styles of employees – the aggregate measure of organizational cognitive climate (Kirton and McCarthy 1988) – was adaptive
- The new managing director himself was a strong innovator.
- A significant discrepancy between employees' preferred working styles and required behaviour was observed.

Detailed analysis showed that the prevailing adaptive climate was a result of organizational development in a stable external environment. It was appropriate before the major changes in the company orientation. The new managing director attracted other innovators to join the company while, at the same time, introducing new managing practices within an adaptive system. For most of the adaptors this translated into higher work pressure as they were forced to use behaviours alien to their preferred styles. On the other hand, the innovators who were younger and relative newcomers to the organization, had tended to push new ways of doing things even further than required. They did not get enough support for doing this among their immediate adaptor-supervisors. The situation resulted in communication problems, job dissatisfaction, higher work pressure, and isolation of the innovator group.

There was also a marked difference, in the perception of their roles in the organization, between adaptors and innovators. The latter had a clear tendency to define it in broader terms including contributing also to strategic issues. The adaptors' view of their role was consistent with their job descriptions, i.e. they focused more on the immediate task than on the context.

The personnel department and the personnel director, without having a deeper insight into these processes in the period of the organizational transition, were able only to record signs of dysfunction of the whole system. From the HRM viewpoint it was important to stress during the feedback sessions, that organizational changes towards a more flexible system required the participation and commitment of all employees.

Programme example

According to Pedler *et al.* (1991), a learning organization facilitates the learning of all its members and continuously transforms itself. We cannot find a better example of a desperate need for the transformation of a company than the transformation from a state-owned organization into a private one. This programme is the main part of the training course 'Stimulating creativity in an organization'. A typical sequence of activities looks like this. Eighteen managers of all levels (from the CEO to the foreman) of one organization take part in the programme. All meet in one room and create groups of six, each containing representatives from each level of the hierarchy. Using the '6–3–5 technique', each group generates ideas about the biggest problems in the organization. Participants are asked to be as specific as they can. The 6–3–5 technique requires 6 people to generate 3 ideas in 5 minutes. After five minutes each person passes a list of ideas to the person to the right and receives the list from the person on the left. He/she adds three more ideas and the procedure continues until all those involved have received their original papers back. Each group has to summarize and categorize all its ideas. The problems usually identified concern strategy, policy-making and decision-making, communication, organizational structure, culture and climate, motivation, finance, power, training and development, and human resource management. The most serious problems in each category are selected by voting or ranking. The results are presented on flipcharts to be read by all eighteen participants. Each group chooses a different category and generates ideas about how to solve the most serious problem from that category. The 6–3–5 technique is used again. The ideas are again summarized and presented on flipcharts and read by all eighteen participants. The ranking of ideas follows. All participants evaluate all the ideas generated by the three groups. Five to seven ideas, i.e. the best suggested solutions are selected for a more sophisticated weighting procedure (e.g. using paired comparison analysis, Isaksen 1991). Each group works on its solutions. The result of each group's work is the list of five to seven solutions of the biggest problems, ordered according to several criteria. Presentation on flipcharts and discussion about the results follow. The final step requires each participant to elaborate a detailed plan of the implementa tion of every solution at his/her level of competence and responsibility.

This procedure has several advantages. First of all this is very often the first occasion when top and bottom-line managers identify and solve problems of the organization together. Second, the participants recognize that they are able, not only to identify the problems, but also to suggest many workable and acceptable solutions. The last, but not least, benefit is that participants can see that almost all problems and solutions have a human resource basis and that almost everybody in the company can contribute.

CONCLUSION

In conclusion, we find these times of great change very exciting. The challenge to HRM is obvious. Already we can see striking differences in the response of newly privatized organizations, as compared to state-owned firms. In the latter case we find management willing to talk about HRM, but only within normal working hours. The private firms will not let us go home. They do not want just to talk about HRM; they want to participate in actual training activities, preferably at weekends. We find this difference to be symbolic of the coming times. As Charles Handy (1991) says, discontinuity is a great learning experience, but only if we survive it. Our efforts in HRM theory and practice in Czechoslovakia aim at not only surviving, but also at learning as much as possible from this natural experiment of political paradigm shift.

We think that researchers as well as practitioners in HRM, industrial and organizational psychology and OD must pay more attention to the topics which have been neglected for decades in their work and which are crucial for transformation of our society: organizational culture, training and development of people in order to stimulate and manage changes at all levels.

ACKNOWLEDGEMENTS

We owe much to all the scholars and practitioners who have worked with us, formally or informally, during the last few years to help us to leapfrog in the fields of our interest.

We wish to thank the following colleagues for licensing us to use their training and development programmes: Scott Isaksen and Brian Dorval for the Creative Problem Solving Program; Harry Schroder for the High Performance Managerial Competencies Developmental Program; and Maurice Dubras for the Flying Starship Factory simulation, a product of Block, Petrella and Weisbord, Inc.

We have had the privilege of taking the first practical lessons in our trainer/ consultant careers from Walter Schwarz whose enthusiasm has been a unique source of inspiration and energy for us.

Special thanks are owed to Michael Kirton who not only stimulated us to look for a productive connection of theory to practice, but who was also courageous enough to do so in times when the Iron Curtain still divided the world. His support and stimulating thinking are greatly appreciated here.

The assistance of Sam Mudd in the preparation of this material is also greatly appreciated and our thanks are due to Malcolm Peel and George Hardy for their constructive comments on an earlier draft.

All these colleagues, and many others not named here, shared with us, not only their professional expertise, but also their friendship in the hope for a better future for all of us.

NOTE

1 This chapter was completed prior to the split of Czechoslovakia into separate Czech and Slovak Republics in 1993.

REFERENCES

Handy, C. (1991) *The Age of Unreason*, London: Business Books.

Isaksen, S.G. (1991) *Basic Approaches to Creative Problem Solving*, Buffalo: Center for Studies in Creativity.

Kirton, M.J. (1976) 'Adaptors and innovators: A description and a measure', *Journal of Applied Psychology*, 61: 622–9.

—— (1989) 'A theory of cognitive style', in Kirton, M. J. (ed.) *Adaptors and Innovators: Styles of Creativity and Problem Solving*; London: Routledge.

Kirton, M.J. and McCarthy, R. (1988) 'Cognitive climate and organizations', *Journal of Occupational Psychology*, 61: 175–4.

Kubeš, M. (1992) 'Adaptors and innovators in Czecho-Slovakia: cognitive style and paradigm shift', unpublished manuscript.

Pedler, M., Burgoyne, J. and Boydell, T. (1991) *The Learning Company*, London: McGraw-Hill.

Schroder, H.M. (1989) *Managerial Competence: The Key to Excellence*, Dubuque, Iowa: Kendall/Hunt.

Senge, P.M. (1990) *The Fifth Discipline*, London: Century Business.

Toffler, A. (1980) *The Third Wave*, New York: Bantam Books.

Weisbord, M.R. (1987) *Productive Workplaces*, San Francisco: Jossey-Bass.

Part IV

Creating the pan-European manager

12 Creating international managers
Recruitment and development issues*

Hugh Scullion

INTRODUCTION

While the effective management of human resources is increasingly being recognized as a major determinant of success or failure in international business (Tung, 1984) in practice many organizations are still coming to terms with the human resources issues associated with international operations (Dowling 1986). In the international arena the quality of management seems to be even more critical than in domestic operations (Tung 1984: 129). This is primarily because the nature of international business operations involves the complexities of operating in different countries and employing different national categories of workers (Morgan 1986: 44). Yet while it is recognized that HRM problems become more complex in the international arena there is evidence to suggest that many companies underestimate the complexities involved in international operations. The field of international HRM is, however, only slowly developing as a field of academic study and has been described by one authority as being in the infancy stage (Laurent 1986: 91). Moreover, there is relatively little empirical research which documents international HRM strategies and practices of international firms – particularly firms which have their headquarters outside North America.

This article reports some of the findings from a recent study of international HRM in British and Irish based international firms. One particular feature of the study was the exclusive focus on managing international managers. Particular attention is given to three key issues in the area of international HRM: international staffing, international recruitment and the variety of issues surrounding the problem of shortages of international managers. It will also briefly consider the nature of the HRM challenges facing companies in the light of the internal European market.

A study of how companies deal with the international HRM issues outlined above is particularly appropriate for the following reasons:

*This chapter is based on an article 'Strategic recruitment and development of the international manager' which was published in the *Human Resource Management Journal*, Winter 1992.

1 The international staffing process is of considerable importance to an international firm.

Virtually any type of international problem, in the final analysis, is either created by people or must be solved by people. Hence, having the right people in the right place at the right time emerges as the key to a company's international growth. If we are successful in solving this problem, I am confident we can cope with all others.

(Duerr 1968: 43)

The staffing problems facing international firms are more complex than in domestic firms and inappropriate staffing policies may lead to difficulties in managing overseas operations. The international literature indicates that expatriate failure is a persistent and recurring problem, particularly for US multinationals (Mendenhall and Oddou 1985; Desatnick and Bennett 1978; Tung 1981). Frequently the human and financial costs of failure in the international business arena are more severe than in domestic business. In particular indirect costs such as a loss of market share and damage to overseas customer relationships may be considerable (Zeira and Banai 1984).

2 Shortages of international managers is becoming an increasing problem for international firms. A survey of 440 executives in European firms claimed that a shortage of International managers was the single most important factor constraining corporate efforts to expand abroad. Almost one third of the executives surveyed had experienced difficulties in finding managers with the necessary international experience and orientation (*International Management*, November 1986). The findings of the survey suggest that the successful implementation of global strategies depends, to a large extent, on the existence of an adequate supply of internationally experienced managers (Hamill 1989: 18).

3 There is little empirical research on the international HRM issues associated with the management of managers in British and Irish international firms, especially in relation to the considerable literature on international HRM in US firms.

4 The advent of the internal European market and the rapid growth of British direct investment abroad since the early 1980s means that issues of international staffing, recruitment and development are increasingly important concerns in a far wider range of organizations than the traditional giant multinationals. International HRM problems are becoming increasingly important for a growing number of smaller and medium sized companies who have significantly internationalized their operations in recent years.

RESEARCH METHODOLOGY AND SAMPLE

The principal research method was structured interviews with each company's corporate personnel or human resources director or alternatively with a senior corporate HR executive. The majority were conducted in 1990 with the remainder in 1991. The duration of interviews varied from two hours to three and a half hours. During each interview information on company structure and international operations was sought. The interviewer also asked questions concerning international staffing, expatriate performance, international HRM policies and international management development.

These questions were adapted from a study by Tung (1981) and through consultation with a number of international HRM practitioners. The purpose of the questions was to provide a structured basis for each interview and responses to questions were noted by the interviewer. Interviewees were not asked to fill in a questionnaire. Additional information was obtained from company reports, company documents such as international personnel policies and newspaper articles.

Forty-five international companies participated in the study. Forty companies were UK owned and five were Irish owned international firms. The sample was specifically chosen to include companies from both the manufacturing and the service sector. Twenty-six companies in the study were primarily manufacturing firms and sixteen were service sector firms. Two oil companies and one mining company also participated. The size of the companies in this international firm sample ranges from medium to very large. The total number of employees ranges from 9,500 to 240,000. The smaller size of the Irish international firms and their relatively recent internationalization were two principal reasons for their inclusion in the study. For the sample as a whole there was a wide range in the number of countries the companies operated in and in the length of time of international operations.

INTERNATIONAL STAFFING POLICIES AND PRACTICES

International firms face three alternatives with respect to the staffing of management positions abroad; the employment of parent country nationals (PCNs), host country nationals (HCNs) or third country nationals (TCNs). Much of the existing research focuses on the advantages and disadvantages of using expatriates as opposed to local managers and identifies a range of host country, company and individual factors as important to consider in international staffing decisions. Most studies are, however, largely inconclusive on the question of when parent country nationals should be sent abroad (Boyacigiller 1990).

The findings of the present study on staffing practices in UK and Irish international firms reveal that a majority of the companies continued to rely heavily on expatriates to run their foreign operations. The research findings showed that while almost 50 per cent of companies had formal policies which favoured using host country managers to run their foreign operations, in practice just over a third operated with HCNs in senior management positions in their foreign operations. In other words, two-thirds of the companies relied primarily on expatriates to run their foreign operations. Furthermore, the trend has moved in the direction of greater use of expatriates. Half of the companies in the sample (22 out of 45) reported an increase in the use of expatriates over the previous decade and only 20 per cent indicated that they had reduced their use of expatriates. The remainder reported no significant change.

These findings raise serious questions about the ability and commitment of some British multinationals effectively to identify and develop host country managers in their foreign operations. Therefore the recruitment, selection and development of host country managers emerges as a vital issue for British and Irish multinationals given the need to develop global teams with a variety of different perspectives and competencies. The findings of the present study on staffing practices in British and Irish firms reveal sharp differences with American experience. Indeed recent work by Kobrin suggested that the tendency of American multinationals to reduce the numbers of expatriates had gone too far. He argued that American firms have tended to substitute HCNs to replace expatriates primarily in response to the difficulties American managers have experienced in adjusting to other cultural environments (Kobrin 1988: 66). Kobrin recognized that increased use of host country managers may in part reflect the cost of maintaining expatriates abroad, the greater sensitivity of local managers to local culture and local market needs and the growing international maturity of some multinationals. It is suggested however that expatriate reduction may result in American multinationals facing reduced identification with the world wide organization and its objectives, difficulties in exercising control and a lack of opportunities for American managers to gain international experience abroad. The principal concern is that American multinationals could face major strategic management control problems where managers identified with local units rather than with global corporate objectives (Kobrin 1988: 68–73).

The present study identified a number of principal reasons for employing expatriates. The first was the lack of availability of management and technical skills in some countries. There was a greater tendency for companies to use expatriates in less developed countries due to the weak pool of available local management talent. This was also true for those companies who used host country managers to run their foreign operations in advanced countries. The second major reason cited for using expatriates was the objective of control of local operations. Thirty-three out of forty-five firms in the present study identified control as a key reason for their use of expatriates. Expatriates were felt to be more familiar with the corporate culture and the control system of headquarters, and this was felt to result in more effective communication and coordination. Indeed, a key role for senior expatriates was to train local managers to understand corporate financial and control systems. This point is illustrated by the following comment from the human resource director of a financial services company:

The main advantage of using expatriates is that they understand our (corporate) culture and reporting systems and they teach the locals how to relate to the centre. This is vital when you are establishing a new foreign business.

This finding on the importance of control is consistent with previous research on European multinationals which shows control to be an important reason for expatriate transfers (Torbiorn 1985, Brewster 1988). Yet in previous research only rarely has control been identified as an important aim of expatriate assignments. This probably reflects the North American origin of much previous research and the tendency of some managers and researchers to view control as a rather disreputable rationale for using expatriates (Brewster 1991: 34).

A further key reason for using senior expatriates was to maintain trust in key foreign businesses following large international acquisitions. This finding is particularly interesting because previous research has suggested that the employment of expatriates will be lower in acquisitions by comparison with greenfield sites (Hamill 1989: 22). The emergence of trust as a major factor is related to the rapid growth in the number and scale of foreign acquisitions by British companies in the 1980s. For example, in the late 1980s a UK brewing and leisure company emerged as one of the world's leading hotel groups following a massive £2 billion acquisition of a global hotel chain. In this example a major reason given for using expatriates to run the acquisition was 'the need to have the peace of mind which comes from having our people running such a large and strategically important investment'. There was often an unwillingness to allow newly acquired foreign businesses to be run by the existing host country national management primarily because they were not known well enough and their loyalty to the business was not proven.

The research also found that using expatriates for management development purposes was important and was increasing in significance for British multinationals. Thirty-four out of forty-five companies reported that expatriates were used for development purposes and twenty-five of these firms claimed that use of expatriates for this purpose was becoming more important. This reflects the tendency of British companies to see expatriation as part of the career development process. In this context, it is interesting to note that in most cases the management of expatriates was the responsibility of the corporate human resource function. This was the case even in some highly decentralized organizations (e.g. engineering companies) where the corporate human resource role was rather limited.

One very recent trend identified by the research was the tendency for companies to give younger managers international experience much earlier in their career than previously. Over half of the companies in the sample (26 out of 45 companies) reported significant changes in this respect. This was linked to the growing problems of mobility (spouse's job, children's education, etc.) for older managers. This also reflects the strategy of some companies to broaden the opportunities for international development and the growing recognition in some quarters that the payback on the investment of a developmental assignment may well be greater with a younger manager.

The performance of foreign subsidiaries also emerged as a significant factor influencing the use of expatriates. There was a greater tendency for the companies in the sample to use senior expatriates where the acquired business had been under-performing before the foreign acquisition. Similarly, poor performance by host country managers in the post-acquisition phase was cited as an important reason for them being replaced with expatriates. This is well illustrated by the case of a major UK food and drinks company which made two very large acquisitions in the USA in the late 1980s. The first acquisition was a global drinks business with its headquarters in the USA, and the second was a large US food business. The staffing policy differed sharply in the two acquisitions. In the former case the existing management team (composed entirely of host country managers) continued to run the business. In the words of a corporate HR executive: 'In this case, we inherited an excellent management team who were achieving first-class results. Why change a winning team and upset morale by introducing expatriates?' In the second case, by contrast, the entire US management team was replaced by expatriates, 'mainly due to poor financial results and weak managerial performance'.

Another factor influencing the approach adopted by companies was a strong expectation on the part of major foreign customers (and sometimes foreign governments) that the top managers in their country should be parent country nationals. Thirteen of the sixteen international firms in the service sector and a minority of manufacturing firms (6 out of 26) said they had taken this into account in deciding their policy. Public relations and marketing were usually the key roles in this context. Previous research has largely ignored this factor because it has concentrated on the very largest multinationals and tended to neglect the service sector (Brewster, 1991: 33).

For example, two Irish banks operating in the USA felt there were considerable marketing and public relations advantages in using expatriates, given their marketing strategy of targeting the ethnic Irish population. In the banking, insurance and finance areas, British companies reported that in many countries major foreign customers frequently had a strong preference for their senior executives to be British expatriates.

There is also strong evidence from the present research that expatriates are more likely to be used in the early stages of new foreign operations. This is consistent with previous research which shows this practice is common in the early stages of internationalization where a company is setting up a new business, process or product in another country and prior experience is considered essential (Zeira 1976). A majority of firms indicated that control and trust were particularly important in the early stages of internationalization. In the present study this factor had become more significant due to the rapid growth of international business in the last decade.

Nearly half of the companies (21 out of 45) also cited weaknesses in their training and development of host country national and third country national managers to explain their continued use of expatriates, despite their having a formal policy to replace expatriates with host country managers after the start-up phase. A typical comment in this respect came from a pharmaceutical company:

The training and development of host country nationals and third country nationals is a major weakness in achieving our objective of localising management in our operating companies.

SHORTAGES OF INTERNATIONAL MANAGERS

It was argued above that the successful implementation of global strategies depends, to a large extent, on the existence of an adequate supply of internationally experienced managers. In the present study two-thirds of the companies (30 out of 45) said that they had experienced shortages of international managers and over 70 per cent indicated that future shortages were anticipated.

While the faster pace of internationalization was cited as the primary reason for shortages by thirty-four out of forty-five firms in the sample, the findings suggest that over half the firms (24 out of 45) reported that failures to effectively recruit, retain and develop host country managers was another key reason to explain why shortages exist. A number of factors make the recruitment of host country managers more difficult and costly compared to recruiting in the home country. These include the following: lack of knowledge of local labour markets; ignorance of the local education system and the status of qualifications; language and cultural problems at interviews; trying to transfer recruitment methods which work well in the UK to foreign countries.

Many international firms have tended to neglect the training and development needs of their host country managers and focus virtually all of their managerial development efforts on their parent country national managers (Shaeffer 1989: 29). Twenty-six out of forty-five firms in the sample reported that weaknesses in their training and development in respect of host country managers had contributed to shortages of international managers. The failure to develop local managers effectively was frequently given by British multinationals as a reason for continuing to use UK expatriates in similar management positions rather than using local managers. Alternatively this could be interpreted as something of an excuse for their preference to use expatriates beyond the development phase of international operations.

The present research highlighted three important lessons for those international firms who are seriously attempting to provide management training and development for HCNs and TCNs. First, is the need to avoid the mistake of simply exporting parent country training and development programmes to other countries. This point is illustrated by the following comment from the personnel director of a large chemical firm:

> We have learned from some tough experiences that training and development programmes for local managers must be culturally adapted to local conditions.

Second, the management development programmes for HCNs and TCNs need to be linked to the strategic situation in each country as well as to the overall strategy of the firm. This need to take account of a variety of foreign product market situations superimposed upon the overall strategic thrust of the firm adds considerably to the complexity of devising appropriate management development programmes. Third, is the need to utilize much further the practice of developing host country managers through developmental transfers to corporate headquarters. It has been argued that this type of international transfer exposes HCNs and TCNs to the headquarters corporate culture and facilitates their developing a corporate perspective rather than simply reflecting their own local interests (Dowling and Schuler 1990: 109).

It has also been argued that this approach to development can be very effective in helping to develop global management teams and a necessary part of successfully operating a truly global firm (Edstrom and Galbraith 1977, Prahalad and Doz 1981). The present research indicated however that, a majority of British companies were still failing to recognize the need to develop high potential HCN managers beyond the opportunities which exist in their own countries and this exacerbates the problem of attracting and retaining high potential young managers in the host countries.

RESPONSES TO THE SHORTAGES OF INTERNATIONAL MANAGERS

Nineteen of the forty-five companies had responded to the shortage of international managers by attempting to identify managers of high potential at an earlier stage in their career and by giving them international experience at a much younger age. Over one third of the companies reported that they were sending young managers of high potential on international assignments partly for developmental purposes. This was in sharp contrast to the previous practice when many MNCs relied on developing a cadre of career expatriates who moved from one international position to the next. The trend towards giving younger managers the opportunity for international experience earlier in their careers was often part of a more general trend to give international experience to a wider range of managers and not just to a relatively small group of expatriates. Increasing numbers of international firms were also using short term developmental assignments in order to develop larger pools of employees with international experience.

Another significant response to the shortage of international managers was the rapid growth in importance of external recruitment to fill management positions abroad. Until a few years ago the majority of firms had relied almost exclusively on internal recruitment for foreign management posi tions. British MNCs traditionally had a strong preference for internal managers for expatriate management positions, as they had well known track records and their loyalty to the company was proven. Over a quarter of the firms (13 out of 45) in the study had, in the past five years, introduced external recruitment to fill management positions abroad and several others were planning to do so. Financial services companies were a good example of this. Some of these companies had rapidly internationalized relatively recently and felt they had to recruit externally at senior level to establish their foreign operations.

A third response to the shortages of international managers by fourteen of the forty-five companies was to attempt to sell themselves more effectively to graduates through various types of marketing designed to highlight the international nature of their activities (e.g. in graduate recruitment bro- chures and in national press advertising). This type of marketing highlighted the prospects of early international experience to attract graduates seeking an international career. This can be illustrated by the example of the two textile companies who had a policy of sending young graduates on inter- national assignments within three or six months of joining the firm. This policy was very effective and was designed specifically to recruit high potential young graduates who were particularly interested in an inter- national career. The corporate human resources director of one of the textile companies commented:

> Textiles is not a particularly fashionable industry. We are competing for the best graduates with companies who enjoy a more glamorous image. The fact that we can offer the opportunity of very early international experience is the main reason we can attract some high potential graduates when the big guns, such as Shell, BP, and ICI, are fishing in the same pool.

A minority of companies (8 out of 45) were also broadening their sources of graduate recruitment to include some continental European countries and this reflected their anticipation of a growth in the competition for high potential graduates following the advent of the internal market in 1993. Two computer companies had recently introduced Euro-graduate management development programmes. A feature of these programmes was that graduates were recruited from several European countries for a two-year period of training and development in the UK. On completion of their training graduates were transferred to a management position in a third country. The need to develop more flexible succession planning systems to support the development of Euro-graduates was identified as an important issue by both firms operating this type of programme.

There was also growing recognition of the importance of developing effective international management development programmes to help secure an adequate supply of international managers. The majority of firms reported that they were spending more money and time on international management education, particularly for top and senior management. These firms were using a combination of internal and external international management development programmes. One interesting feature of these programmes was that teachers frequently came from prestigious foreign business schools in Europe and the USA, as well as from internal sources. But, perhaps surprisingly, only three out of the forty-five firms claimed they had effective systems for evaluating their international management development programmes.

The introduction of language training for top, senior and middle levels of management by the majority of companies in the study was seen as an important development in the light of the acute shortages of international managers with language skills. This suggests that the importance of language training is increasingly being recognized by British multinationals. This finding is in sharp contrast with studies of American MNCs which found that only a minority of US MNCs felt that knowledge of foreign languages was necessary for conducting business abroad (Baker 1984; Tung 1981; Brewster 1991). Increasingly it was recognized that language training increased the effectiveness of staff working abroad and helped them relate more easily to a foreign culture. There was also a growing awareness that language training promoted a better image of the MNC in the host country.

There were two areas, however, where the companies were clearly failing to take effective action to ease the acute shortage of international managers. First, there was no evidence that British MNCs were taking serious steps to increase the proportion of women in international management. International management has long been a masculine preserve in Europe and the USA. Adler's study estimates that under 3 per cent of North American expatriates are female (Adler 1984: 81). In the present study no company claimed to have more than 3 per cent female expatriates. Indeed, the evidence suggests that women in British multinationals are not making as much progress in international management as women in American multinationals. For example, in the US banking and financial sector there has been a significant increase in female expatriates (Adler 1984: 83–4). The under-representation of women in international management is illustrated by a quote from a woman HR executive of a UK pharmaceutical company:

> In the UK, the majority of marketing staff are women. By contrast, in our foreign operations, the vast majority of marketing staff are male. Companies still tend to shy away from using female expatriates because of fears that women will not be accepted in some countries and the major problem of disrupting the career of their partner.

The lack of willingness to recruit and develop women as international managers is worrying as recent research suggests that, in many ways, women are well suited to international management. This research suggests that women are more sensitive to cultural differences and are therefore more able to work effectively with managers from other countries (Barham and Devine 1991: 24).

The second area which impacts on the supply of internationalists is the failure by many companies adequately to address repatriation problems. The repatriation of managers has been identified as a major problem for multinational companies in the UK and North America (Adler 1986; Harvey 1989; Hamill 1989; Johnston 1991). Over 70 per cent of the firms (33 out of the 45) in the present study said they faced significant problems regarding re-entry. Further it was generally recognized that this may lead to low morale and a higher turnover of expatriates. For example, only three of the firms claimed that repatriates had no difficulty reintegrating into the UK organization. A key problem for the majority of companies was finding suitable posts for repatriates of similar status and responsibility to those they held abroad. For many UK MNCs this problem had become more acute in recent years because, for many of the companies, expansion of overseas operations had taken place at the same time as the rationalization of UK operations, thereby reducing the number of senior posts in the UK. Other problems associated with reintegrating into the UK, are loss of status, loss of autonomy, loss of career direction and a feeling that international experience is undervalued by the company.

Further there was growing recognition that where companies are seen to deal unsympathetically with the problems faced by expatriates on re-entry, managers will be more reluctant to accept the offer of international assignments. Research in North America indicates that 20 per cent of all managers who complete foreign assignments wish to leave their company on return (Adler 1986). This was a growing problem for UK multinationals, particularly when many companies are willing to pay a premium to attract the experienced international manager. Yet while it is widely accepted that the costs of expatriate turnover are considerable, very few firms had introduced formal repatriation programmes to assist managers and their families with repatriation difficulties. Similarly, very few companies had introduced mentor systems to check the career progression of the international manager. Many expatriate managers were concerned about losing out on opportunities at home and in some companies this was a constraint on their willingness to go abroad. Clearly UK companies need to give a higher priority to the issue of repatriation in order to encourage international mobility and to help secure an adequate future supply of international managers.

BARRIERS TO INTERNATIONAL MOBILITY

This section will briefly consider the reasons why shortages of international managers are expected to continue in the future. In particular it will examine the growing restrictions on international mobility and their significance for the international capability of the firm. Over 70 per cent of the firms (34 out of 45) reported that they anticipated shortages of international managers over the next five-year period. There was a growing concern on the part of many firms that the pace of internationalization would further outstrip the supply of international managers. The demographic time-bomb, the growing internationalization of European firms, and the advent of the internal European market in 1993, led firms to expect a more international and competitive market for managers and graduates. For example, one financial services corporate HR executive expressed the problem like this:

> Attracting and retaining high potential graduates and managers with international experience is vital if we are going to implement our corporate objective of achieving a much stronger presence in Europe. The problem is that the pool of available talent is not growing fast enough to meet demand.

The same executive commented:

> In the short run we have to ensure that our reward package becomes internationally competitive, but this will not be enough. We need to look at new sources of labour supply such as women, host country managers, third country nationals and reduce our dependency on expatriates.

The problem of ensuring an adequate supply of international managers is further exacerbated by growing resistance to international mobility. Indeed it was suggested by twenty-six out of forty-five firms in the sample that individuals were becoming less internationally mobile just at the time when there was a growing need for international managers because of expansion abroad. The reduction in international mobility was attributed to several factors including continued rationalization in the UK which created uncertainties regarding re-entry; the growing unwillingness to disrupt the education of children; the growing importance of quality of life considerations and finally, continued uncertainty regarding international terrorism and political unrest. Indeed concerns about dual career problems and disruption to children's education were seen as major barriers to future international mobility by many companies. In the past working spouses were less common, generally female, and were prepared to follow their partners' career transfers. More frequently now however, spouses must also leave a job or career in order to follow their partner to the foreign country (Hall and Richter 1988; Hall and Hall 1987). The growing significance of the dual career problem is well illustrated by a quote from the HR corporate executive of a large oil company: 'Nowadays families are less willing to disrupt personal and social lives even where they accept that international experience will enhance the manager's career prospects.' And a banking HR executive described the problem in these words:

> More and more women have careers and not just jobs. For many it would be impossible to continue their careers in a foreign country. Increasingly international mobility is limited by the dual-career factor. Also we need to

recognize that dual career problems can seriously affect career development plans for our international managers.

Two further restrictions on international mobility are illustrated by the following quote from an HR executive of a chemical firm:

It's becoming more common for offers of foreign assignments to be rejected because the location does not appeal to the family and when managers are willing to go abroad they are much more demanding about all aspects of the remuneration package.

The above discussion would suggest that restrictions on international mobility appear to be growing just at the time when the need for international mobility is becoming vital for the internationalization of UK business. Indeed the problem of international mobility could emerge as a key factor in determining the international capability of a firm.

1993 – THE HRM CHALLENGES

In the present study companies were asked to identify the main HRM challenges they faced arising from the advent of the internal European market in 1993. For 80 per cent (36 out of 45) of firms that the main challenge was felt to be securing an adequate supply of international managers. A majority of firms said they needed to upgrade management skills and competencies in order to compete effectively in Europe and many companies were concerned about the poaching of graduates and managers by firms based in continental Europe.

Over 70 per cent of companies (33 out of 45) identified recruitment as a priority area. It was felt that the SEM would intensify competition for labour, increase mobility of labour and increase pressure on UK salaries. While some companies identified a number of positive opportunities presented by 1992, namely an increase in opportunity to recruit labour and management from other European countries, the majority of firms felt there would be a net loss of staff to continental Europe. A small minority of companies were seeking to develop a pan-European approach to recruitment but were facing many practical problems such as which journals to advertise in and which qualifications to ask for. In addition there is a problem of the profile of a company abroad, because a company which is well known in the UK may be much less well known in other countries.

The need to develop a more international top management team to reflect the growing international nature of the business was increasingly recognized as a major challenge because, at the present time, very few British companies could claim to have a truly international top management team. Similarly a growing concern was the need to assess what new knowledge, skills and competencies are required to operate effectively in the internal European market. There was also growing anxiety about the managerial skills and competencies needed to deal with the complex HRM issues and problems associated with the growth of international joint ventures (e.g. the evaluation and promotion of managers and the problem of conflict of loyalty of managers to the joint venture or to the parent companies).

There was also a growing recognition by the companies of the need to understand the importance of cultural differences within Europe. This is particularly interesting in the light of the finding that only a very small minority (3 out of the 45) of companies currently use cross-cultural training to help prepare managers for international transfer within Europe. By contrast, it was much more common for firms to provide cultural training for transfers to countries in the Far and Middle East, where the culture gap was seen to be greater. Specialist external courses were often used but not for international transfers within Europe.

The above discussion suggests that the most formidable task facing British companies wishing to operate across Europe is the recruitment and development of a cadre of managers and executives who understand and can operate effectively in the international environment. In practice, the impact of the SEM on HRM strategy varied according to the stage of internationalization and the overall strategy of the firm. Most multinational firms traditionally pass through various stages of internationalization between the evolution from a domestic to a truly global organization.

For some well established international firms '1992' intensifies and sharpens the focus of problems associated with internationalization rather than creates new problems. A small number of highly internationalized businesses who regarded themselves as transnationals (companies with the ability to manage across national boundaries, retaining local flexibility while achieving global integration) felt the nature of the HR challenge of 1992 would be marginal rather than central. Such companies (e.g. the oil companies) tended to see pan-European recruitment and language training initiatives as a response to 1992 but they stressed that fundamental issues such as the supply of managers and management development issues should be related to the broader international strategy of the business rather than '1992'.

'1992' did, however, represent a major HR challenge for 'new' international firms who had internationalized in the recent past and for firms who were significantly shifting the focus of their international activities towards Europe. International HRM strategy, like HRM strategy generally, must be linked to the strategic evolution of the firm. This chapter has highlighted some of the HRM issues and challenges which such firms will face as they undergo the internationalization process. It also suggests that, for British international firms, the recruitment and development of international managers will be the key challenge of the 1990s.

REFERENCES

Adler, N. J. (1984) 'Women in international management; where are they?', *California Management Review* 26 (4): 78–89.
—— (1986) *International Dimensions of Organizational Behavior*, Boston: PWS Kent.
Baker, J.C. (1984) 'Foreign language and departure training in US multinational firms,' *Personnel Administrator*, July, 68–70.
Barham, K and Devine, M. (1991) *The Quest for the International Manager: A Survey of Global Human Resource Strategies*, Special Report No. 2098, Berkhamsted/London: Ashridge Management Research Group/Economist Intelligence Unit.
Boyacigiller, N. (1990) 'The role of expatriates in the management of interdependence, complexity and risk in multinational corporations', *Journal of International Business Studies* 21 (3): 357–81.
Brewster, C. (1988) 'The management of expatriates', Human Resource Research Centre Monograph 2, Cranfield Institute of Technology.
—— (1991) *The Management of Expatriates*, London: Kogan Page.
Desatnick, R.L. and Bennett, M.L. (1978) *HRM in the Multinational Company*, New York: Nichols.
Dowling, P.J. (1986) 'Human resource issues in international business', *Syracuse Journal of International Law and Commerce* 13 (2): 255–71.
Dowling, P.J. and Schuler, R.S. (1990) *International Dimensions of Human Resource Management*, Boston: PWS Kent.
Dowling, P.J. and Welch, D.E. (1988) 'International human resource management: an Australian perspective', *Asia Pacific Journal of Management* 6 (1): 39–66.
Duerr, M.G. (1968) 'International business management: its four tasks', *Conference Board Record*, October.
Edstrom, A. and Galbraith, J. (1977) 'Transfer of managers as a co-ordination and control strategy in multinational organizations', *Administrative Sciences Quarterly* 22: 248–63.
Hall, F.S. and Hall, D.T. (1987) 'Dual careers – how do couples and companies cope with the problems?', *Organizational Dynamics*, Spring, 57–77.
Hall, D.T. and Richter, J. (1988) 'Balancing work and home life: what can organizations do to help?', *Academy of Management Executive* 2 (3): 213–23.
Hamill, J. (1989). 'Expatriate policies in British multinationals', *Journal of General Management* 14 (4): 18–33.
Harvey, M.G. (1989). 'Repatriation of corporate executives: an empirical study', *Journal of International Business Studies* 20 (1): 131–44.
International Management (1986) 'Expansion abroad: the new direction for European firms', 41 (11): 21–5.
Johnston, J. (1991). 'An empirical study of repatriation of managers in UK multinationals', *HRM Journal* 1 (4): 102–8.
Kobrin, S.J. (1988) 'Expatriate control and strategic control in American multinationals', *Human Resource Management* 27 (1): 63–75.
Laurent, A. (1986) 'The cross-cultural puzzle of international human resource management', *Human Resource Management* 25 (1): 91–102.
Mendenhall, M. and Oddou, G. (1985) 'The dimensions of expatriate acculturation: a review', *Academy of Management Review* 10: 39–47.
Morgan, P.V. (1986) 'International human resource management: fact or fiction', *Personnel Administrator* 31 (9): 43–7.
Prahalad, C.K. and Doz, J.L. (1981) 'An approach to strategic control in MNCs', *Sloan Management Review* 22 (4): 5–13.
Shaeffer, R. (1989) 'Managing international business growth and international management development', *Human Resource Planning*, March, 29–36.

Torbiorn, I. (1985) 'The structure of managerial roles in cross-cultural settings', *International Studies of Management and Organization* XV (1): 52–74.

Tung, R.L. (1981) 'Selection and training of personnel for overseas assignments', *Columbia Journal of World Business* 16 (1): 18–78.

—— (1984) 'Strategic management of human resources in the multinational enterprise', *Human Resource Management* 23: 129–43.

Zeira, Y. (1976) 'Management development in ethnocentric multinational corporations', *California Management Review* 18 (4): 34–42.

Zeira, Y and Banai, M. (1984) 'Present and desired methods of selecting expatriate managers for international assignments', *Personnel Review* 13 (3): 29–35.

13 Developing the middle manager for globalization
The case of Electrolux

Mike Regan

It is very often the case that the HR implications of globalization start to be considered at group executive management level and that same examination concludes with the impact of global organizations on senior executive level. Less often do such examinations lead to a focus on middle management despite their importance for globalization. This chapter concerns the necessity to develop middle managers to perform effectively in businesses which have moved through a local, national and regional context, and are increasingly operating on a world stage. The chapter will describe some of the Electrolux experiences, thoughts, and initiatives that we have taken to more readily equip our middle managers to come to terms with the demands placed on organizations during the final part of the twentieth century and into the twenty-first century. We have all, from time to time, used the catchphrase 'think global, act local'. Unfortunately, in many respects, this catchphrase is interpreted by staff within organizations as if the global thinking is undertaken by the top executive group whilst the middle management group act in the same local way that they have always done. We would like to describe how Electrolux has tried to address these issues and to prepare members of local management to play not just an on-going local role, but to understand how important a cog they are in the global whole.

ELECTROLUX: HISTORY AND STRATEGY

Although Electrolux has existed for most of the twentieth century, the foundations of the current structure can more readily be traced to the mid-1960s. From about that period, through the 1970s and early 1980s, a somewhat moribund company was enlivened by a series of acquisitions and the foundation for international expansion established.

In 1962, Electrolux was on a downward curve. Profits were falling and the company had not developed any significant in-house research and development capability. Compared with other appliance manufacturers such as Philips, Siemens, GEC and Matsushita, it had a limited range of products: the core business was made up of vacuum cleaners and absorption-type refrigerators. These refrigerators were increasingly unable to compete with the new compressor-type refrigerators developed by the competitors, and sales of the once highly successful lines of vacuum cleaners were rapidly declining. . . . In 1967 Hans Werthen was appointed CEO of Electrolux. In the next two decades he and the other two members of what was known as the 'Electrolux Troika', Anders Scharp and Gasta Bystedt, would manage to develop the company from a relatively small and marginal player in the business into the world's largest manufacturer of household appliances.

(Ghoshal and Haspeslagh 1990: 415)

The policy in this period was to acquire a series of troubled companies, generally in mature markets but not necessarily synergistic, and to turn them around by cost cutting and allowing local management considerable autonomy, with the emphasis being placed on bottom line achievement. In the period from the mid-1960s until the start of the 1980s there were a multitude of such acquisitions (see Figure 13.1).

The strategy of the time was reflected in the culture and core values of the business which could be identified through the considerable freedom that was given to local managers: a significant amount of decentralization even before it became a generally fashionable concept; organization of the business on a country basis; a lack of bureaucracy and interference from the centre other than concentration on the bottom line; a pragmatic, open, down-to-earth, task-orientated management style, with, not surprisingly, a constant attention to costs and day-to-day basic issues.

By the early 1980s, the disadvantages of such a policy were becoming apparent with the potential peril of being an average player, rather than being a market leader. It was clear that many of the industries in which the group operated, while all being mature, were highly fragmented and ready for restructuring as global buying trends increased.

A change in strategic direction was initiated; to become global leaders in chosen core businesses. The objective was to become number one or two in core areas either in volume or niche markets or to depart the business. This ambition has been achieved in a number of key sectors. In certain sectors, such as household appliances, this development has significantly altered the ground rules of the business game by encouraging other competitors to seek out acquisitions, mergers or joint ventures.

A further series of acquisitions was therefore embarked upon during the mid and late 1980s which, while they followed some of the previous tried and tested routes from earlier days, now followed what can, perhaps, most aptly be described as a structured purposeful approach to the rationalization of certain industries. Hence, in white goods, Zanussi (Italy), White Consolidated (USA) and the Thorn EMI Appliance interests (UK) were all acquired. Similar movements took place in other sectors (see Figure 13.1).

In consumer goods, and to a lesser but a marked degree in industrial

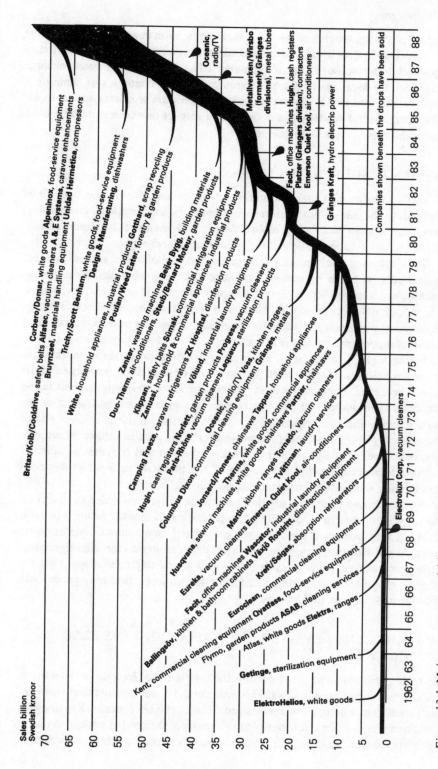

**Sales billion
Swedish kronor**

Britax/Kolb/Cooldrive, safety belts Alfatec, vacuum cleaners A & E Systems, caravan enhancements
Corbero/Domar, white goods Alpeninox, food-service equipment
Bruynzeel, materials handling equipment Unidad Hermética, compressors

Tricity/Scott Benham, white goods, food-service equipment
Design & Manufacturing, dishwashers

White, household appliances, industrial products
Poulan/Weed Eater, forestry & garden products

Duo-Therm, air-conditioners. Steub/Bernard Moteur, garden products
Gotthard, scrap recycling

Zanker, washing machines Beijer Bygg, building materials
Zanussi, household & commercial refrigeration, industrial products
Klippan, safety belts Sümak, commercial refrigerators
Camping Freeze, caravan refrigerators ZK Hospital, disinfection products
Völund, industrial laundry equipment
Hugin, cash registers Norfett, garden products Leqeaux, sterilization products
Paris-Rhône, vacuum cleaners Gränges, metals
Columbus Dixon, commercial cleaning equipment
Oceanic, radio/TV Voss, kitchen ranges

Jonserd/Pioneer, chainsaws Tappan, household appliances
Therma, white goods, commercial appliances
Husqvarna, sewing machines, white goods, chainsaws Partner, chainsaws
Martin, kitchen ranges Emerson Quiet Kool, vacuum cleaners
Eureka, vacuum cleaners Tornado, vacuum cleaners
Facit, office machines Wascator, industrial laundry equipment Tvättman, laundry services
Ballingsöv, kitchen & bathroom cabinets Växjö Rostfritt, disinfection equipment
Kent, commercial cleaning equipment Kreft/Seiges, absorption refrigerators
Euroclean, commercial cleaning equipment
Flymo, garden products Oyatfass, food-service equipment
Atlas, white goods ASAB, cleaning services
Elektra, ranges

Getinge, sterilization equipment

ElektroHelios, white goods

Oceanic,
radio/TV

Metallverken/Wirsbo
(formerly Gränges
divisions), metal tubes

Facit, office machines Hugin, cash registers
Platzer (Gränges division), contractors
Emerson Quiet Kool, air conditioners

Gränges Kraft, hydro electric power

Electrolux Corp. vacuum cleaners

Companies shown beneath the drops have been sold

| 1962 | 63 | 64 | 65 | 66 | 67 | 68 | 69 | 70 | 71 | 72 | 73 | 74 | 75 | 76 | 77 | 78 | 79 | 80 | 81 | 82 | 83 | 84 | 85 | 86 | 87 | 88 |

70
65
60
55
50
45
40
35
30
25
20
15
10
5
0

Figure 13.1 Major company acquisitions and divestments since 1962

products, the approach has been to reduce duplication in manufacturing effort by sourcing on a regional and/or a global basis accompanied by a multi-brand approach to attract segments of the market. The clear aim is to cater for local tastes within local markets while exploiting mass economies of scale on a regional (such as pan-European) or, in certain product segments, global basis. This evolution of strategy has a significant impact on the requirement for a particular type or types of managers.

HUMAN RESOURCE IMPLICATIONS

While it can be seen that the culture of the business from the late 1960s through to the mid-1980s required entrepreneurs and independent business-men and women who were self-sufficient and resented interference, new skills are required in the new strategic and structural order.

The new approach requires managers to collaborate across national boundaries with the prerequisite of accepting, contributions, to decision-making at all levels. The style of management needed for the entrepreneurial phase did not necessarily fit such new requirements. The new strategy demands, in contrast, coordination from management and an integration of effort and cooperation across boundaries.

Increasingly it necessitates an awareness of the pressures of working in different cultures, together with the evolution of a common language and the development of a set of common values, but not necessarily limited to the financial core which had previously been the glue which had acted as the adhesive for the old organization. The evolution of the previous lack of bureaucracy into a more positive networking approach is further inherent in the new strategy. A far greater flexibility of mind and cooperative spirit is needed to accompany the breakdown of the previous national or sectorial boundaries and to overcome some of the cultural barriers.

By the change of the decade the framework of the new order in structural terms was already in place, which further indicated that the future would be typified as much by organic growth as through acquisition. This move to organic growth accelerated and heightened as the world recession tightened. The promotion of a new president who had previously been responsible for the development and implementation of the strategy in white goods only further underpinned the changes.

MANAGEMENT DEVELOPMENT INITIATIVES: THE EXEC PROGRAMME

In anticipation of these developments the International Executive Programme (Exec) was introduced in 1988. This is an annual development programme for selected high potential managers, aged 33–43, who are already in senior jobs involving international responsibilities usually at the level of general manager of a significant business unit. Apart from developing general management skills, the programme attempts to harness motivation and energy to speed the development of a common corporate international identity and culture, thereby progressing the evolution of international networks. As with all our programmes, the educational exercise can be seen as a byproduct to the main objective of the programme in terms of aiding corporate development and generating common values and energy.

Although this programme successfully cuts a swathe across the younger new breed of senior executives in the top 450 managers, the question needed to be posed as to whether this initiative could develop sufficient momentum to empower change in the new direction. While the corporate strategy dictates that companies in the group have to operate, at least, on a regional basis in those product lines that have gone global, it could be queried whether the managers reporting to managing directors are equipped to do this. No longer are management teams being asked to implement policies to supply markets in which they reside. Instead these top teams are being asked to devise, implement and control projects and units that are dependent on markets outside their home base. For instance, blue collar workers in the north-east of England are now supplying European markets and their management are being asked to motivate such staff to understand issues that are happening in the economies of Germany, Italy, Finland and others when previously they had been focused on their home base.

The critical organizational questions to be posed are whether the issues for a regional focus are essentially the same as supplying a domestic market or whether there are subtleties that, for example, a manufacturing unit should be aware of when its customer base is across Europe or a sales and marketing team should consider when sourcing from manufacturing units across Europe. Our conclusion to the question is that there are such subtleties and it is important that people are exposed to them openly rather than stumble across them.

MANAGEMENT DEVELOPMENT INITIATIVES: THE INTERNATIONAL BUSINESS LEADERSHIP PROGRAMME

For this reason the International Business Leadership (IBL) programme was created with Ashridge Management College in the UK. This programme is specifically aimed at top team members of business units in Europe (not the managing directors for whom the Exec programme is available) to give them an appreciation, in as real life a setting as possible, of what it actually means to operate on a truly international basis.

For cost and practical reasons it was decided that such programmes should be administered on a regional or a continental basis. Thus there is a sister programme to the European IBL programme, running in Pacific Asia, with comparable programmes being in a development stage in both North and Latin America.

In terms of design it is important that the programme reflects our core values and heritage, but at the same time moves forward our international culture and framework. Thus the programme is highly practical. While the participants are to be exposed to theoretical concepts these concepts must be experienced on a pragmatic basis. The programme content has to evolve directly in step with the way that the business and managers are developing. It would be the kiss-of-death to bring people to the programme and teach them concepts that they never practise when they are back at base. The programme is structured in a multinational, multicultural, and multi-functional way to underpin the international aspects of our business.

In the past, with strong autonomous entrepreneurs *in situ*, top team members have been 'doers' with little involvement in development of the business strategy. This developed a functional orientation which needs to be broken down by expecting all managers to contribute to decision-making in a commercial way. The programme must at the same time support the transition from national to global markets and underpin the movement from a functional to a general management focus.

It is equally important that the programme leads to the attainment of the skills of leading a winning team where cost economies require the breakdown of the old hierarchical structures, leading to fewer decision-making levels and a more 'hands on' style from middle managers. In other words, they are required to undergo a transformation from managers to operational leaders.

As with the Exec programme, IBL is a further building block in the development of common values and language. It is anticipated it will further foster networks throughout the organization. Finally, it is important in this dynamic world to ensure that the programme itself is in a constant state of flux. This aspect recognizes the transitory nature of business. Put simply, if the programme became institutionalized it should be stopped.

In order to deliver such demanding objectives we had to develop a close partnership with Ashridge. It would not have worked with a traditional 'arms-length' buyer–supplier relationship. Ashridge spent a year before the first programme learning about Electrolux by background research, in-depth discussions, visiting important facilities and gaining exposure to current issues facing the major business units. This process, and the resulting accumulation of relevant knowledge and data, substantially enhanced the credibility of the Ashridge tutorial staff in the eyes of programme participants.

In addition, from the inception of the programme, senior staff from both Ashridge and Electrolux worked very closely in terms of planning each programme, orchestrating programme delivery, and reviewing and evaluating programme design and participant reaction in order to make changes for subsequent iterations. Special attention was paid to the need to present a 'European' face to the programme, rather than it be seen as either 'British' or 'Swedish' and the need to ensure the integration and meshing of both Ashridge and Electrolux presenters.

The programme is designed into two week-long segments, divided by a six-month break, which is used to undertake an in-company project. The first week of the programme is held at Ashridge in the UK and the second week at a location in mainland Europe. The split is designed to ensure that the learning experience of the programme can be applied in practice. The project is the bridge back to the operation which reflects our desire that the programme does not become too academic. More important, exchange of information about the individual's project is a real-time example of the benefits of networking. It demonstrates to participants the wealth of knowledge that is around them in the organization and opens up this untapped resource. This exchange of experience is at the very heart of the networking organization that we aim to develop.

At the time of writing three waves of the programme have been completed with a further two to be undertaken before the summer of 1994. Each new wave now consists of approximately twenty-five people from across Europe. So what have been the results? Perhaps the best summary is that provided by one of the participants on the first programme who said:

> A well designed programme for people such as myself who have been trained or worked in a particular discipline but who are now working outside their own field ... A key benefit is the international aspect, in particular the ability to mix and exchange views with other Europeans over an extended period in informal surroundings. This tends not to happen in the normal work context.

Clearly it is too early to quantify our success or lack of it at this stage. The real question must be: 'are we helping the businesses to become more flexible and responsive and by so doing fully exploiting our strategic initiatives?' The anecdotal evidence suggests that the programme is achieving its aims. The people who have undertaken the programme are the best ambassadors for it and we have significant demand and waiting lists. Those who have been through the programme have champions in their bosses back at base. People who have examined the programme, like what they see, and want more.

The programme must be further developed in line with business requirements. In this respects the second module was some 20 per cent different in content from the first, with further changes planned for the next wave. At this stage we are satisfied with the programme to a certain extent, but not totally. We can always improve but it has been an excellent start and is a good underpinning of what we are trying to do in the business at large.

LESSONS LEARNED AND PROVISIONAL CONCLUSIONS

It is abundantly apparent that in any structural or strategic change the competence level of managers in the body of the organization lags behind the requirements of the organizational thrust. While there is a deep fund of goodwill amongst such middle managers in terms of both the desire for change and the excitement of the opportunities offered by globalization, these very same managers, however young or however experienced, feel increasingly uncertain in this changing panorama. Increasingly, they become small fishes in larger ponds and their confidence levels need to be increased by their ability to interface with colleagues in a similar position on programmes such as these. There is strength in numbers.

Despite excellent communications on the business strategy and initiatives it is still surprising that a lack of awareness exists about the intent and potential of future directions brought about by such global thrusts. Using development programmes such as the IBL to underpin and complement other communication strategies is essential, particularly in an organization such as Electrolux with its patchwork history and its heritage of independent operators, who are both used to and adept at controlling the communications process.

Different national identities clearly emerge. It is manifest that Europe is far from being one nation (see Chapters 2 and 3). Set against a framework where such differences are highlighted, this exploration in a multicultural context tends to be most rewarding for those involved. If this was the only outcome of such a programme, it would still be worthwhile running it.

Finally, such programmes, as with any development activity, give visibility to the participants. Visibility both in terms of exposure for group management ideas, initiatives and personalities and also in the respect that the participants can see themselves being more visible in what can become an increasingly amorphous and extensive organization. Multinational organizations should not lose sight of the fact that as they move increasingly to international structures and organizing businesses on a sectoral basis across continents that they can lose sight of important players on a local level. Such programmes enable both the participants and the organization to bridge that gap.

In conclusion, any transnational organization entering the twenty-first century will need to maximize the contribution of its middle managers throughout the world by managing and exploiting the differences in culture rather than submerging those differences. This internal development process has some parallels with the marketing of consumer products across different markets. Just as the most global consumer products such as microwaves, personal audio equipment and other brown goods tend to be those new products which have developed in the last decade, then perhaps future generations of managers will automatically veer towards operating on a global stage. However, that generation has not yet arrived and the generation who are currently 35-plus still need some considerable assistance in managing the implications of globalization at a local level. Such programmes as the IBL programme offer this assistance and boost the confidence of middle managers in this new era.

For the foreseeable future these programmes will be a permanent feature of the landscape of businesses that are going through evolution towards global levels, such as Electrolux. Whether the programmes should be organized as ours on a group basis or whether they should be organized at a sectoral level depends to a considerable degree on the history, heritage and stage of evolution of the particular organization. Such programmes continue to offer a reinforcement, if not a realignment of managerial focus at middle management level.

REFERENCE

Ghoshal, S. and Haspeslagh, P. (1990) 'The acquisition and integration of Zanussi by Electrolux: a case study', *European Management Journal* 8 (4): 414–33.

14 Competences for the pan-European manager

Kevin Barham
Ariane Berthoin Antal

INTRODUCTION

Advertisement in *The Economist*, January 1999

CREATING EUROPE'S MANAGERS FOR THE 21ST CENTURY

Applications are invited from young men and women graduates of European nationality to join the European Economic Area's newly-established Multinational Marriage project (MuM). This project aims to produce a pool of multilingual, multicultural children from which the high potential Euromanagers of the future will be drawn.

Following initial screening in Brussels, a successful applicant will be given the opportunity to contract a marriage with an applicant from another European country. Couples will enjoy a honeymoon at a holiday resort of their choice and will thereafter receive fully-funded assistance with child rearing, including education fees. Couples will be expected to alternate periods of residence between each parent's home country to ensure that their children are exposed to both cultures. Children conceived in this project will be given preferential access to places at leading European business schools.

Please apply enclosing a full c.v. and a recent photograph . . .

This Orwellian scenario of how to breed international managers to meet the needs of global competition may be all that companies will have to resort to, if we do not succeed in designing more appropriate approaches to the development of such people than are currently available. Neither the 'sink or swim' approach traditionally used by some companies to making managers international nor the focused grooming of a few elite expatriates used by other corporations can respond to the expanded quantitative and qualitative demands for international managers today.

Firms of all sizes are recognizing that 'global competition and globalization of the firm's operations' represent the greatest change they have to deal with (Barham and Rassam 1989; Harper 1992: 11). The implications for human resources are significant: in order to exploit the removal of economic and political barriers, firms need many more people in all manner of functions who are capable of working across cultural boundaries. Top managers in multinational companies with headquarters in Europe confirm that this is one of the highest priorities on their agenda (Barham and Berthoin Antal 1992).

Since there is a growing awareness that 'the complexity of international business does not point to standard packages and solutions' for developing international managers (Reid 1991: 2), this chapter explores three dimensions before proposing approaches for management development. First, the strategic and organizational contexts in which international managers are working are outlined briefly, for the differences in setting have a significant impact on the expectations placed on managers. Second, the wide variety of international roles and responsibilities that exist or are required are illustrated in order to provide a sense for the large numbers and the different types of international managers who need to be developed. Third, key components that need to be considered in the identification of management competences for international responsibilities are described. When these three dimensions are brought together, clear implications for appropriate ways of developing international managers emerge.

ORGANIZATIONAL DESIGNS FOR EUROPEAN AND GLOBAL BUSINESS

The competences needed by pan-European managers will be partly determined by the strategic and organizational context in which they operate. For many firms, Europe is part of a wider global gameplan. While the turmoil in European currency markets and political relations that occurred in the autumn of 1992 may have given some firms pause in their plans for expansion in Europe, we assume the longer-term trend towards economic unity will continue.

The desire to exploit the possibilities of the single market is pushing some companies in a 'transnational' direction as advocated by Bartlett and Ghoshal (1989). These authors assert that businesses need to organize themselves in a very different way if they are to compete effectively in the international business arena of the 1990s. Firms can no longer build their international operations around one strategic focus, as they have done in the past. Rather, if they are to cope with the complex international environment, they must have an equally complex and multi-faceted business strategy. They must be able to pursue simultaneously three types of international strategy: 'global' (strategic coordination and economies of scale and scope), 'multinational' (responsiveness to local conditions), and 'international' (exploiting and adapting parent company knowledge).

Bartlett and Ghoshal argue that international business now demands every part of the organization to collaborate, share information, solve problems and collectively implement strategy. The way that the transnational corporation achieves this is to form itself into an integrated network which shares decision-making and where components, products, resources, information and people flow freely between its interdependent units.

The transnational corporation must win the agreement and commitment of every individual employee to the overall corporate agenda. Through a process of 'co-option', each individual must understand, share and 'internalize' the company's purpose, values and key strategies. The transnational firm also allocates international product responsibilities to different national subsidiaries according to their relative skills and strengths. This not only taps the particular expertise of the business unit but also confirms its identity with the company's international operations.

Adler and Bartholomew (1992) have proposed a similar model of international organizational evolution whereby companies develop from a 'domestic' stance via 'multi-domestic' and 'multinational' phases to a 'transnational stage'. In the latter phase, companies are both globally integrated and locally responsive and depend on worldwide organizational learning. Rather than cultural differences being minimized through assimilation into the dominant organizational culture, as in previous phases, they are recognized throughout the organization and are valued and used to the firm's advantage.

Our own research indicates that many firms are indeed trying to implement more complex, multi-dimensional organizations, such as matrix or network structures, at both the global and European levels. They are, however, at various stages of the process and there is no one model to which they all aspire. For some, the first step is to rationalize their European operations. For instance, those that in the past have had to build separate facilities in each country because of customs barriers may now have the opportunity to achieve greater efficiency by building one plant to serve the whole of Europe.

But it sometimes seems that the more that economic barriers come down, the more cultural barriers go up as local managers seek to protect local interests. As one manager in a company that is rationalizing its European operations told Ashridge researchers:

> Your people in, say, Italy will tell you 'We have this business because we are a local producer. If you ask us to import from France or the UK, we will lose half the business'. And, if the local organization believes that it won't work, they can damn well make sure it won't work. They find all the reasons why the French don't know what the Italians want and why they don't know how to ship it.
>
> (Barham and Wills 1992)

Some firms have gone further in restructuring their European businesses. The international operations of Unilever, the Anglo-Dutch food giant, used to be highly decentralized. It has now modified the structure of its European business in a transnational direction. The aim is to be able to plan marketing in the framework of the single market without having to reinvent the wheel in different countries. For instance, instead of fourteen European detergent businesses strongly coordinated at the centre in London, the company now has one European business with headquarters in Brussels and presences in each country (Barham and Devine 1991).

The matrix structure introduced by Unilever had three aims. The first was the need for flexibility, the second the need to transfer good practice across countries and groups, and the third was the encouragement of innovation from all possible sources. Unilever's chairman believed that the company's matrix structure had improved its decision-making process:

> In my view, when the matrix fails, it is normally because people aren't trained to work within it. We are very fortunate in that we have a cadre of various nationalities that have been trained and developed to work within it.
>
> (Barham and Oates 1991)

SKF, the Swedish bearings manufacturer, is another company that has turned to a matrix solution with country managers combining a local, geographical responsibility with cross-border product responsibilities. An SKF manager described the effects to Ashridge researchers:

> What we will see is the end of the 'King of Germany' and the 'King of Italy' as the massive local organizations start to break down into world-wide product divisions and segments. So it is not enough in SKF any more to be just a local manager. The trend is for many of our businesses to have a matrix organization where a country manager could be responsible not just for his country but also for products in other countries and where his product range might be the responsibility of somebody else outside his own country. While the local pull is historically stronger, it might hurt managers in their product division capacity. It's a tough game for them to play because basically they need two heads.
>
> (Barham and Wills 1992)

One of the boldest attempts to combine the benefits of international co-ordination and economies of scale with local responsiveness is that of ABB Asea Brown Boveri, the Swedish-Swiss electrical engineering group and the biggest pan-European merger yet. It describes itself as a 'multi-domestic' federation of national companies. Along one dimension, the company is a dispersed global network in which managers around the world make decisions on product strategy and performance 'without regard for national borders'. Along a second dimension, it is a collection of national companies and profit centres serving their home markets. The aim is that each unit should be able to capitalize on the knowledge and expertise of all its global partners. The managers who run the fifty business areas into which ABB divides its products hold both global and local roles, so that a manager may be responsible for a whole range of products in his own country but will also have a global responsibility for a particular product.

Percy Barnevik, ABB's president and chief executive, has described his company's operating philosophy as follows:

You want to be able to optimize a business globally – to specialize in the production of components, to drive economies of scale as far as you can, to rotate managers and technologists around the world to share expertise and solve problems. But you want to have deep local roots everywhere you operate – building products in the countries where you sell them, recruiting the best local talent from the universities, working with the local government to increase exports. If you build such an organization, you create a business advantage that's damn difficult to copy.

(Taylor 1991)

A striking feature of the ABB approach is the way that it brings together managers from different units in different countries to find solutions to problems. Such teams might, for example, be working on pan-European products to replace products previously designed for national markets. The result is that many more managers are having to look outside their units and to work across borders.

INTERNATIONAL MANAGERS: THE NEED FOR AN APPRECIATION OF DIFFERENT ROLES

Managers and scholars now agree that 'there is no such thing as a universal global manager' (Bartlett and Ghoshal 1992: 124), but there is less agreement on how to identify the different kinds of international managers either currently operating in organizations or needed for the future. Clearly, the international manager is no longer simply the expatriate who is based abroad, nor the jetsetter who travels extensively from one country to the next. Companies need both managers who can physically operate across national boundaries and managers who, although they may not work or travel abroad, in their minds can also travel across boundaries by understanding the international implications of their work. Studies increasingly show that companies need to develop both the internationally-mobile and the internationally-thinking manager (Barham 1991).

A number of different approaches can be taken to identifying international managers. Here we will look at Bartlett and Ghoshal's typology (1992), the analytical model proposed by Adler and Ghadar (1990), and an internal study conducted by Fiat in this area (Auteri and Tesio 1990).

Bartlett and Ghoshal (1992) identify four types of international manager: business managers, country managers, functional managers, and the top executives at corporate headquarters who manage the interactions between the three. Their approach is useful because it highlights the richly varied roles each of these types of managers has to play in shaping and implementing the international strategy of an organization.

1 They characterize the business manager as 'strategist + architect + co-ordinator' and point out that 'many traditional multinational companies have made the mistake of automatically anointing their home country

product-division managers with the title of global business manager' (ibid.: 127).

2 The country manager is described as 'sensor + builder + contributor', a person who:

> Must be good at gathering and sifting information, interpreting the implications, and predicting a range of feasible outcomes. More important, this manager has the difficult task of conveying the importance of such intelligence to people higher up, especially those whose perceptions may be dimmed by distance or even ethnocentric bias',
>
> (Bartlett and Ghoshal 1992: 128)

3 The third type of international manager is the functional manager who serves as a 'scanner + cross-pollinator + champion'. Their role is to scan for specialized information worldwide and promote the transfer of best practice and innovation between different parts of the organization. According to the authors, the role of the functional manager is particularly important for achieving organizational learning.

4 Last, the corporate manager is 'leader + talent scout + developer' who is seen as 'playing perhaps the most vital role in transnational management' (ibid.: 131) as coordinators of the first three types and developers of new talent.

The colourful descriptions of the multiple roles these four types need to fulfil contribute to differentiating our understanding of international managers. However, there are two important drawbacks to this typology. First, it is based solely on the 'transnational' type of corporation as defined by Bartlett and Ghoshal (1989), and which is rarely found in practice. Second, their approach focuses on top managers. They mention other managers only in passing, and assign them very little significance in international management. This view is not shared by many managers today, who see a much greater distribution of international responsibilities deeper into the organization (Barham and Berthoin Antal 1992). The Fiat case documents this well, but before turning to it, it is useful to consider the Adler and Ghadar model, which sheds some light on why it may be so difficult for companies to see beyond a small group of elite international managers.

Adler and Ghadar (1990) propose looking at different kinds of international managers by applying their four-phase model of international corporate strategies (see also Adler and Bartholomew 1992). Rather than exploring the variety of types of international managers in one firm in depth, their conceptual model highlights the fact that different international strategies require different kinds of international managers. They point out that each phase implies a particular level and focus of cultural sensitivity, with which particular management roles are associated.

In Phase One, in which the company operates primarily domestically, few (if any) managers are sent abroad. The authors cite a manager from such an ethnocentric firm who commented, 'It is best to get your international experience standing next to the globe in the president's office' (Adler and Ghadar 1990: 247).

In Phase Two, when the company expands from domestic to international operations, cultural sensitivity becomes very important for managers in a variety of functions: 'Phase Two firms frequently select and send home country sales representatives to market products overseas, technical experts to transfer technology to overseas production sites, and managing directors and financial officers to control overseas operations' (Adler and Ghadar 1990: 247). The number of managers with international responsibilities therefore increases significantly in this phase, but the flow is only from headquarters out to the countries in which the company is operating. The spread of international interaction is often circumscribed by having overseas personnel reporting to an international division, rather than integrating them in the mainstream business structure.

A further shift is observed in Phase Three, when firms develop a multinational rather than a multi-domestic strategy. In these firms, international management roles are focused on top managers who are drawn from all parts of the worldwide organization. 'The international cadre of executives takes on the central role of integrating the firm' (Adler and Ghadar 1990: 250). As the authors note, 'having hired people from around the world and integrated them into the overall organization' these firms have a very high number of managers in many functions whose work entails international interaction.

A significant transition occurs in Phase Four, in which a truly global view is taken of markets and resources. Since the competitive strategy is based on the concept of mass customization, they must 'develop global R&D, production, and marketing networks' which 'forces them to manage cultural diversity within the organization as well as between the organization and its supplier, client, and alliance networks' (Adler and Ghadar 1990: 243). In companies of this kind the old distinctions between local and expatriate managers become obsolete because people from all over the world must constantly communicate and work with each other and consciously manage their cultural diversity. Thus, in a fully blown Phase Four organization, the overwhelming majority of managers has international dimensions to their responsibilities.

This typology is useful not only because it highlights the key differences between the stances to international management implied in each of the four corporate product and market strategies. Perhaps more importantly, it is useful because it reveals how companies overlook many international management responsibilities actually being fulfilled in their midst. For example, in Phase One companies domestic managers may have contact with foreign clients, but this does not appear to be considered international management. This may be because 'cultural differences are absorbed by the foreign buyers, rather than by the home country's product design, manufacturing, or marketing teams' (Adler and Ghadar 1990: 242).

The international dimension of the work of host country managers in the multiple locations who interface with the managers from headquarters is not recognized in Phase Two companies. In Phase Three a different kind of blinders is in place. 'Phase Three firms often attempt to assume away the culture differences by choosing to believe that organizational culture overrides differences in national perspective and behavior' (Adler and Ghadar 1990: 251). Again, therefore, these firms tend to underestimate the amount of international management being done by their employees and they focus attention on a relatively narrow band of types of international responsibilities.

The purpose of this discussion is not to recommend that all companies shift as rapidly as possible to a Phase Four position. Neither this typology, nor the one proposed by Bartlett and Ghoshal (1989), should be interpreted in a prescriptive fashion as a necessary progression towards an ideal end state for all companies. Rather, the intention here is to point out the need to overcome the blindspots inherent in each model in order to recognize the full range of international responsibilities actually exercised in the course of daily business. Instead of restricting the definition of who is an international manager to the limited types inherent in each of the models, it is worth developing a practical overview of the international tasks and responsibilities managers really do fulfil. On the basis of this, then, the actual competences required for each job can be analysed, and this can be reflected in more appropriate development approaches.

Some companies have conducted job analyses with an eye to identifying the international dimensions they involve. The results are startling. For example, when Fiat, the Italian car manufacturer, introduced its 'internationalization of management' project, it discovered that more than 40 per cent of the managerial jobs in the company deal with international matters (Auteri and Tesio 1990). Fiat found that the international jobs correspond not only to expatriates but to all jobs, wherever they are, that have to contend with a 'pluralistic context', that is to say they involve managing social, political, cultural, linguistic and technical differences and differences in standards. As a Fiat human resource director said:

> We discovered a simple truth. At the beginning of the research we thought that our international managers were the people that we sent abroad. But we found that the real problem of the international manager is not linked to the people sent abroad. It is the people at home who have to manage the international structure. The problem was not how to handle and care about the 'foreign legion'. The problem was here [in Italy]. How international can our managers here be?

> (Barham and Devine 1991)

Fiat identified four types of management position, each of which was exposed to the international business environment to a greater or lesser degree:

1 Transnational positions: operating over the whole geographic area covered by the business.

2 Multinational positions: operating in the context of several different countries.
3 Open, local positions: operating within the context of a single country, with significant links, reference points and dependence on elements outside the country (generally head office).
4 Local positions: operating within a single country, influenced by locally-determined variables, without significant interaction with other countries.

In its analysis, Fiat found that the most internationally exposed jobs are its commercial, administrative, planning, and organization and personnel functions. This may be a function of its particular industry or of its current business strategy. Other international companies may come up with a different distribution.

This kind of distinction between types of international exposure of jobs has been found useful by other companies as well. For example, Price Waterhouse Europe, the international accounting and management consultancy firm, applies a similar three-fold typology to differentiate between its international managers: those who manage across national boundaries from their native country; the managers based abroad; and managers managing in their home country but needing to stay abreast of international trends (Barham and Devine 1991).

Drawing the insights together from the approaches described here, we propose the following practical steps:

1 Managers may find it helpful first to look at the current and future international business strategy of their company and understand the international human resource implications, along the lines proposed by Adler and Ghadar.
2 Building on this, managers can in a second step review the different degrees of international exposure that jobs at all levels either do or should entail in order to achieve the strategy, as done by Fiat.
3 Managers can then expand on the approach used by Bartlett and Ghoshal and attempt to characterize the combination of international roles that the different managers need to be able to play throughout the organization. Companies may find it helpful to stimulate the exploration of these roles by encouraging the use of such colourful terms as those used by Bartlett and Ghoshal to depict their top managers. The purpose is not to engage in a dry academic exercise to produce exhaustive lists, but rather to arrive through the roles to an appreciation of the variety of competences needed by individuals and groups of individuals in the organizations.

PAN-EUROPEAN COMPETENCES

While we need to consider the development needs of people with different types of international exposure, one particular type of international manager is coming into increasing prominence. With barriers coming down and organizations trying new forms of international coordination and integration, the international manager is coming to be someone who can manage across a number of countries and cultures simultaneously, either globally or regionally, such as at the pan-European level. To find out about the competences needed by such key people, Ashridge Management Research Group interviewed managers in companies as diverse as ABB Asea Brown Boveri, Airbus Industrie, Barclays Bank, Cathay Pacific, Nokia-Maillefer, Rohm & Haas, Skandia International, SKF, and Tiphook (Barham and Wills 1992).

'Doing competences'

The interviews revealed two sides to international management competence. The first involves active 'doing' competences consisting of four main roles:

- Championing international strategy.
- Operating as cross-border coach and coordinator.
- Acting as intercultural mediator and change agent.
- Managing personal effectiveness for international business.

Champion of international strategy

As champions of international strategy, international managers work with managers from other countries to envision the future and formulate strategies to take the organization forward. They set up forums for crafting strategy to draw upon the knowledge and expertise of local managers and to spread ownership of the international strategy. As an executive from Barclays Bank said:

> We want to get our European partners to buy into some ideas about what we need to do on a common basis and about the common problems that we need to solve. We are not going to tell the French how to run a French bank, or the Italians an Italian bank. But there are some common issues that we all need to address.

In an age of accelerating product life cycles, one of the international manager's tasks is to speed up business development where possible by exploiting and adapting learning between different countries and markets. Barclays described its approach in Europe:

> The real trick is transferring skills step by step from country to country. The methodology is to migrate your technologies but emphasize the local flavour and use local advertising. It depends on lots and lots of research. You must understand the different buying habits and patterns of the different countries and regions. The Spanish want to see and touch the product, it is the same with banking – they want to see the bank manager. Germans on the other hand buy a lot by mail order so the way that you reach people in Germany will be different from the way that you reach people in Spain or Portugal.

The international manager will take care to educate people at the corporate centre about international initiatives and to secure the support of top management for international initiatives. Said one manager:

> You can spend 50 per cent of your effort convincing people behind you. It means that people in head office must be internationally-minded themselves. My international management starts at home because a lot of the initiatives and a lot of the drive can only come from the support and compliance of head office.

To underpin the role of international strategy champion, the international manager must also ensure that he or she stays globally aware. For the pan-European manager, this means looking out beyond Europe, staying abreast of the world standard of competition and what it takes to match and beat it. Maintaining global awareness and implementing international strategy will depend greatly on the international manager's ability to build strong personal networks both internally and externally:

> I have been around a long time and have worked in different countries and management positions so I've created a network of contacts both outside the company with customers and inside the company in various countries. Without this network it would be very difficult to be successful, particularly in a matrix organization. It provides a lot of information and makes it much easier to get things fixed and agreed when you know the people you are dealing with.

Cross-border coach and coordinator

As cross-border coaches and coordinators, international managers are increasingly working with local management teams in a way that emphasizes collaboration as equals, encouraging local managers to contribute their own ideas and helping them to extract the learning from their experiences. Two Swedish managers explained their approach:

> The question I ask is how can we at the corporate centre help you to build up your business? We are there to help. It's your company but we want to collaborate and work together to build up your operation.

> I spend time talking with them and exchanging ideas. I am the coach – I tell them you are running the company, not me. I coach them by providing a lot of ideas. The point is to get them to start thinking in a different way.

While such an approach fits particularly well with Scandinavian norms of consensus, it is also an ideal espoused by international managers of other nationalities. For example, one French manager explained a similar view:

> I don't travel to control, I travel more to coach. My task is to set the direction and to do whatever is possible to help my people succeed. I do this

through coaching rather than a rigorous type of control. My job is also to make sure that what is being done in one part of the world is in line with something in another part of the world. So I also act as a communication link.

What such international managers want from local management is early warning of problems that are brewing. Said one manager:

I have established a policy of transparency, a rule of no surprises, so that whenever there is a problem, they have to call me or send me electronic mail to let me know that there is a problem, so that there is no surprise. This means I don't get a call from the field on a product which is in trouble and I am not aware it is in trouble. It works because when they do that I don't blame them and beat them up every time they tell me they have a problem.

The same manager explained why controlling local managers rigidly and penalizing failure can undermine strategy:

If management is there to beat up everybody about every problem then people don't take risks any more. There are cover-ups, and the transparency disappears. The traditional management culture was delegate and control, but with the acceleration of the development cycle, you want your people to shoot for the absolute best can-do schedule. If you beat them up every time they miss their schedule, next time they will build in some contingency. If they do that, they will not be able to meet the best can-do schedule. So you may lose three months of time to market because of your personal attitude as a manager.

An open, collegiate coaching style of this sort is essential in managing the transnational matrix or network with which some firms are experimenting. The international manager has to rely on persuasion rather than formal authority and must help local managers to understand that they are complementing each other rather than competing. The task is to turn local managers into internationally-thinking managers who will look outside their own subsidiaries and understand that they are interdependent with the rest of the company. According to an international banking manager:

We are trying to create an organization that is greater than the sum of the parts and to entice a flow of business between the different businesses. That can only come through making us feel that we are part of one group and that is the role of international management.

Intercultural mediator and change agent

Creating flexible yet cohesive international organizations involves considerable change and demands new ways of thinking and working. These may sometimes run counter to cultural norms in some countries, as recognized by an Italian manager in ABB's Italian operations:

We Italians are very individualistic. But this can be a problem in a company like this. We have to learn to listen more to other people's opinions.

As intercultural mediators and change agents, international managers are able to switch their frame of reference rapidly between different cultures. They are able to drive in different gears, rather than just one gear. They are not only aware of their own cultural underpinnings and of the need to be sensitive to cultural differences. They are also able to manage change in different cultural contexts and to push the boundaries of different cultures, although they will beware of assuming that approaches to change that work in one culture will work in another one.

Many international managers are well aware of time imperatives in rapidly-changing markets. A Finnish manager from one company that had been rationalizing its international operations following a large merger with another group claimed that:

Decisions taken early are normally the good decisions. Things that drag on are normally not so good. We have lots of examples of things that have gone well and not so well and the difference is mainly to do with time and speed, where good intentions have not materialized in actions.

The need for speed, however, must be weighed against the need to manage change sensitively. Another manager pointed to the need to build on what already exists rather than trying to impose a totally different approach:

As an international manager trying to introduce change, you must be aware of current reality in cultural terms and try to add on to it. You can't get them to do somersaults. If you are trying to introduce change, you have to get *them* to do it, and sit back and have faith in them.

In the past, companies have assumed that managers will acquire international skills by giving them international assignments. If change is a central component of the international manager's work, this may not be sufficient in itself in future. We were struck by what one British manager told us about his extensive international experience:

My overseas experience has certainly made me more flexible and adaptable but that has a downside. It means that one is prepared to take things as given rather than perhaps working to change them.

Managing personal effectiveness for international business

A further critical competence is the individual's ability to manage his or her personal effectiveness for international business. The international manager's job involves a great deal of travelling and a lot of stress. The average number of days that the managers interviewed spend away from their home base was about 120 days a year. In other words, they spend a third of their life away from home. This makes it very difficult to achieve a satisfactory balance between home and private life and the costs imposed on the family can be considerable. A Swedish manager said:

My family has had to be very understanding. We have been married for 26 years. But we joke that we have only been married for 13 years because I have been away half the time. My son was growing up just when I was doing the maximum travelling. I think that he lost his father.

Another tension is that working at a distance from the scene of operations threatens the manager's sense of control over events. According to a British manager working in a Swedish company:

What causes stress is that you can't spend the time to really go into things the way that you would like to. Sometimes you would like to get more involved than you can. The inability to influence certain things causes stress because you cannot really go in there and do it yourself. You can only work through people. Sometimes you feel that life goes too slowly and that things are not happening in the way that you would like them to.

'Being competences'

The job of the international manager is challenging and makes heavy demands on both the individual and the family. It is clear, however, that many people thrive on the challenges. Successful international managers have a philosophy of life or 'being' that enables them to do so. This second side to international competence underpins the active side of the job and concerns the way that the manager thinks and reasons, the way that they feel, and the beliefs and values that motivate them. It consists of three mutually sustaining parts: cognitive complexity, emotional energy, and psychological maturity.

Cognitive complexity

Cognitive complexity is the ability to see several dimensions in a situation rather than only one and to identify relationships and patterns between different dimensions. This is particularly significant 'wherever uncertainty and situational flux prevail, especially where multifaceted task components and environmental demands require frequent re-adaptation' (Streufert and Nogami 1989: 107). In the international arena, managers need to be able to enter into the minds of people operating out of different perspectives from their own. This facility depends critically on the capacity for active listening which is related to the insight provided by another study on international managers: 'For the "most international", things are assumed to be not what they seem, and need to be constantly checked and rechecked against the new data' (Ratiu 1983: 144). Psychological studies have found that cognitively complex people 'tend to search for diverse (not only confirmatory) information and are more sensitive to and more able to utilize minimal cues'

(Streufert and Nogami 1989: 115). As Ratiu notes, the emphasis of the other managers in his study was 'less on data collection and more on early explanation and rapid conclusions' (Ratiu 1983: 144).

The Ashridge research (Barham and Wills 1992) shows that among successful international managers, cognitive complexity is related to two additional features: a certain sense of humility and fluency in at least one other language. The first point may seem surprising, for such individuals may be perceived as having little to be humble about. The explanation by one manager serves to illustrate the concept of humility in practice:

> Initially, I rely on the local people to guide me. I'm not embarassed about this, quite the contrary. I tell the local people: 'Help me so that I don't make a mistake'.

This attitude contrasts strongly with the image of the 'know-it-all' international manager who imposes his or her way of doing things on each location.

The second point, language fluency, is related to the concept of cognitive complexity because it can contribute to a deeper understanding of culture and thereby promotes a greater 'quality and quantity of hypotheses about the behavior of others' (Streufert and Nogami 1989: 114). In addition, psycholinguistic studies have shown that individuals who speak more than one language are exposed to a number of alternative ways of seeing things, not only because each object and concept has a different word in each language, but also because 'every language offers to its speakers a ready-made interpretation of the world, truly a Weltanschauung' (Kaplan 1972; see also Price-Williams and Ramirez 1977). Finally, and most obviously, language fluency is an important factor in the success of international managers because it helps to create the trust on which international relationships depend. An American manager working in Europe who recognized these various aspects of language said:

> I've insisted that in all the countries I've been in, I do my daily work in the language of that country. It would be very easy for me to do it in English because I work for an American company and English is the language of this company. But I've insisted everywhere I've gone that people speak to me in the language of that country, so meetings, memos, and everything are done in the local language.

Emotional energy

International managers bring to their work a great deal of emotional energy. They have developed an emotional resilience that allows them to take risks and deal with personally uncomfortable or stressful situations. This is often fostered through earlier career experience abroad. One British manager described the 'dreadful psychological hardness' that he had encountered when working in the USA:

People offering business are two-a-penny and it is only those who stick the course who succeed. Those of our people who have worked in the US and learnt the hard way at the coal face come back here far better business getters because they have been exposed to that really harsh environment.

The willingness and ability of international managers to express and reflect upon emotions appears to be an important distinguishing feature. As Indrei Ratiu found in his study, 'the ease and readiness with which they [the most international managers] can recall and discuss the stress symptoms indicative of culture shock' contrasted with the other managers who 'claim never to have experienced culture shock or else refer to it only obliquely, and with discomfort' (Ratiu 1983: 143).

Psychological maturity

International managers have also developed a psychological maturity that depends on three core values. First, they have a strong curiosity to learn that stays vibrant throughout their career. As one Swiss manager put it:

You have to have a willingness to learn, you cannot operate internationally thinking you know everything about everything.

Second, they believe in living fully in the 'here and now'. This allows them to apply a great deal of psychological energy into unravelling the current complexity. This contrasts strongly with the 'backward looking' approach to making sense of a situation found to be characteristic of less international managers who tend to perceive and use only data that confirm their previous conclusions (Ratiu 1983: 145).

Third, many successful international managers have also developed a strong personal morality. They believe in respect for all persons regardless of nationality or race. They also believe in contributing to the wider organization rather than focusing only on their own bottom line. This is particularly important in companies that are trying to implement transnational matrix or network structures. One Swedish manager in ABB said:

I am paid to run my own local operation in ABB in Sweden but I think I also have a mission to contribute knowledge so that we can improve the overall activity of ABB in my Business Area. There is not very much payback in my pocket for that; in fact, it probably takes money out of my pocket.

A collective international competence

All the roles described here – champion of international strategy, cross-border coach and coordinator, and intercultural mediator and change agent – depend on relationships with other people. A focus on individual competences alone will therefore not build the highly responsive international organization that will be needed in future. Companies operating in fast-moving and interdependent European and global markets will depend as never before on their capacity for promoting organizational learning and feedback across borders, on cross-border teamwork, and on the ability to distribute ownership of strategy across the organization. As one senior manager told Ashridge researchers:

> We have many very able and talented individuals. The problem is that we do not work together very well.

Developing the organization's collective international competence will be of critical importance for the future.

THE IMPLICATIONS FOR MANAGEMENT DEVELOPMENT

What are the implications for management development of the review of organizational structures and strategies for international management, the highlighting of the variety of international managers, and the study of competences? The greatest constraint companies are grappling with in achieving their international strategies is the shortage of managers capable of meeting these challenges (e.g. Bartlett and Ghoshal 1992 and Scullion, Chapter 12, this volume). There are more debates than solutions in this area. In order to move on to productive ideas, we will first briefly summarize the state of the discussion.

One of the debates to which academics and managers alike have contributed without coming to a useful conclusion is whether the competences sought in international managers are significantly different from those sought in good managers (for a review of some of the arguments, see Reid 1991). The question can be framed as 'does the global arena merely reduce the margin of error for mediocrity in management?' (Lobel 1990: 39). The spread of international management responsibilities deeper and broader in organizations makes this debate redundant.

A second point of contention is about the extent to which the desired competences can actually be developed (see for example the reviews by Canney Davison 1991; Lobel 1990; and for cognitive complexity in particular, Streufert and Nogami 1989). A glance at the current fragmented state of approaches to the selection and development of international managers in organizations explains why this debate remains unresolved. Some companies have operated on the theory that 'if you move enough people around the world then the benefits of increased understanding of other's cultures, values, beliefs and assumptions would automatically accrue. What has happened in many cases has been quite the reverse' (Neale 1991: 30). Others have invested in intercultural training courses, but little else. As long as approaches to development are themselves 'underdeveloped', the question as to whether the competences needed for international management can be developed cannot be adequately answered.

We would therefore like to propose a framework for an integrated approach to developing international managers. The three major stumbling blocks to designing appropriate approaches to development are, first, the short term and *ad hoc* view often taken to career development; second, the tendency to think in bipolar terms of 'experience' versus 'training'; and third, the individualistic focus of management development. Companies and the managers themselves have to start taking a much longer term view of development: they need to think in terms of 'becoming' rather than simply 'being' international managers. This is because the kinds of competences discussed above cannot be developed overnight. It is important to stress that taking a more systematic and long-term approach to identifying and developing the potential of international managers does not imply imposing a cumbersome and rigid process on organizations. Maintaining flexibility and taking advantage of opportunities as they arise are essential in developing these managers. The point here is that learning opportunities are used more effectively when embedded in a developmental perspective.

The kind of learning that can be provided for in training programmes, whether in-company or at a business school, is different from the learning afforded by on-the-job experience. There is little mileage to be gained in debating whether one is more useful than the other. Both have their advantages, and, fortunately, innovative programmes are being designed to combine the best of both kinds of learning for international managers (e.g. Ashridge Management College, IMD, University of Michigan). A danger inherent in the debate on 'experience' vs. 'training' is that a key element in the learning process, as modelled by Kolb (1984) receives almost no attention: the need for reflection in order to understand an experience, draw out the learning and assimilate it in new behaviour. It is this that hampers managers in their ability to learn from the experiences on the job (Berthoin Antal and Gonin 1992). They do not have the time or opportunity to extract the learning in an experience because they are constantly moving on from one activity to the next. At worst, 'superstitious' learning (Levitt and March 1988) occurs because the various factors that impinge on a situation are not explored, and conclusions are drawn without being challenged. A key challenge for management development, therefore, is to build opportunities for reflection into the work of managers, rather than creating additional 'activities' for them to experience. The opportunity to reflect in dialogue is particularly valuable, whether it be through discussions with peers, coaches or mentors, because they allow the manager to explore different interpretations of events and behaviours.

The third barrier to management development that needs to be overcome is the individualistic focus. There are several aspects to this point. First, management development needs to be embedded in the strategic development of the organization in which an individual works in such a way that the individual learns what is actually needed. This implies developing a clarity of organizational purpose and linking it with an analysis of required competences at the individual level. Second, the learning achieved by the individual needs to be reabsorbed by the organization: ideally, the organization should benefit from individual learning by changing itself. Third, a fresh look needs to be taken at the 'learning unit' so that the development needs of project groups, departments, or other organizational units are targeted, rather than the isolated manager. It is becoming increasingly obvious to organizations that work needs to be organized in groups and teams, and the ability to work in teams is a key competence required of international managers (Barham and Wills 1992; Canney Davison 1991; Neale 1991). It is therefore more logical to provide team-based management development than to try to develop 'team players' individually. A further reason for shifting to a team or group focus is that the range of competences needed is greater than most individuals can reasonably be expected to develop. Instead of seeking the elusive 'superman' composite of desirable competences for international management, it is advisable to compose and develop teams whose strengths can be pooled and weaknesses balanced.

Only if companies can take a 'becoming' view to the long-term development of international managers as members of working units will they actually have the qualified people they need. The horror vision of breeding grounds for elite international managers can then be relegated to the closet in which it belongs.

REFERENCES

Adler, N. J. and Bartholomew, S. (1992) 'Managing globally competent people', *Academy of Management Executive* 6 (3): 52–65.

Adler, N.J. and Ghadar, F. (1990) 'Strategic human resource management: a global perspective' in Pieper, R. (ed.) *Human Resource Management: An International Comparison*, Berlin, New York: de Gruyter, pp. 235–60.

Auterio, E. and Tesio, V. (1990) 'The internationalization of management in Fiat', *Journal of Management Development* 9 (6): 6–16.

Barham, K. (1991) 'Developing the international manager' in Reid, P. (ed.) *Global Management: Culture, Context, Competence*, Berkhamsted: Ashridge Management Research Group, pp. 3–16.

Barham, K. and Berthoin Antal, A. (1992) 'Setting the international agenda', *Ashridge Management Review*, Summer: 18–20.

Barham, K. and Devine, M. (1991) *The Quest for the International Manager: A Survey of Global Human Resources Strategies*, Special report No. 2098, Berkhamsted/London: Ashridge Management Research Group/Economist Intelligence Unit.

Barham, K. and Oates, D. (1991) *The International Manager*, London: Business Books.

Barham, K. and Rassam, C. (1989) *Shaping the Corporate Future*, London: Unwin Hyman.

Barham, K. and Wills, S. (1992) *Management Across Frontiers*, Berkhamsted: Ashridge Management Research Group and Foundation for Management Education.

Bartlett, C.A. and Ghoshal, S. (1989) *Managing Across Borders*, London: Hutchinson Business Books.

—— (1992) 'What is a global manager?', *Harvard Business Review*, Sept–Oct: 124–32.

Berthoin Antal, A. and Gonin, D. (1992) 'Rethinking management: what the participants think', *efmd Forum*, 2: 9–12.

Canney Davison, S. (1991) 'Mapping the issues for training the international manager', in Reid, P. (ed.) *Global Management: Culture, Context, Competence*, Berkhamsted: Ashridge Management Research Group, pp. 37–50.

Harper, S.C. (1992) 'The challenges facing CEOs: past, present and future', *Academy of Management Executive* VI (3):7–25.

Kaplan, R.B. (1972) 'Cultural thought patterns in intercultural education' in Allen, H.B. and Campbell, R.N. (eds), *Teaching English as a Second Language: A Book of Readings*, 2nd edn, New York: McGraw-Hill, pp. 294–309.

Kolb, D.A. (1984) *Experiential Learning: Experience as the Source of Learning and Development*, Englewood Cliffs, New Jersey: Prentice Hall.

Levitt, B. and March, J.G. (1988) 'Organizational learning', *Annual Review of Sociology* 14: 319–40.

Lobel, S.A. (1990) 'Global leadership competencies: managing to a different dream-boat', *Human Resources Management* 29 (1): 39–47.

Neale, R. (1991) 'Establishing and developing multicultural teams in BP', in Reid, P. (ed.), *Global Management: Culture, Context, Competence*, Berkhamsted: Ashridge Management Research Group, pp. 29–35.

Price-Williams, D.R. and Ramirez, M. (1977) 'Divergent thinking, cultural differences and bilingualism', *Journal of Social Psychology* 103: 3–11.

Ratiu, I. (1983) 'Thinking internationally: a comparison of how international executives learn', *International Studies of Management and Organization* XIII (1–2): 139–50.

Reid, P. (1991) 'Introduction', in Reid, P. (ed.), *Global Management: Culture, Context, Competence*, Berkhamsted: Ashridge Management Research Group, pp. 1–2.

Streufert, S. and Nogami, G.Y. (1989) 'Cognitive style and complexity: implications for I/O psychology', in Cooper, C.L. and Robertson, I. (eds), *International Review of Industrial and Organizational Psychology*, Chichester: John Wiley, pp. 93–143.

Taylor, W. (1991) 'The logic of global business: an interview with ABB's Percy Barnevik', *Harvard Business Review*, March–April 1991: 91–105.

Part V
Conclusions

15 Current trends, future prospects and a research agenda

Paul S. Kirkbride

The chapters in this volume have, in their various ways, sought to illuminate the context, processes and key concerns of HRM in Europe in the 1990s. They have done so from a series of individual perspectives and utilizing broad definitions of both Europe and HRM. It is not our intention here to summarize or rehearse these chapters, but it is probably worthwhile to attempt to extract some common trends and to identify prospects for the future and critical areas for future research.

One key trend which has been identified by several contributors in this volume is the 'transfer' of various forms of HRM theory, processes and practices. We have seen reference to two forms of such transfer. The first, and oldest, form is the transfer of managerial theory and HR knowledge from the USA to Europe. It is widely acknowledged that the majority of modern managerial theory in many diverse fields has its origins in the United States. Historically business and management education, and thus an academic business profession, occurred much earlier, and on a much greater scale, in the USA than in anywhere in Europe. As a result the bulk of management thought currently taught in business schools throughout Europe is either directly American in origin or is indirectly heavily influenced by American work. There is very little which is distinctly 'European' or indigenous to a particular European country.

Examples of this process of 'transfer' from the USA to Europe would include leadership theory (Chapter 3), HRM models (Chapter 5), and HRM practices (Chapter 8). Of course, there is nothing intrinsically *wrong* with such transference. Indeed, the transfer of a model or practice from one context to another which shares the same environment can be applauded as a learning process and a refusal to 'reinvent the wheel'. However, the key issue is that the environmental contexts have to be the same. Yet, as several contributors to this volume have argued, neither the cultural (Chapters 1, 3, 4) nor political, economic and legal (Chapters 5, 7, 8) environments are the same in Europe as they are in the United States. Indeed, they are not even the same *within* Europe. Thus either the models and practices have to be adapted for use in a new environment or indigenous models and practices have to be developed within the new environmental contexts.

The second, and most recent, form of such transference is that which is increasingly occurring between 'West' and 'East'. Here we appear, with a sense of *deja vu*, to be witnessing history repeat itself. Several contributors (Chapters 9, 10, 11) have identified an explosion in terms of 'American' and 'Western European' theories, models and practices being transferred to Eastern Europe. While this process may be seen as a necessity, given the rapid collapse of the Eastern bloc system and the serious economic problems which Eastern European nations find themselves with, there is obviously still a need for both cultural and environmental sensitivity in the process. Put simply, solutions to a set of issues and problems pertaining in one context do not necessarily resolve very different sets of issues and problems in another context.

Another key trend concerns the development of new organizational structures. Several commentators (Chapters 4, 5, 6, 7, 12, 13, 14) have identified the increased incidence of European joint ventures and what are variously referred to as 'European multinational corporations', 'pan-European companies' and 'transnational' or 'global' organizations. It may be suggested that such organizations have distinct and different sets of problems and issues to those which are domestic in orientation. Of particular relevance to HRM are the problems of cultural compatibility between European joint venture partners and the difficulties in sourcing and developing the new breed of 'international' or 'European' managers required to operate in this complex cultural context and new structural configurations.

What of the prospects for the future? A key theoretical debate running through this volume is that of cultural convergence versus cultural divergence. To what extent are European countries beginning to coalesce towards a common 'European' culture? Or are the very different cultures of Europe proving resistant to pressures to change? On the one hand we have seen evidence of the strong pressures to convergence which include the economic and political pressures of the EC, the development of a European labour market, and the increased incidence of European MNCs and IJVs. There is some evidence that it may be possible, at the appropriate level of abstraction, to delineate the contours of a European theory of management or a European model of HRM. On the other hand we have heard evidence of the problems caused by the clash of different European cultures for pan-European operation. It has also been suggested that it is at the level of cultural 'clusters' that the key implications for differences in HRM practices and leadership styles are located. Overall the balance of evidence and argument seems to favour the latter view over the former. This would accord with our own views on this issue.

As a result many of the contributors to this volume have identified as a key issue the management of the cultural diversity which exists within Europe. This imperative applies at the European infrastructural, pan-European organizational, European joint venture, and individual managerial levels. It is interesting to note that most of the contributors see cultural diversity as a strength rather than a weakness. Thus they tend to stress the positive advantages created by different cultural perspectives, such as innovation and creativity, and thus the need to maintain and increase cross-cultural inter-actions while searching for culturally synergistic solutions to organizational issues and problems.

The chapters in this volume represent one of the first steps on the road to our increased understanding of the processes and issues of HRM in Europe. They are often as interesting for the gaps they identify in our knowledge as for the data they provide. From a study of these chapters it is possible to identify a number of key areas for further study and future research work. An obvious first point is our paucity of knowledge and data concerning the cultural, economic, political and social contexts of Eastern Europe. Partly because of language difficulties and partly because of the lack of 'Western' research access (until recently), our knowledge of Eastern Europe remains limited. We need to rapidly increase our knowledge of this key area whether as academics, researchers, HR practitioners or management trainers.

Second, we have identified a need to develop cluster or country-specific theories of both HR practice and managerial behaviour. This is easier said than done, particularly in view of the hegemony of American theory and the investment required to develop such indigenous models and theories. Third, we need to gather more data on HR practice in Europe, both West and East. The Price Waterhouse Cranfield Project under Chris Brewster has proved extremely valuable in this regard, but more detailed work remains to be done in Western Europe and similar work needs to be developed with Eastern Europe. Fourth, there is a need to track the impact of the SEM (or EU1992) on HRM practices within the EC. Much has been written predicting de-velopments; more now needs to be done to describe the reality. Fifth, more research work needs to be done on the emergence of the European MNC and on European IJVs. Particular areas of interest concern how such companies are structured; how they seek to exert control across national boundaries; how they create a global culture, how they 'fit' systems to local contexts; and how they develop a European management capability and cadre.

Finally we return full circle to the beginning of this volume and the conference from which the majority of contributions were taken. While the conference was extremely 'international' with participants from over fifteen countries and papers on over twenty-five countries or regions, it was perhaps not as 'European' as it could have been. This may be a result of language barriers both to the marketing of such events in Europe and to the willingness to present papers in English. Yet, it is obvious that the research agenda listed above can only be addressed by pan-European research collaboration. This is therefore a plea for the increased use of European research teams, collabor-ative research projects, and specifically European conferences. This is not a call for an academic 'Fortress Europe', but for a much closer integration of research activities with Europe while retaining existing links outside the European domain. It will be interesting to watch these developments through the last half of this decade and into the next century.

Index